中英文对照

Resources Retrieval and Utilization On International Medical Licensing Examination

国际执业医师考试资源检索与利用

庄善洁 于静 王杰 主编

知识产权出版社

全国百佳图书出版单位

图书在版编目（CIP）数据

国际执业医师考试资源检索与利用 / 庄善洁, 于静, 王杰主编. —北京：知识产权出版社, 2017.7
ISBN 978-7-5130-4879-8

Ⅰ.①国… Ⅱ.①庄… ②于… ③王… Ⅲ.①医师－资格考试－信息检索 Ⅳ.①G252.7

中国版本图书馆CIP数据核字（2017）第093806号

内容提要

本书分上下两篇。上篇介绍了医学电子图书、电子期刊、电子会议文献、医学视频资料及MOOC资源的获取途径；下篇介绍了各国和地区的执业医师考试资源的获取和利用，主要介绍了美国、加拿大、中国香港、澳大利亚、新西兰、英国等国家和地区的医学资格考试内容及考试所用资源。本书为想在其他国家和地区做执业医师的中国学生及留学生提供了参考资料。

This book is divided into two parts.The first part is about introduction for medical electronic books, electronic journals, electronic conference papers, medical video materias and MOOC resource and acquisition approach to them. The second part is about introduction for the acquisition and utilization of practicing physician examination resources all over the world. The book mainly introduces the contents of medical qualification examination and the resources use in the United States, Canada, Chinese Hongkong SAR, Australia, New Zealand, and the United kingdom. The book provides reference for Chinese students and foreign students to be practicing physician in other countries and area.

责任编辑：许 波　　　责任出版：孙婷婷

国际执业医师考试资源检索与利用
GUOJI ZHIYE YISHI KAOSHI ZIYUAN JIANSUO YU LIYONG
庄善洁 于静 王杰 主编

出版发行：知识产权出版社 有限责任公司		网　　址：http：//www.ipph.cn	
电　　话：010－82004826		http：//www.laichushu.com	
社　　址：北京市海淀区西外太平庄55号		邮　　编：100081	
责编电话：010－82000860转8380		责编邮箱：xubo@cnipr.com	
发行电话：010－82000860转8101/8029		发行传真：010－82000893/82003279	
印　　刷：北京中献拓方科技发展有限公司		经　　销：各大网上书店、新华书店及相关专业书店	
开　　本：720mm×1000mm　1/16		印　　张：22.25	
版　　次：2017年7月第1版		印　　次：2017年7月第1次印刷	
字　　数：345千字		定　　价：66.00元	

ISBN 978-7-5130-4879-8

本书编委会

主　审：陈廷玉　孙秀斌

主　编：庄善洁　于　静　王　杰

副主编：朱　翃　孙丽丽　郭　妍

前　言

　　资格考试评定一个人的综合性职业能力，包括理论能力考试和实践能力考试。医师资格考试是行业准入考试，是对医生所必需的专业知识与技能的评估。随着全球一体化的发展，各国执业医师临床技能逐渐标准化，考试科目逐渐综合化，考试内容逐渐扩大化，仅仅掌握医学专业知识是不够的，这也从另一方面对医生的知识结构提出了新的要求。特别是目前，世界各国以各种方式对行医执照互认政策的实行，促使医师在各国之间互相流动。要想取得在别国或地区的行医资格，就必须明晰该国或地区的执业医师标准，通过其执业医师考试。

Preface

　　The qualification examination is used to assess a person's comprehensive professional ability, includung theoretical ability test and practical ability test. Physician qualification examination is an industry admittance examination, which is the evaluation of the professional knowledge and skills of doctors. With the development of globalization, practicing physician clinical skills all over the world gradually tend to standardization, test subjects gradually integrated, test contents gradually expanded, so it is not enough only to master medical professional knowledge, which puts forward new requirements for the knowledge structure of doctors on the other hand, especially at present, countries all over the world implement the policy of mutual recognition of license in various ways which urges physicians to flow between countries. In order to obtain medical practice in other countries and areas, examinees must clarify about the country's physician practice

如何获得该国或地区的执业医师考试信息及考试所用参考资料是非常重要的，而电子资源是快速了解和掌握相关医学信息的重要途径。正是基于这个原因，本书的作者搜集了各国大量的与考试有关的医学电子资源，从上下两篇讲述了国际医师执业考试涉及的电子资源。

本书以英汉对照的形式对各国或地区的执业医师考试资源做了详细介绍。佳木斯大学、吉林大学和黑龙江中医药大学的老师和学生共同参与编写本书。

陈廷玉负责审校英文部分的内容；孙秀斌负责审校中文部分内容，庄善洁主编第六章的第二、三、四、五节；于静主编第七章、第九章和第十章；王杰主编第四章、第五章；朱翀主编了第一章及从 A~K 的 SCI 收录的期刊整理，孙丽丽主编第六章的

standards, and pass through its practicing physician examination.

It is very important to get the information of the medical examination and reference materials for examination of the country and areas, and the electronic resource is an important way to quickly understand and master the relevant medical information. It is for this reason that the author of the book collected a large number of different countries relevant medical electronic resources. From the two chapter describes the international physician practice examination involving electronic resources.

The book gives a detailed introduction to the resources of practicing physician examination in different countries and areas in the form of English–Chinese contrast. Teachers and students in Jiamusi University, Jilin University and Heilongjiang University of Chinese Medicine work together to write this book.

Chen Tingyu checked for English contents part, Sun Xiubin checked for Chinese part, Zhuang Shanjie wrote the second, the third, the 4th, the 5th of chapter 6; Yujing wrote the chapter7, chapter 9,chapter 10; Wangjie wrote the chapter 4 and chapter 5; Zhuhong wrote the chapter 1 and arranged journals SCI included

第一节和第六节及从 L~Z 的 SCI 收录的期刊整理；郭妍主编第二章、第三章、第八章及从 I~K 的 SCI 的收录期刊整理。吉林大学白求恩医学部学生薛鸿萌做了大量的国外医学相关网站资料的前期搜集工作。

from A to K; Sunlili wrote the first and the 6th of chapter6, arranged journals SCI included from L to Z; Guoyan wrote the chapter 2, chapter 3, chapter 8 and arranged journals SCI included from I to K. Xue hongmeng in Bethune Medical School of Jilin University has done a lot of preparatory work to collect foreign websites related to medicine resources.

目　录

上 篇
Part one

中外电子资源
Chinese and Foreign
Electronic Resources

第一章　电子图书
Chapter one　Electronic Books

电子图书是以各种磁或电子介质为载体的一种无形的，以电子文件形式存在的图书，与传统纸质图书相比，具有方便、快捷的特点。阅读电子图书时，只需借助一定的阅读设备和特定的软件就可以随时随地阅读。电子图书是超文本的，内容包含文字、图片、声音、动画等丰富的信息。电子图书支持超文本链接，阅读很方便。电子图书还具有任意复制、剪切、方便传递等功能。一本电子图书可以同时被多个读者使用，这是与传统纸质图书最大的区别，电子图书能够实现信息共享。电子图书优于纸质图书的另一个特点是快捷查找信息，提高了信息检索的效率。

The electronic book is a kind of intangible item, which is based on various magnetic or electronic media. It has the characteristics of convenience and quickness. When reading electronic books, you can read them at any time with the help of certain reading equipment and specific software. Electronic books are hypertext, which contains rich information such as text, picture, sound, animation and so on. E-books support hypertext links, and they are easy to read. It also has the functions of copy, cut, transfer and so on. An e-book can be used by multiple readers at the same time, which is the biggest difference from the traditional paper books. Electronic books can realize information sharing. Another feature that the electronic book is better than the paper book is to find information quickly, and to improve information retrieval efficiency.

1.1 免费中文电子图书的网站

1.1 Free Chinese E–book Website

1.1.1 超星数字图书馆

1.1.1 Chaoxing digital library

超星数字图书馆由北京世纪超星信息技术发展有限责任公司开发，包含社会科学、自然科学、工程技术、医药卫生等多个专题的电子图书。目前超星数字图书馆拥有数字图书十万多种，并在以每天数百种的速度增加。在超星数字图书馆中在线阅读图书是免费的，如果想下载电子图书，需要凭超星读书卡下载，才可进行离线阅读。目前，大多数高校图书馆都购买了超星数字图书馆，在校学师生可以免费下载。

Chaoxing digital library is developed by Beijing Century Information Technology Development Co. Ltd., which contains social science, natural science, engineering, medicine and health e–books. Now, it has more than one hundred thousand kinds of digital books, and it is increasing with hundreds of books speed per day. Reading online is free in Chaoxing digital library, if you want to download the e–book, chaoxing reading card is needed, then reading offline. At present, Most university libraries have purchased chaoxing digital library, teachers and students can download they need freely.

1.1.2 方正 Apabi 数字图书馆

1.1.2 Founder Apabi digital library

方正 Apabi 数字图书馆是由北大方正集团有限公司开发的数字图书系统，提供中国出版的电子新书，学科涉及文学艺术、语言、历史、经济、法律、政治、哲学、计算机等多个类别，利用该数字图书馆可检索 30 种年鉴（国际性年鉴、全国性年鉴、省直辖市年鉴、城市年鉴、区县年鉴）。

Founder Apabi digital library is a kind of digital library system developed by Peking University Founder. The new e–books in this system are published in China. The books' subject involves many categories, such as literature, art, language, history, economy, law, politics, philosophy, computer and so on. The digital library can be used to search for 30 kinds of Yearbook (International Yearbook, national Yearbook, provincial and municipality directly under the central government, city Yearbook, county and district Yearbook).

阅读方正 Apabi 电子书，需先下载并安装 Apabi 阅读器。目前，多数高校图书馆都购买了该数字图书馆，在校园网内的用户直接点击 IP 用户登录，就可以免费阅读方正 Apabi 电子书了。

Reading founder Apabi e-book, you need to download and install Apabi Reader. Download and install the founder of the Apabi reader. At present, most university libraries have purchased this digital library, the campus network users can directly click on the IP user login and read founder Apabi e-book freely.

1.2 免费的外文电子图书网站

1.2 Free Foreign E-book Website

1.2.1 FreeBookSpot 网站

1.2.1 FreeBookSpot website

在该网站上有近5000个免费资源可供下载，用户可以使用搜索功能或分类功能查找所需图书。该网站对英语学习和专业知识学习有很大帮助。

There are more than 5000 free resources available for download. Users can use the search function, or classification function to find the required books. This website is also great helpful to English learning and professional knowledge learning.

1.2.2 4 eBooks 网站

1.2.2 4 eBooks website

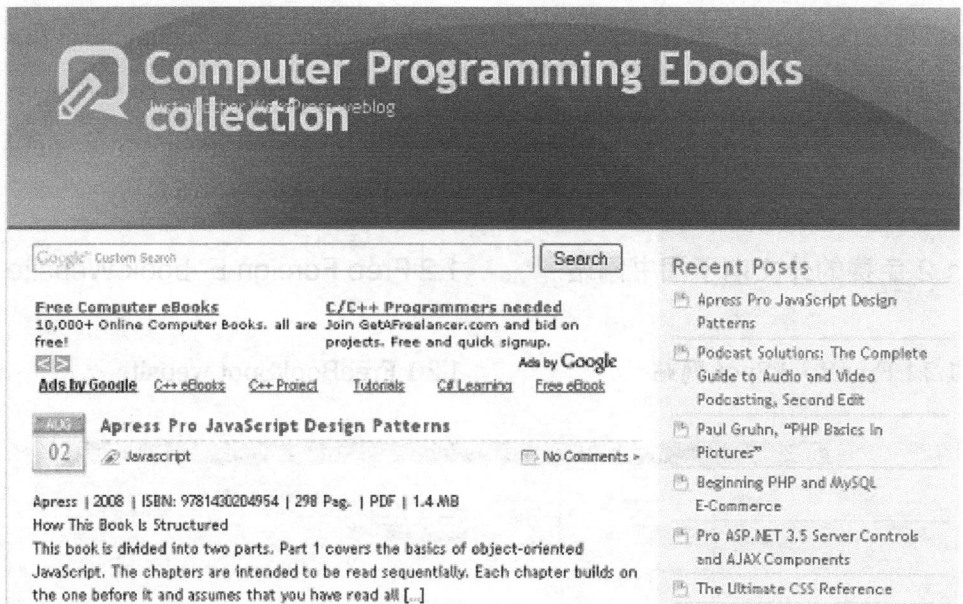

4ebooks 网站图书内容主要是涉及电子计算机相关专业的。每种电子书有如何下载的简短介绍，在这里，用户可以找到计算机相关的英文书籍，如.NET, ActionScript, Ajax, Apache等。

The content of 4eBooks website is mainly about computer-related professions. Each ebook has a brief introduction about how to download, on this website, you can find thousands of computer-related professions English books, such as.Net, ActionScript, Ajax, Apache, and so on.

1.2.3 Free-ebooks 网站

1.2.3 Free-ebooks website

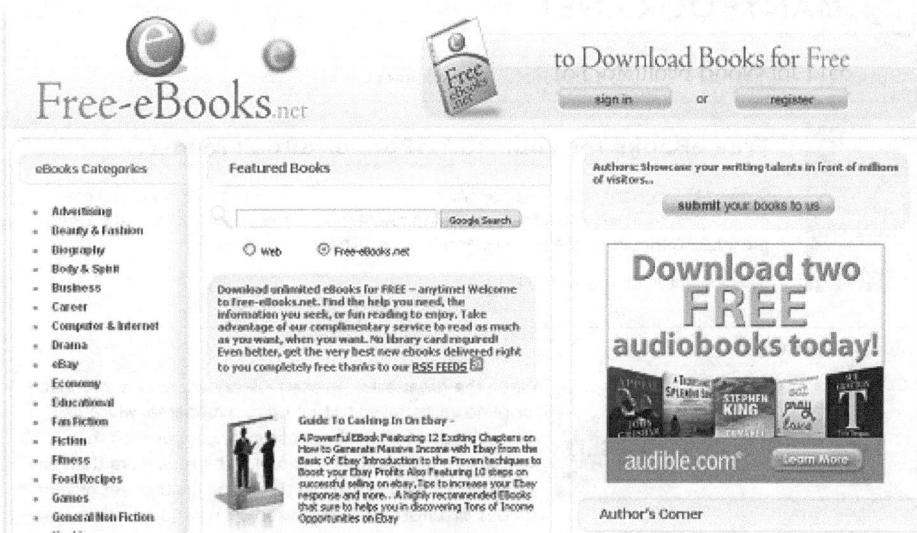

　　该网站提供了很多电子书籍来下载，并且有英文杂志。用户不仅可以阅读和使用网站上的电子图书，而且还可以分享和上传自己喜欢的电子书或文章。

　　This website provides a lot of electronic books to be downloaded, and it also provide English magazines. Users can not only read and use the electronic books on the site, but also can share and upload their favorite e—books or articles.

1.2.4 ManyBooks 网站

1.2.4 ManyBooks website

　　该网站拥有两万多种电子图书可供下载，可免费为 PDA、iPod 和其他电子图书阅读器提供服务；另外，用户可以浏览最流行的电子书下载，也可以看到编辑推荐的书籍。

　　The site has more than twenty thousand kinds of electronic books available for download, free ebook is for your PDA, iPod and other electronic book reader; in addition, you can browse the most popular e—book download and also see the recommended books editor.

MANYBOOKS.NET

| AUTHORS | TITLES | CATEGORIES | LANGUAGES | |

Free eBooks for your PDA, iPod, or eBook reader.

Browse through the most popular titles, recommendations, or recent reviews from our visitors. Perhaps you'll find something interesting in the special collections. There are 21,287 eBooks available here and they're all *free!*

NEW Recent Additions to the library.

Books of the Week

Scarhaven Keep
J.S. Fletcher

When the great actor, Bassett Oliver, who was a martinet for punctuality, failed to turn up to a rehearsal which he himself had called, his business manager guessed that something had happened. It had. But it took more than one set of brains to discover the truth, and another set of very curious circumstances was mixed up in it. Copplestone, the young dramatist, helping to solve the mystery, found himself suddenly in love; and the solution and his happiness were discovered together.

1.2.5 GetFreeEBooks 网站　　　1.2.5 GetFreeEBooks website

getfreeebooks
ALL THE EBOOKS YOU NEED

| Ads by Google | Free eBooks | Download Book | C++ eBooks | eBooks Library | | Search... | GO |

Pages: ABOUT SUBMIT YOUR EBOOKS　　　Page 1 of 20 [1] 2 3 4 5 » ... LAST »

Free Ebooks Download
Grab Your Free Ebooks Today
Download Now And Make Money
117network.com

Free Ebooks
Download eBooks for Free Download
Now!
www.FreeEbookSearch.net

Ads by Google

Free Ebooks Recommendation

Heaven for public domain resources
can be found here.

Spots Blind

Short Stories

Spots Blind

Linda A. Lavid

Spots Blind
by Linda A. Lavid
http://www.lindalavid.com

Spots Blind is a collection of short fiction by award-winning author, Linda A. Lavid. The eleven stories in this collection address those unexpected events that change lives. "Regardless of foresight, planning, preparation, you can't always see what's coming. The trajectory is misinterpreted, misconstrued, minimized. On the other hand someone could be blocking your view, on purpose, with malice. No matter what, something is heading your way."

Read more and download the ebook »

Google Search

Subscribe to RSS Feeds

Popular Topics

Babies Business children coloring Computers and Internet craftsmanship Do It Yourself Education electronics Family and Kids fantasy Fiction Food and Health gym Health and Fitness Hobbies and Interest Household Humour internet Internet Marketing Interviews japanese Language list building mathematics membership sites muscle Non Fiction novel Personal Development PPC Marketing Religion resumes romance Science Fiction Self Help short stories sports success Various viral Web Design working world world Writing

| Categories | Pages | Archives | Links |

• **Categories**
  • Agricultural (1)
  • All In One (9)
  • Architecture and Design (1)
  • Arts and Drawing (4)
  • Audio Ebooks (3)
  • Blogging (2)

该网站是一个提供免费下载图书、拥有大部分电子图书下载的网站。

This site is a free download books place, with most of the e-books download site.

1.2.6 FreeComputerBooks 网站

1.2.6 FreeComputerBooks website

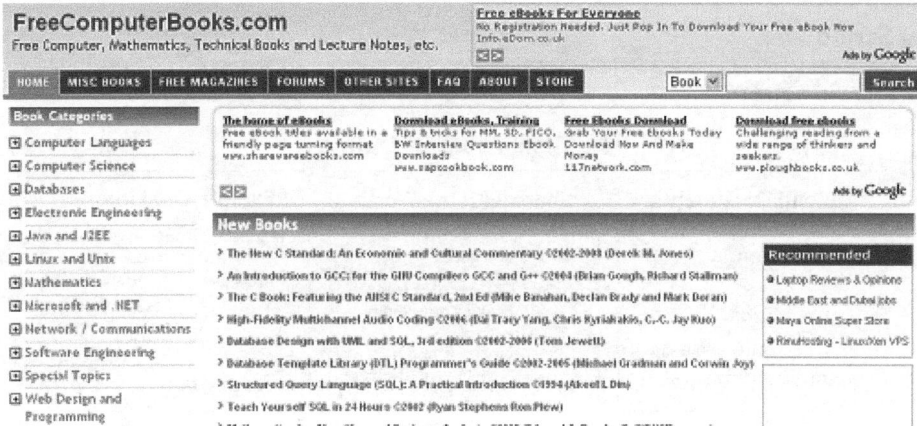

从该网站的名称可以看出，它主要是获取与计算机相关的图书。

From the name of the site , we can know this site is mainly to obtain computer-related books.

1.2.7 FreeTechBooks 网站

1.2.7 FreeTechBooks website

这个网站是关于科学与技术方面电子图书的网站，包括工程规划与设计。

This web site is about science and technology, including engineering planning and design.

1.2.8 Scribd 网站

1.2.8 Scribd website

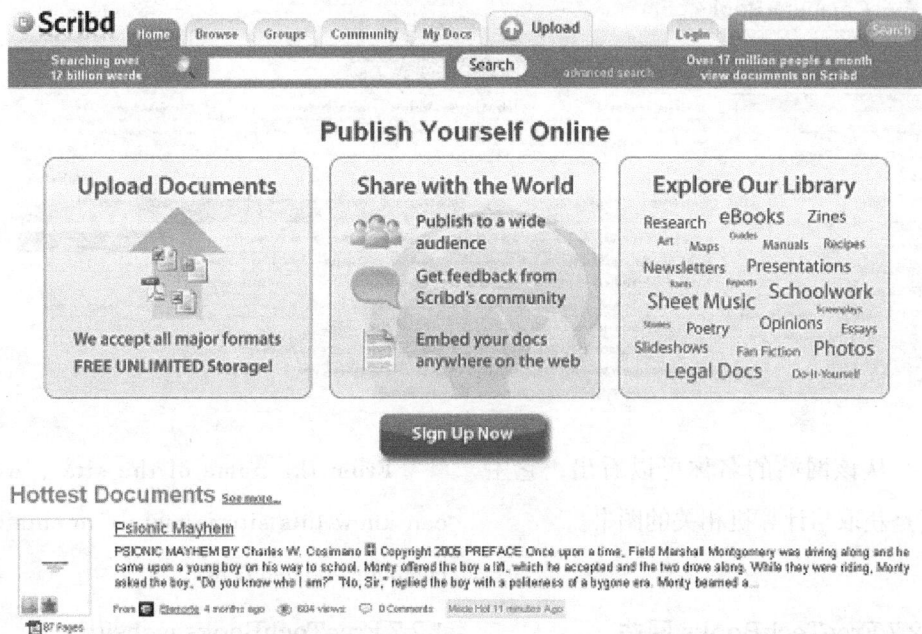

此网站提供关于办公格式方面的电子图书，包括 word、Excel，PowerPoint，PDF 和目前流行的格式，用户可以去下载需要的格式。

This site provides electronic books on the office format, including word, Excel, PowerPoint, PDF and other current formats, you can download the format you need.

1.2.9 KnowFree 网站

1.2.9 KnowFree website

KnowFree 不仅提供电子图书，而且还提供视频教程，全部资源免费下载，同时也提供生活知识。

KnowFree not only provides electronic books, but also provides video tutorials. All resourses are free to be downloaded, and it also provide you with life knowledge.

Securing Windows Server 2008: Prevent Attacks from Outside and Inside Your Organization

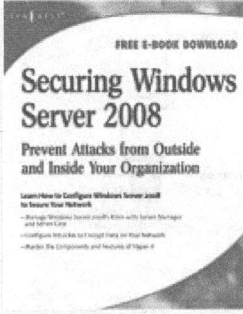

Microsoft hails the latest version of its flagship server operating system, Windows Server 2008, as "the most secure Windows Server ever". However, to fully achieve this lofty status, system administrators and security professionals must install, configure, monitor, log, and troubleshoot a dizzying array of new features and tools designed to keep the bad guys out and maintain the integrity of their network servers. This is no small task considering the market saturation of Windows Server and the rate at which it is attacked by malicious hackers. According to IDC, Windows Server runs 38% of all network servers. This market prominence also places Windows Server at the top of the SANS top 20 Security Attack Targets.

1.2.10 Onlinefreeebooks 网站

此网站提供的电子书种类较多，包括自动化、商业、工程、小设备、硬件、医疗保健、业余爱好、规划设计、科技、体育、艺术等方面的书籍。

1.2.10 Onlinefreeebooks website

This site offers a wide variety of e-books, including automation, business, engineering, small equipment, hardware, health care, hobbies, planning and design, science and technology, sports, arts and so on.

1.2.11 OnlineComputerBooks 网站　　1.2.11 OnlineComputerBooks website

　　此网站提供免费的计算机电子书，涉及技术、应用服务、网络、商业、市场营销、数学、物理等科学书籍。

　　This site gives us free computer electronic books, involving technology, application services, network, business, marketing, mathematics, physics, and so on science books.

1.2.12 BookYards 网站　　1.2.12 BookYards website

此网站涉及教育信息、信息、上网等方面的电子书。

This site involves e-books about educational information、information、internet access, etc.

1.2.13　AskSam Ebooks 网站

1.2.13 AskSam Ebooks website

该网站提供莎士比亚作品电子书，也包括各种法律等。

This site provides e-books of Shakespeare works, also includes a variety of laws and so on.

1.2.14　Baen Free Library 网站

1.2.14　Baen Free Library website

这是一个小说类电子图书的网站，其中包含科幻小说等。

It is a novel class of electronic books site, which includes science fiction.

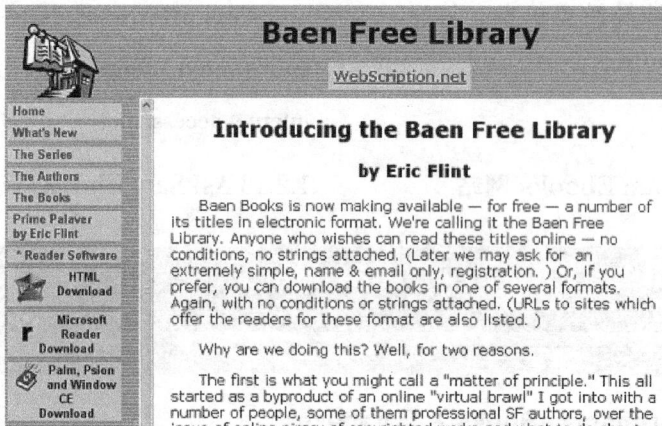

1.2.15 eBookLobby 网站

此网站的电子书种类包括商业、计算机、教育等。

1.2.15 eBookLobby website

The ebooks on this site include business, computer, education, etc.

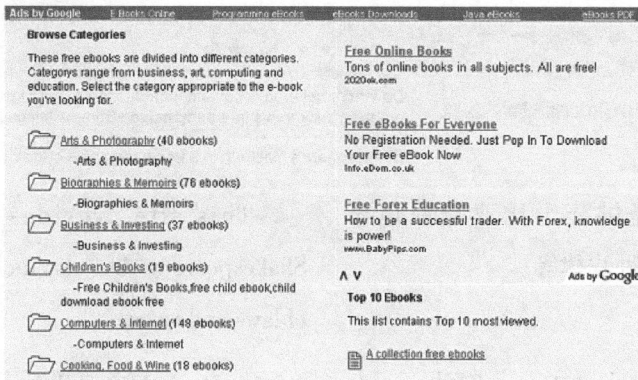

1.3 购买电子图书网站

1.3 E-books Purchasing Website

1.3.1 淘宝网（taobao network）http://re.taobao.com

淘宝网是中国最大的网购平台，是亚洲第一大购物网站。

Taobao.com is the largest online shopping platform in China, and also is the largest shopping website in Asia.

1.3.2 苏宁易购（suning network）http://list.suning.com/

苏宁易购是苏宁云商网上商城，是领先的综合网上购物商城。

Suning.com is the online mall of Suning cloud business, it is a leading integrated online shopping mall.

1.3.3 亚马逊（Amazon）Amazon.cn

亚马逊是综合网购商城，是全球最大的网上书店。

Amazon is a comprehensive online shopping mall, and it is the largest online bookstore all over the world.

1.4 医学类外文电子图书

1.4 Medical Foreign E-books

1.4.1 基础医学电子图书

1.4.1 E-books of basical medicine

分子克隆—实验室手册（第 3 版）（1）	Molecular Cloning–A Laboratory Manual 3rd (1).djvu
分子克隆—实验室手册（第 3 版）（2）	Molecular Cloning–A Laboratory Manual 3rd (2).djvu
分子克隆—实验室手册（第 3 版）（3）	Molecular Cloning–A Laboratory Manual 3rd (3).djvu
生理学彩色图谱（第 6 版）	Color Atlas of Physiology 6th.pdf
遗传学彩色图谱	Color Atlas of Genetics.pdf
格氏解剖学（第 39 版）	Gray's Anatomy 39th.chm

疾病的病理生理学（第 3 版）	Pathophysiology of Disease 6th.chm
生理学图谱	Atlas of Physiology.pdf
功能解剖学	Functional Anatomy.pdf
神经病学局部诊断	Duus Topical Diagnosis in Neurology.pdf
袖珍人体解剖学图谱	Pocket Atlas of Human Anatomy.pdf
医学免疫学（第 5 版）	Medical Immunology Fifth Edition.pdf
病理学彩色图谱	Color Atlas of Pathology.pdf
基础病理学（第 8 版）	Robbins Basic Pathology 8th.chm
神经解剖学和神经生理学图谱（特种版本）	Atlas of Neuroanatomy and Neuro-physiology (Special Edition). pdf
强磁场脑 MRI	High field brain MRI.pdf
MRI 完全版	MRI From A to Z.pdf
人类大脑和脊髓的图谱（第 2 版）	Atlas of the Human Brain and Spinal Cord 2nd.chm
简单病理学（第 3 版）	Concise Pathology 3rd.chm
质谱和基因组分析	Mass Spectrometry and Genomic Analysis.pdf
膜蛋白结构测定方法和实验指南	Membrane Protein Structure Determination–Methods and Protocols.pdf
非洲爪蟾和斑马鱼发育生物学分子方法（分子生物学方法）	Molecular Methods in Developmental Biology Xenopus & Zebrafish (Methods in Molecular Biology). pdf
PCR 技术的应用	PCR Applications.pdf
自身免疫性神经系统疾病	Autoimmune Neurological Disease.pdf
细胞因子与自身免疫性疾病	Cytokines and Autoimmune Diseases.pdf

实用免疫学（第4版）	Practical Immunology 4th.pdf
中枢神经系统中神经保护的分子和细胞生物学	Molecular and Cellular Biology of Neuroprotection in the CNS
学生用解剖学	Gray's Anatomy for Students.chm
细胞学、组织学和显微解剖学彩色图谱（第4版）	Color Atlas of Cytology, Histology and Microscopic Anatomy 4th.pdf
骨和软组织病理学	Bone and Soft Tissue Patholgy.pdf
骨免疫学	Osteoimmunology.pdf
医学与生物学中级物理	Intermediate Physics for Medicine and Biology.pdf
激光组织相互作用原理与应用（第3版）	Laser–Tissue Interactions Fundamentals and Applications 3rd.pdf
生物物理中的基本概念	Fundamental Concepts in Biophysics.pdf
非蛋白编码RNA	Non–Protein Coding RNAs.pdf
荧光光谱原理（第3版）	Principles of Fluorescence.Spectroscopy 3rd.pdf
脂蛋白的相互作用	Protein–Lipid Interactions.pdf
单分子和纳米技术	Single Molecules and Nanotechnology.pdf
生物物理学	Biophysics.djvu
微生物与免疫学世界 I	World of Microbiology and Immunology I.pdf
微生物与免疫学世界 II	World of Microbiology and Immunology II.pdf

解剖学和生理学基础　　　　　　　　Delmar's Fundamentals of Anatomy and Physiology.pdf

脊柱、脊髓和 ANS 的基础和临床解剖学　　Basic and Clinical Anatomy of Spine, Spinal Cord and ANS.pdf

解剖与生理学原理（第 12 版）　　　　Principles of Anatomy and Physiology 12th.pdf

免疫学（第 11 版）　　　　　　　　Kuby Immunology 11th.pdf

LWW 解剖学图谱　　　　　　　　　Lippincott Williams & Wilkins Atlas of Anatomy 1st.chm

基础解剖学　　　　　　　　　　　　Fundamental Anatomy 1st.chm

解剖学速学　　　　　　　　　　　　Quick Study Anatomy.pdf

临床解剖基础（第 4 版）　　　　　　Essential Clinical Anatomy 4th.pdf

骨科图谱　　　　　　　　　　　　　Osteopathic Atlas 1st.pdf

腰椎、骶骨临床解剖　　　　　　　　Clinical Anatomy of the Lumbar Spine and Sacrum.pdf

临床解剖学（第 6 版）　　　　　　　Clinical Oriented Anatomy 6th.chm

颈椎　　　　　　　　　　　　　　　The Cervical Spine.chm

基础医学术语速学　　　　　　　　　QuickStudy–Medical Terminology Basics.pdf

人体医学术语速学　　　　　　　　　QuickStudy–Medical Terminology The Body.pdf

中枢神经系统冰冻切片文库　　　　　Frozen Section Library–Central Nervous System.pdf

组织学教材及图谱（第 4 版）　　　　Histology–A Text and Atlas 4th.pdf

脑干及小脑图谱	Duvernoy's Atlas of the Human Brain Stem and Cerebellum.pdf
组织学基础（第 12 版）	Junqueira's Basic Histology 12th.chm
人类解剖学	Human Anatomy.pdf
临床影像鉴别诊断图谱（第 5 版）	Clinical Imaging An Atlas of Differential Diagnosis 5th.chm
解剖照片抽认卡	Rohen's Photographic Anatomy Flash Cards 1st.chm
医学术语指南	Medical Terminology An Illustrated Guide by Barbara J. Cohen.djvu
解剖病理学彩色图谱（第 3 版）	Colour Atlas of Anatomical Pathology 3rd.pdf
格氏解剖学（第 40 版）	Gray's Anatomy 40th.chm
彩色解剖学图谱（第 7 版）	Color Atlas of Anatomy 7th.pdf
临床骨科检查（第 5 版）	Clinical Orthopaedic Examination 5th.pdf
牛津临床医学手册（第 7 版）	Oxford Handbook of Clinical Medicine 7th.chm
牛津临床诊断手册	Oxford Handbook of Clinical Diagnosis 1st.chm
牛津临床检验及实践技能手册	Oxford Handbook of Clinical Examination and Practical Skills 1st.chm
牛津临床专业手册（第 7 版）	Oxford Handbook of Clinical Specialties 7th.chm

牛津临床手术手册（第 3 版）	Oxford Handbook of Clinical Surgery 3rd. chm
临床医生医学论文写作指导	The Clinician's Guide to Medical Writing.pdf
奈特骨科学	Netter's Orthopaedics.chm
脊柱推拿	Manipulation of The Spine.djvu
脊髓损伤（第 2 版）	Spinal cord injury 2th.pdf
颈椎和胸椎的机械方法诊断和治疗（第 1 卷）	The Cervical & Thoracic Spine Mechanical Diagnosis & Therapy–Vol 1.pdf
颈椎和胸椎的机械方法诊断和治疗（第 2 卷）	The Cervical & Thoracic Spine Mechanical Diagnosis & Therapy– Vol 2.pdf
腰椎的机械方法诊断和治疗（第 1 卷）	The Lumbar Spine– Mechanical Diagnosis and Therapy Vol 1.pdf
腰椎的机械方法诊断和治疗（第 2 卷）	The Lumbar Spine– Mechanical Diagnosis and Therapy Vol 2.pdf
脊髓损伤后的自主神经功能障碍	Autonomic Dysfunction After Spinal Cord Injury.pdf
临床医学类	Contents of Clinical Medicine
糖尿病的干细胞治疗	Stem Cell Therapy for Diabetes.pdf
临床骨科检验（第 5 版）	Clinical Orthopaedic Examination 5th. pdf
急救学基础	Essentials Emerg Medicine.chm
心电图学	Electrocardiography.chm
利平科特护理实践手册（第 8 版）	Lippincott Manual of Nursing Practice 8th.chm

牛津美国临床诊断手册（第 8 版）	Oxford American Handbook of Clinical Diagnosis 8th.pdf
慢性病及残疾的医学及社会心理学	Medical and Psychosocial Aspects of Chronic Illness and Disability.pdf
个性化医疗教材	Textbook of Personalized Medicine.pdf
贝茨身体检查及病史指南	Bates' guide to physical examination and history taking.chm
你永远需要的心电图手册（第 5 版）	The Only EKG Book You'll Ever Need 5th.chm
卡普兰临床高血压（第 10 版）	Kaplan's Clinical Hypertension 10th.chm
核磁共振成像实践（第 2 版）	MRI in Practice 2nd.pdf
实用临床计	Clinical Calculations Made Easy.chm
电子病历——初级保健实用指南	Electronic Medical Records—A Practical Guide for Primary Care.pdf
护理常规	Nursing Care Procedures.pdf
按摩	Reflexology.pdf
马里奥特实用心电图学	Marriott's Practical Electrocardiography.pdf

1.4.2 内科电子图书

1.4.2 Contents of inernal medicine e-books

| 哈里森实用内科学（第 16 版） | Harrison's Principles of Internal Medicine 16th.pdf |

希氏内科学（第 23 版）	Cecil Medicine 23rd.chm
哈里森实用内科学（第 17 版）	Harrison's Principles of Internal Medicine 17th.chm
盖尔医学百科（第 3 版）	The Gale Encyclopedia of Medicine 3rd. pdf
心血管疾病流行与预防的全球挑战（第 2 版）	Epidemiology and Prevention of Cardiovascular Diseases a Global Challenge 2nd.pdf
实用心脏病学	Practical Cardiology.chm
高血压和中风的病理生理学和管理	Hypertension ans Stroke-Pathophysiology and Management.pdf
哈里森心血管医学	Harrison's Cardiovascular Medicine.pdf
哈里森内分泌学（第 2 版）	Harrison's Endocrinology 2nd.pdf
哈里森胃肠病学与肝病学	Harrison's Gastroenterology and Hepatology.pdf
哈里森血液学与肿瘤学	Harrison's Hematology and Oncology. pdf
哈里森传染病学	Harrison's Infectious Diseases.pdf
哈里森肾脏学与酸碱紊乱	Harrison's Nephrology and Acid-Base Disorders.pdf
哈里森临床神经学（第 2 版）	Harrison's Neurology in Clinical Medicine 2nd.pdf
哈里森肺及重症监护学	Harrison's Pulmonary and Critical Care Medicine.pdf
哈里森风湿病学（第 2 版）	Harrison's Rheumatology 2nd.pdf

1.4.3 神经科电子图书

脑部检查新技术

系统神经学中的 23 个问题

神经解剖学临床实例

神经学诊断标准

弗兰特 H. 奈特神经解剖学和神经生理学图谱

脑损伤学

亚当斯和维克托神经学原理（第 8 版）

失语及其治疗

临床神经生理学（第 2 版）

急性缺血性卒中的影像与介入（第2版）

神经内科与临床神经学

神经科学——脑的探索（第 3 版）

神经内科彩色图谱（第 2 版）

神经传导研究手册（第 2 版）

神经科学学科数学

1.4.3 Contents of neurology e-book

New Techniques for Examining the Brain.pdf

23 Problems in Systerms Neuroscience.pdf

Neuroanatomy Through Clinical Cases.pdf

Diagnostic Criteria In Neurology.pdf

Atlas of Neuroanatomy and Neurophy-siology–Frank H. Netter.pdf

Brain Injury Medicine.pdf

Adams & Victor's Principles of Neurology 8th.chm

Aphasia and Its Therapy 1st.chm

Clinical Neurophysiology 2nd.pdf

Acute Ischemic Stroke Imaging and Intervention 2nd.pdf

Neurology and clinical neuroscience.pdf

Neuroscience—Exploring the Brain 3rd.pdf

Color Atlas of Neurology 2nd.pdf

Manual of Nerve Conduction Studies 2nd.pdf

Mathematics for Neuroscientists.pdf

神经反射与调节，技术与应用	Neurofeedback and Neuromodulation Techniques and Applications.pdf
神经内科——皇后广场教科书	Neurology—A Queen Square Textbook.pdf
神经系统中氯化物转运体和通道的生理学与病理学	Physiology and Pathology of Chloride Transporters and Channels in the Nervous System.pdf
肌肉骨骼检查特殊试验	Special Tests in Musculoskeletal Examination.pdf
临床神经解剖学（第 7 版）	Clinical Neuroanatomy 7th.chm
迪韦努瓦脑干小脑图谱	Duvernoy's Atlas of the Human Brain Stem and Cerebellum.pdf
神经系统自身免疫性疾病	Autoimmune neurological disease.pdf
吉兰—巴雷综合征	Guillain–Barré Syndrome.pdf
实验神经科学中的生物医学成像	Biomedical Imaging in Experimental Neuroscience.pdf
阿尔茨海默病	Alzheimer's Disease.pdf
神经学基础	Essential Neuroscience.chm
临床神经学教科书（第 3 版）	Textbook of Clinical Neurology 3rd.chm
神经病学与临床神经学	Neurology and Clinical Neuroscience.pdf
神经系统（第 2 版）	The Human Nervous System 2nd.pdf
癫痫中的神经信息学	Computational Neuroscience in Epilepsy.pdf

脑老化和神经退行性病变中的星形胶质细胞	Astrocytes in Brain Aging and Neurodegeneration.pdf
实验神经科学中的生物医学成像	Biomedical Imaging in Experimental Neuroscience; Nick van Bruggen, Timothy Roberts (CRC, 2003). pdf
大脑的事实——大脑和神经系统入门	Brain Facts—A Primer on the Brain and Nervous System (The Society for Neuroscience).pdf
意识与医学	Brain Mind and Medicine.pdf
大脑视觉记忆	Brain Vision Memory. pdf
神经学研究中的细胞和分子方法	Cellular and Molecular Methods in Neuroscience Research; Adalberto Merighi, Giorgio Carmignoto (Springer, 2002). pdf
神经学临床试验	Clinical Trials in the Neurosciences.pdf
神经系统学，神经解剖学，神经病理学彩色图谱 2000	Color Atlas of Neuroscience Neuroanatomy and Neurophysiology 2000.pdf
神经信息学——一个全面的方法	Computational Neuroscience—A Comprehensive Approach; Jianfeng Feng Chapman & Hall, 2004). pdf
脑功能活体光学成像	*In Vivo* Optical Imaging of Brain Function 1st.pdf
脑功能活体光学成像（第 2 版）	*In Vivo* Optical Imaging of Brain Function 2nd.pdf
大鼠脑卒中模型手册	Manual of Stroke Models in Rats.pdf
脑缺血新概念	New Concepts in Cerebral Ischemia.pdf

发展精神病理学（第2版）	Developmental Psychopathology, 2nd – Volume Two – Developmental Neuroscience; D. Cicchetti, D. Cohen (Wiley, 2006).pdf
神经科学中的动力系统——兴奋性突的几何形状	Dynamical Systems in Neuroscience—The Geometry of Excitability and Bursting; Eugene M. Izhikevich (MIT Press, 2007).pdf
进化认知神经科学	Evolutionary Cognitive Neuroscience; Steven M. Platek, Julian Paul Keenan, Todd K. Shackelford (MIT Press, 2007).pdf
临床神经病理学——教材及彩色图谱	Clinical Neuropathology—text and color atlas.pdf
从计算机到大脑——神经信息学基础	From Computer to Brain—Foundations of Computational Neuroscience; William W. Lytton (Springer, 2002).pdf
从分子到网络——细胞与分子神经科学导论	From Molecules to Networks—An Introduction to Cellular and Molecular Neuroscience – John H. Byrne, James L. Roberts (Elsevier, 2004).pdf
从神经科学到神经病学——神经科学、分子医学和神经病学的治疗转变	From Neuroscience to Neurology—Neuroscience, Molecular Medicine, and the Therapeutic Transformation of Neurology; Stephen Waxman (Elsevier, 2005).pdf

功能与功能失调性行为：神经科学与比较心理学的综合	Functional and Dysfunctional Sexual Behavior–A Synthesis of Neuroscience and Comparative Psychology; Anders Agmo (Academic PRess, 2007).pdf
发展认知神经科学手册	Handbook of Developmental Cognitive Neuroscience; Charles A. Nelson, Monica Luciana (MIT Press, 2001).pdf
生物医学非线性光学显微镜手册	Handbook of Biomedical Nonlinea Optical Microscopy.pdf
神经化学与分子神经生物学神经信号机制手册	Handbook of Neurochemistry and Molecular Neurobiology Neural Signaling Mechanisms.pdf
神经病理检查	Neuropathology Review.pdf
钾通道：机制与治疗方案	Potassium Channels: Methods And Protocols.pdf
综合神经学	Integrative Neuroscience.pdf
基因组学方法	Methods in Genomic Neuroscience; Hemin R. Chin, Steven O. Moldin (CRC, 2001).pdf
神经科学中的行为分析法	Methods of Behavior Analysis in Neuroscience; Jerry J. Buccafusco (CRC, 2001).pdf
敞开心灵	Mind Wide Open.pdf
脑的两个半球	The Two Halves of the Brain.pdf
神经分析	Neuro Analysis.pdf

认知神经学的神经生物学基础	Neurological Foundations of Cognitive Neuroscience; Mark D'Esposito (MIT, 2003).pdf
神经学：考前自测与复习（第 6 版）	Neuroscience – PreTest Self–Assessment and Review, Sixth Edition; Allan Siegel (McGraw–Hill, 2007).pdf
浅谈神经科学	Neuroscience at a Glance; Roger A. Barker, Stephen Barasi (Blackwell, 1999).pdf
神经科学学家	Neuroscience for Neurologists; Patrick F. Chinnery (Imperial College Press, 2006).pdf
精神活性物质的使用和依赖及神经科学	Neuroscience of Psychoactive Substance Use and Dependence (World Health Organization, 2004).pdf
神经科学（第 3 版）	Neuroscience, Third Edition; Purves, Augustine, Fitzpatrick, Hall, Lamantia, McNamara, Williams (Sinauer, 2004).pdf
神经科学与心理学	Neuroscience and Philosophy.pdf
脑神经科学	Neuroscience Science of the Brain.pdf
脑风景	Brain Landscape.pdf
创立现代神经科学革命性的 50 年代	Creating Modern Neuroscience the Revolutionary 1950s.pdf
神经学基础	Essential Neuroscience.chm
神经体征词典（第 3 版）	A Dictionary of Neurological Signs 3rd.pdf

中枢神经系统再生——基础与临床进展（第2版）	CNS Regeneration—Basic Science and Clinical Advances 2nd.pdf
脑活动手册	Handbook of Brain Activity.pdf
自由意志和意识——他们如何工作	Free Will and Consciousness—How Might They Work.pdf
脑中的离子	Ions in the Brain.pdf
脑与社会意识中的自控	Self Control in Society Mind and Brain.pdf
脑科学的未来	The Future of the Brain.pdf
脑的突触组织（第5版）	The Synaptic Organization of the Brain 5th.pdf
神经科学原理	Principles of Neural Science.pdf
神经科学下的精神病学	Psychiatry as a Neuroscience; Juan Jose Lopez-Ibor, Wolfgang Gaebel, Mario Maj, Norman Sartorius (Wiley, 2002).pdf
精神分析与神经科学	Psychoanalysis and Neuroscience; Mauro Mancia (Springer, 2006).pdf
浦肯野视觉研究	Purkinje's Vision.pdf
奇点已近	The Singularity is Near.pdf
先进神经模型	Spiking Neuron Models.pdf
高等生物物理技术	Advanced Techniques in Biophysics.pdf
阿尔茨海默病与帕金森病研究进展	Advances in Alzheimer's and Parkinson's Disease.pdf
焦虑症中的神经科学及其治疗	Behavioral Neurobiology of Anxiety and Its Treatment.pdf

跨膜信号传导中的生物物理层　　　　　Biophysical Aspects of Transmembrane Signaling.pdf

脑缺氧与缺血　　　　　　　　　　　Brain Hypoxia and Ischemia.pdf

脑－机接口　　　　　　　　　　　　Brain–Computer Interfaces.pdf

神经信息学　　　　　　　　　　　　Computational Neuroscience.pdf

脑的协调活动　　　　　　　　　　　Coordinated Activity in the Brain.pdf

阿尔茨海默病的研究成果与当前的假说　Current Hypotheses and Research Milestones in Alzheimer's Disease.pdf

动态脑成像　　　　　　　　　　　　Dynamic Brain Imaging.pdf

神经科学百科全书　　　　　　　　　Encyclopedia of Neuroscience.pdf

兴奋性毒性的神经化学层次　　　　　Neurochemical Aspects of Excitotoxicity.pdf

神经干细胞　　　　　　　　　　　　Neural Stem Cells.pdf

神经解剖学研究者指导　　　　　　　Neuroanatomy for the Neuroscientist.pdf

神经科学：数学入门　　　　　　　　Neuroscience: A Mathematical Primer.pdf

离子通道传感　　　　　　　　　　　Sensing with Ion Channels.pdf

神经中央处理器——生物神经网络的集成接口　The NeuroProcessor An Integrated Interface to Biological Neural Networks.pdf

认知神经科学全景　　　　　　　　　Perspectives from Cognitive Neuroscience; Lynn C. Robertson, Noam Sagiv (Oxford University Press, 2005).pdf

新的认知神经科学（第2版）　　　　　The New Cognitive Neurosciences, Second Edition; Michael S. Gazzaniga (MIT, 2000).pdf

平行脑-胼胝体认知神经科学	The Parallel Brain – The Cognitive Neuroscience of the Corpus Callosum; Eran Zaidel, Marco Iacoboni (MIT, 2003).pdf
视觉神经科学卷（第 1 卷、第 2 卷）	The Visual Neurosciences, Volumes 1 & 2; Leo M. Chalupa, John S. Werner (MIT, 2004).pdf
血脑屏障	The Blood Brain Barrier.pdf
脑理论与神经网络手册	The Handbook of Brain Theory and Neural Networks.pdf
缺血半影区	The Ischemic Penumbra.pdf
杜丝神经局部诊断	Duus Topical Diagnosis in Neurology.pdf
人脑地图的基本问题	Foundational Issues in Human Brain Mapping.pdf
意识的认识神经科学	The Cognitive Neuroscience of Mind.pdf
神经科学理论	Theoretical Neuroscience.pdf
脑的替换零件	Toward Replacement Parts for the Brain.pdf
感官：综合的参考	The Senses: A Comprehensive Reference.pdf
同情的社会神经科学原理	The Social Neuroscience of Empathy.pdf
理解的意识（第 2 版）	Understanding Consciousness 2nd.pdf
理解和模拟大脑功能需要的计算	What Should be Computed to Understand and Model Brain Function.pdf
生化系统信息处理	Information Processing By Biochemical Systems.pdf

记忆与计算脑	Memory and the Computational Brain.pdf
光学成像和光谱学	Optical Imaging and Spectroscopy.pdf
光学（第4版）	Optics 4th.djvu
认识神经科学发展进展（第3版）	Developmental Cognitive Neuroscience 3rd.pdf
麦卡尔平多重硬化症（第4版）	McAlpine's Multiple Sclerosis 4th.pdf

1.4.4 康复医学类

1.4.4 Contents of rehabilitation medicine

腰椎力学诊断与治疗（第2卷）	The Lumbar Spine–Mechanical Diagnosis and Therapy Vol 2.pdf
疼痛治疗的植入疗法图谱	Atlas of Implantable Therapies for Pain Management.pdf
肌肉骨骼检查中的特殊试验——临床医生循证指南	Special tests in Musculoskeletal Examination—an evidenced based guide for clinicians.pdf
七步除痛（如何使用麦肯锡方法快速缓解背部和颈部疼痛）	7 Steps to a Pain Free Life (How to Rapidly Relieve Back & Neck Pain Using the Mackenzie Method) by Robin McKenzie.pdf
人体四肢机械诊断与治疗	The Human Extremities–Mechanical Diagnosis and Therapy.pdf
颈椎与胸椎机械诊断与治疗（第1卷）	The Cervical & Thoracic Spine Mechanical Diagnosis & Therapy Vol 1.pdf
颈椎与胸椎机械诊断与治疗（第2卷）	The Cervical & Thoracic Spine Mechanical Diagnosis & Therapy Vol 2.pdf

腰椎——机械诊断与治疗（第1卷）	The Lumbar Spine—Mechanical Diagnosis and Therapy Vol 1.pdf
腰椎——机械诊断与治疗（第2卷）	The Lumbar Spine—Mechanical Diagnosis and Therapy Vol 2.pdf
脊髓损伤后自主神经功能障碍	Autonomic Dysfunction after Spinal Cord Injury.pdf
颈椎综合征的保守治疗	Conservative Management of Cervical Spine Syndromes.pdf
肌肉骨骼康复的病理与干预	Pathology and Intervention in Musculoskeletal Rehabilitation.pdf
急性脑卒中护理（第2版）	Acute Stroke Care 2nd.pdf
疼痛管理手册（第2版）	Handbook of Pain Management.pdf
骨质疏松症	Osteoporosis.pdf
疼痛学教材（第5版）	Text Book of Pain 5th.pdf
背部疼痛革命（第2版）	The Back Pain Revolution 2nd.pdf
脊柱推拿	Manipulation of The Spine.djvu
循证物理疗法	Practical Evidence–Based Physiotherapy.pdf
临床基础推拿手册	Handbook of Basic Clinical Manipulation.pdf
疼痛医学麦格劳希尔委员会评论	McGraw–Hill Specialty Board Review Pain Medicine.pdf
脑卒中康复	Stroke Rehabilitation.pdf
肌肉疼痛	Muscle Pain.pdf
卒中后的脑修复	Brain Repair After Stroke.pdf
物理治疗与康复委员会评论	Physical Medicine and Rehabilitation Board Review.pdf

神经心理康复——理论与实践　　　　Neuropsychological Rehabilitation—
　　　　　　　　　　　　　　　　Theory & Practice.pdf

脑性瘫痪物理治疗 2007　　　　　　Physical Therapy Of Cerebral Palsy
　　　　　　　　　　　　　　　　2007.pdf

理疗先进新技术 2007　　　　　　　Recent Advances in Physiotherapy 2007.
　　　　　　　　　　　　　　　　pdf

脑性瘫痪　　　　　　　　　　　　Cerebral Palsy.pdf

运动治疗——基础与技巧（第 5 版）　Therapeutic Exercise—Foundations And
　　　　　　　　　　　　　　　　Techniques 5th.pdf

本体感神经肌肉易化法实践（第 3 版）　PNF In Practice 3rd.pdf

筛查要点　　　　　　　　　　　　Screening Notes.pdf

康复中的疼痛管理　　　　　　　　Pain Management In Rehabilitation.pdf

健身——力量训练解剖（第 2 版）　Bodybuilding—Strength Training
　　　　　　　　　　　　　　　　Anatomy 2nd.pdf

威德拉 - 斯帕克曼职业治疗法（第 11　Willard & Spackan's
版）　　　　　　　　　　　　　　Occupational Therapy 11th.chm

物理医学与康复要点（第 2 版）　　Essentials Of Physical Medicine &
　　　　　　　　　　　　　　　　Rehabilitation 2nd.chm

运动损伤手册（第 2 版）　　　　　Bull's Sports Injuries Handbook 2nd.
　　　　　　　　　　　　　　　　chm

物理医学与康复原理与实践（第 4 版）　Physical Medicine & Rehabilitation
　　　　　　　　　　　　　　　　Principles & Practice 4th.chm

基础物理医学与康复　　　　　　　Essential Physical Medicine and
　　　　　　　　　　　　　　　　Rehabilitation.pdf

卡拉脑卒中康复先进技术　　　　　Kalra Recent Advances in Stroke
　　　　　　　　　　　　　　　　rehabilitation.pdf

康复影像　　　　　　　　　　　　Imaging in Rehabilitation.pdf

心脏康复	Cardiac Rehabilitation.pdf
神经内科社区康复	Community Rehabilitation in Neurology.pdf
物理康复中的职业治疗依据	Occupational Therapy Evidence in Practice for Physical Rehabilitation.pdf
脑卒中	Caplan's Stroke.pdf
肌肉不平衡的评估与治疗	Assessment and Treatment of Muscle Imbalance.pdf
运动锻炼功能解剖	Functional Anatomy for Sport and Exercise.pdf
伸展解剖学	Stretching Anatomy.pdf
美国运动医学会认证评论（第3版）	ACSM Certification Review 3rd.pdf
美国运动医学会运动测试与运动处方指南（第8版）	ACSM's Guidelines for Exercise Testing and Prescription 8th.pdf
体育与运动科学训练生理学进展	The Physiology of Training Advances in Sport and Exercise Science series.pdf
残疾与康复展望	Perspectives on Disability and Rehabilitation.pdf
脊髓损伤（第2版）	Spinal cord injury 2nd.pdf
关节松动手法（第1卷）	Manual Mobilization of the Joints Vol I.pdf
关节松动手法（第2卷）	Manual Mobilization of the Joints Vol II.pdf
牛津美国运动医学手册	Oxford American Handbook of Sports Medicine.pdf
脊髓运动神经生物学	Motor of Neurobiology of the Spinal Cord.pdf

物理治疗实践专业知识（第 2 版）　　Expertise in Physical Therapy Practice 2nd.pdf

肌肉骨骼检查和关节注射技术　　Musculoskeletal Examination and Joint Injection Techniques.pdf

脊柱骨盆区康复超声影像　　Ultrasound Imaging for Rehabilitation of the Lumbopelvic Region.pdf

肌筋膜扳机点——病理生理学和证据信息的诊断与管理　　Myofascial Trigger Points—Pathophysiology and Evidence—Informed Diagnosis & Management.pdf

物理治疗师的慢性疼痛管理（第 2 版）　　Chronic Pain Management for Physical Therapists 2nd.pdf

康复研究到实践的物理因素（第 2 版）　　Physical Agents in Rehabilitation–From Research to Practice 2nd.pdf

骨科物理治疗（第 4 版）　　Orthopeadic Physical Therapy 4th.pdf

骨科物理治疗（第 3 版）　　Orthopaedic Physical Therapy 3rd.pdf

周围神经手法治疗　　Manual Therapy for the Peripheral Nerves.pdf

膝关节活动度　　Knee's ROM.pdf

运动试验手册（第 3 版）　　Manual of Exercise Testing 3rd.pdf

骨科最新动态（第 4 版）　　Current Orthopedics 4th.chm

麻省总医院疼痛管理手册（第 3 版）　　Massachusetts General Hospital Handbook of Pain Management 3rd.chm

康复咨询手册　　Handbook of Rehabilitation Counseling.pdf

脑卒中恢复与康复　　Stroke Recovery and Rehabilitation.pdf

初级保健和运动医学医师的运动试验	Exercise Testing for Primary Care and Sports Medicine Physicians.pdf
职业治疗教育中的服务学习——哲学与实践	Service-Learning in Occupational Therapy Education—Philosophy and Practice.pdf
临床运动医学	Clinical Sports Medicine 1st.chm
老年人足部问题评估与管理	Foot Problems in Older People Assessment and Management.pdf
运动障碍的临床实践	Movement Disorders in Clinical Practice.pdf
颈部过度屈伸损伤、头痛和颈部疼痛的研究性物理疗法	Whiplash, Headache and Neck Pain-Research-based Directions for Physical Therapies.pdf
神经肌肉技术的临床应用（第1卷）——上身	Clinical Application of Neuromuscular Techniques Volume 1—The Upper Body .pdf
步态分析——介绍（第4卷）	Gait Analysis—An Introduction 4th.pdf
步态障碍——评估与管理	Gait Disorders—Evaluation and Management.pdf
物理原理解释	Physical Principles Explained.pdf
严重和复杂的神经功能残疾——身体状况的管理	Severe and Complex Neurological Disability—Management of the Physical Condition.pdf
疼痛分子机制	Molecular Pain.pdf
腰椎力学诊断与治疗（第1卷）	The Lumbar Spine-Mechanical Diagnosis and Therapy Vol 1.pdf

第二章　电子期刊
Chapter two　Electronic Periodicals

期刊是一种连续出版物，一般有固定的刊名，相对固定的版式、篇幅和内容范围，有连续的卷、期号或年、月顺序号，由多个作者的多篇文章组成。与图书相比，期刊的内容新颖，出版周期短，报道速度快，学科广泛，流通面广，信息量大，约占整个信息量的70%，是主要的情报信息源。期刊反映的多数是最新的科研成果。[①]

本章所列的期刊是医学领域的专业期刊，这些期刊影响因子都比较高，多数都是被 SCI 收录的期刊，或大型专业数据库和综合性数据库收录。本章按医学学科专业列举了一些医学专业电子期刊。

A journal is a kind of serials, which has the relatively fixed journal name, format, length and content.It has continuous volume,issue or year, month serial number, and consists of articles with multiple authors. Compared with the books, its contents of the journal are novel, the publishing cycle is short, the reporting speed is fast, the subject is extensive, the circulation is wide, the information is large, accounting for about 70% of the total amount of information. Most of the journals reflect the latest research results.

In this chapter,the journal listed are the professional journals in the field of medicine, the journals impact factors are higher,and the majority of journals indexed by SCI, or included by large professional database and comprehensive database. According to the specialty of medicine, this chapter lists some medical journals.

---

① 庄善洁等 . 现代信息资源检索与利用 [M]. 哈尔滨：哈尔滨工程大学出版社，2010：39

2.1 外科学电子期刊

2.1 Surgery E-Journal

2.1.1 肝、胰、胆：国际肝胰胆协会杂志

2.1.1 HPB

主编（editor）：Professor O. James Gaeden

2013IF（JCR 2014）:2.050

ISI JCR 学科排名（Discipline ranking）:

47/75（Gastroerology & Hepatology）;59/204（Surgery）

它刊登发表有关肝胆胰科学领域的临床调查及基础研究。外科学电子期刊包括原创论文、综述、小文章等板块，另外还有读者来信及对杂志内容的评价。

The journal published clinical investigation and basic research about Liver and Gallbladder pancreatic Science areas. It includes original papers, reviews, articles, etc. In addition, it also contains readers' letters and evaluation on the content of the journal.

2.1.2 国际创伤杂志

2.1.2 International wound journal

主编（editor）：Keith Harding,Douglas Queen

2013IF（JCR 2014）:2.023

ISI 学科排名（Discipline ranking）:

17/61（Dermatology）;66/202（Surgery）

它涵盖与伤口预防、处理和与皮肤状况相关的所有方面，为涉及伤口护理的所有专业提供重要的、相关的应用研究。本刊涉及外科、皮肤医学、肿瘤学、护理、放射疗法、物理疗法、职业疗法和脚病学领域中与伤

The journal covers all aspects of wound prevention and treatment as well as skin conditions. It provides an important, relevant application study for all professionals involved in wound care, This journal covers issues related to wound

口预防处理方面相关的文章。

management in surgery, dermatology, oncology, nursing, radiation therapy, physical therapy, occupational therapy and foot disease.

杂志包含的主题包括：慢性和急性创伤；组织损伤和修复；伤口预防和处理；伤口愈合疗法；疤痕预防和处理；外科手术伤口；皮肤状况诊断和处理；敷料——管理和治疗；糖尿病伤口；小腿溃疡；创伤病人护理；烧伤创面。

The topics included in the journal are: chronic and acute wounds, tissue injury and repair, wound prevention and treatment, wound healing therapy, scar prevention and treatment, surgical wound, diagnosis and treatment of skin condition, dressing—management and treatment, diabetic wound, ulcus cruris, trauma patient care, burn wound.

2.1.3 结肠直肠疾病

2.1.3 Colorectal disease

主编（editor）：R.J.Nicholls

2013IF（JCR2014）:2.017

ISI JCR 学科排名（Discipline ranking）:

49/74（Gastroenterology & Hepatology）; 67/202（Surgery）

它是刊载结肠直肠病理学原创研究的第一份期刊。本刊对胃肠病学家、外科医师、病理学家、肿瘤科医师和有关胃肠道疾病的其他卫生专家都十分具有吸引力。

It is the first journal of original research on colon and rectum pathobiology. It is very attractive to the gastroenterology, the surgeon, the pathologist, the oncologist, the gastrointestinal diseases; and other health professionals.

2.1.4 临床移植

2.1.4 Clinical transplantation

主编（editor）：Anthony Schapira

2013IF（JCR 2014）:1.486

ISI JCR 学科排名（Discipline ranking）：

18/26（Transplantation）,94/204（Surgery）

本刊为器官或组织移植相关医护人员提供一个沟通桥梁，器官或组织移植包括：肾、肠、肝、胰腺、心脏、心脏瓣膜、肺、骨髓、角膜、皮肤、骨胳。本刊还刊登以下内容的文章：免疫学和免疫抑制、患者准备、人造器官、器官和组织的防腐和贮藏。

This journal provides a communication bridge for medical staff on organ or tissue transplants. Organ or tissue transplants include kidney, intestine, liver, pancreas, heart, heart valve, lung, bone marrow, cornea, skin and bones. The journal also publishes the following area articles:immunology and immunosuppression, patient preparation, preservation and storage of artificial organs, preservation and storage of organs and tissues.

2.2 神经科学电子期刊

2.2 Neuroscience E–Journal

2.2.1 欧洲神经病学杂志

2.2.1 European journal of neurology

主编 :Anthony Schapira

20123IF（JCR 2014）:3.652

ISI JCR 学科排名：36/194（Clinical Neurology）；

79/252（Neurosciences）

它涵盖神经病学临床和基础研究的所有领域。它重点关注具有较大临床意义的疾病（痴呆、卒中、癫痫、头痛、多发性硬化、活动病症和传染病）。它为欧洲临床神经科学和医学实践活动提供了一个论坛，并帮助加强欧洲和世界各地研究工作者与临床医师之间的联系。除了原创论文，本期刊还经常刊载综述和更新论文、致编辑信、书评、报告和新闻。

The journal contains all areas of clinical and basic research in neurology. It focuses on the disease with greater clinical significance (dementia, apoplexy, epilepsy, headache, multiple sclerosis, active disorders and infectious diseases). It provides a forum for European clinical neuroscience and medical practice, and strengthen the connection between researchers and clinicians of Europe and all over the world. In addition to the original papers, the journal publishes review and update papers, letters to the editor, book reviews, reports and news.

2.2.2 神经胃肠病学与自动力

2.2.2 Neurogastroenterology and motility

主编：Gianrico Farrugia, Magnus Simren, Gary Mawe

2013IF（JCR 2014）:3.424

ISI JCR 学科排名：21/75（Gastroenterology & Hepatology）; 46/194（Clinical Neurology）; 99/252（Neurosciences）

它是欧洲神经胃肠病学与自动力协会（ENMS）、美国神经胃肠病学与自动协会（ANMS）和脑肠功能研究小组（BFG）的官方期刊。它出版的文章多为英文，并且都是一些在临床方面的原创性研究和（受聘专家）专题评审，研究内容包括：肠胃蠕动，控制肠胃蠕动的肌原机制、神经机制和化学机制，

The journal is the Official Journal of the European Society of Neurogastroenterology and Motility (ENMS), American Society of Neurogastroenterology and Motility (ANMS), Brain–gut Function Research Group (BFG). Most papers are in English. The Journal publishes original research articles and special review,

脑肠互动以及中枢神经系统，自主神经系统及肠神经系统在肠胃蠕动或者其他肠胃功能（包括吸收、分泌、血管收缩和免疫）的控制下相互作用。此外，期刊的内容还包括热点问题的（受聘专家）社论观点，重要专题研讨会的摘要，会议报道，欧洲神经胃肠病学与自动力协会（ENMS），美国神经胃肠病学与自动协会（ANMS）和脑肠功能研究小组（BFG）的通知。

its contents include: Gastrointestinal motility, the myogenic mechanism of gastrointestinal motility, the neural control of gastrointestinal motility mechanism and chemical mechanism, brain-gut interaction and central nervous system, autonomic nervous system and enteric nervous system in the gastrointestinal peristalsis or other gastrointestinal function (including absorption, secretion, vasoconstriction and immune) under the control of the interaction. The journal also includes hot issues (experts) editorial opinion, abstract of important Symposium, important seminar conference reports, the notice of ENMS, ANMS and BFG.

2.2.3 欧洲疼痛学杂志

2.2.3 European journal of pain

主编：Herman O.Handwerker, Erlangen,Germany

2013IF（JCR 2014）:3.218

ISI JCR 学科排名：6/29（Anesthesiology; 52/194（Clinical Neurology）;112/252（Neurosciences）

它是欧洲疼痛学联合会的官方杂志。这是一个多领域国际性期刊。它旨在成为全球疼痛调查研究管理的论坛。期刊发表和疼痛学有关的各方面基础知识以及临床学术论文，包括：牙科学、神经学、整形外科、麻醉

The journal is the official journal of the European Pain Science Federation. It is a multi-disciplinary and international journal.Its aim is to be a global forum on pain research and management. The journal publishes basic and clinical

学、药理学、姑息治疗、精神病学、生理学、心理学。

academic research papers related to pain, it includes dentistry, neurology, orthopedics, anesthesiology, pharmacilogy, palliativecare, psychiatry, physiology, psychology.

学术论文涉及的领域包括：神经生物学、神经学、实验药理学、临床药理学、心理学、行为治疗、流行病学、癌症痛苦、临床实验。

Areas covered by academic papers include neurobiology,neurology,experiment alpharmacology,clinicalpharmacology,psyc hology,behaviortherapy,epidemiology,canc er pain,clinical trials.

2.2.4 睡眠研究杂志

2.2.4 Journal of sleep research

主编 :Derk–Jan Dijk

2013IF（JCR 2014）:2.949

ISI JCR 学科排名：

62/194（Clinical Neurology）;126/252（Neurosciences）

它主要针对基础及临床睡眠研究，刊载睡眠研究各领域（包括生物节律）的原创性研究论文和特邀评论。该期刊的目标是增进来自各种不同研究背景和学科的基础研究及临床睡眠研究者之间的思想交流。该期刊刊载用多学科新方法解答睡眠问题的论文。

The journal is mainly for the basic and clinical sleeping research. It publishes original research papers and invites comments in the field of sleep (including biological rhythms). It's aim is to enhance the exchange of ideas coming from basic research on various research backgrounds and disciplines and between clinical sleep researchers. This journal publishes the papers that using a new multidisciplinary approach to solve sleep problems.

2.3 肿瘤学电子期刊

2.3 Oncology E-Journal

2.3.1 心理肿瘤学

2.3.1 Psycho-oncology

主编 :Jimmie C. Holland, Maggie Watson

2013IF（JCR 2014）:4.044

ISI JCR 学科排名 :

1/37（Social Sciences Biomedical;11/74（Psychology）;13/129（Psychology Multidisciplinary）;52/203（Oncology）

它主要涉及癌症的心理、社会、行为及道德方面的研究。该期刊主要讨论了癌症的两大心理因素：病人及其家属和护理人员在癌症疾病的各个阶段的心理反应；可能会造成病情恶化的心理、行为和社会因素。心理肿瘤学是一门涉及多学科的领域，与肿瘤学的主要研究方向存在界限，包括：临床学科（外科、内科、小儿科、放射科），流行病科，预防学科，内分泌科，生物学，病理学，生物伦理学，缓和治疗，康复医学，临床试验研究与决策，以及精神病学和心理学。

The journal is concerned with the cancer research of the psychological social behavioral and ethical aspects. It discusses two major psychological factors of cancer: psychological reactions of patients and their family members and caretakers in various stages of cancer, psychological, behavioral, and social factors that may influence the disease process. Psycho-oncology is a multidisciplinary field, which has boundaries with the major specialities in oncology: clinical disciplines (surgery medicine pediatrics radiotherapy), epidemiology, immunology, endocrinology, biology,pathology, bioethics, palliative care, rehabilitation medicine, clinical trials research and decision, psychiatry and psychology.

2.3.2 基因、染色体和癌

2.3.2 Genes, chromosomes and cancer

主编 :Felix Mitelman

2013IF（JCR 2014）:3.836

ISI JCR 学科排名 :

45/164（Genetics & Heredity）;57/202（Oncology）

它涵盖的领域包括：所有良性和恶性疾病中的染色体异常，包括肿瘤进展过程中发生的变化；由于基因组重排造成的基因结构变化和调控；染色体变更涉及与细胞增生与分化的调控有关的基因；基因组异常与细胞表型变化之间的关联性；染色体和 DNA 水平的变化在疾病预后及癌症治疗设计和监测中的预测价值；作为癌症罹患因素的遗传病症的细胞遗传学、分子和流行病学分析；外界因素导致的染色体和 / 或遗传损伤；用于基因组分析的新分子生物学和细胞遗传学方法的描述。

The journal involves the areas: chromosomal abnormalities in all benign and malignant diseases including changes in tumor progression, gene structure changes and regulation due to genome rearrangement, chromosomal alterations involving genes related to the regulation of cell proliferation and differentiation, association between genomic abnormalities and phenotypic changes. The predictive value of alterations at the chromosomal and DNA levels in disease prognosis and in designing and monitoring cancer therapies, cytogenetic, molecular, and epidemiological analyses of genetic disorders as factors of cancer, chromosome and / or genetic damage caused by external factors, description of new molecular and cytogenetic methods for genomic analysis.

2.3.3 癌症细胞病理学

2.3.3 Cancer cytopathology

主编 :Celeste N.Powers,MD,phD

2013IF（JCR 2014）:3.807

ISI JCR 学科排名：

15/76（Pathology）;58/203（Oncology）

它是美国癌症协会的期刊，专注于这些领域研究：分析细胞病理学、免疫细胞化学、细针抽吸术、分子诊断、妇科学细胞病理学。

It is a journal of American Cancer Society, which focus on the following areas: analysis of cell pathology; immunohistochemistry; fine needle aspiration FNA; molecular diagnostics; gynecology cell pathology.

2.3.4 癌科学

2.3.4 Cancer science

主编：Yusuke Nakamura

2013IF（JCR 2014）:3.534

ISI JCR 学科排名：34/204（Surgery）68/203（Oncology）

该刊是日本癌症协会的月刊,于1907年首次出版。该刊刊载原创论文、评论和致编辑的信,描述基础、转化和临床癌症研究领域中的原创研究。该期刊还接受报告和病例报告。

This is a monthly journal of the Japanese Cancer Association, which first was published in 1907. The journal publishes original articles, reviews, and editorial letters, describing original research in the fields of basic, translational and clinical cancer research. The journal also receives reports and case reports.

2.3.5 外科肿瘤学杂志

2.3.5 Journal of surgical oncology

主编 :tephone F.Sener,MD

2013IF（JCR 2014）:2.843

ISI JCR 学科排名：34/204（Surgery）;92/203（Oncology）

这是同行评审类月刊，刊载外科肿瘤学领域及其他相关外科科学方面经同行评审的原创性研究论文，包括与外科肿瘤学相关的实验报告和化验研究报告。除此之外，该期刊还包括"快速交流""近期热点话题深度评论"及"我该怎么做"（技术创新简报）等同行评论栏目。

This is a peer-reviewed monthly journal, which publishes original research papers in the field of surgical oncology and related surgical sciences. The papers include reports on experimental and laboratory studies related to surgical oncology. In this journal, there are also peer review column,such as rapid communications, in-depth reviews on topics of current interest, rief reports about technical innovations（"How I Do It"）.

2.4 胃肠病学和肝脏病学电子期刊

2.4 Gastroenterology and Hepatology E-Journal

2.4.1 螺旋菌

2.4.1 Helicobacter

主编（editor）: David Y Graham,Assistant Editor. Francis Megraud

2013IF（JCR 2014）:2.993

ISI JCR 学科排名（Discipline ranking）:27/74（Gastroenterology & Hepatology）;41/119（Microbiology）

Helicobacter 所指的螺旋菌是消化性溃疡、胃腺癌、原发性胃淋巴瘤内

Helicobacter refers to helicobater pyloripeptic in peptic ulcer, gastric

的幽门螺旋菌。新的幽门螺旋菌物种现在不断被发现，该刊涵盖了螺旋菌的整个领域，旨在增进下述学科间的交流：肠胃病学，微生物学，疫苗开发，实验动物学。同时，Helicobacter会公布在分子生物学和临床实验新发现的治疗方法为病人护理和治疗提供更大可能空间的结果。

adenocarcinoma, and primary gastric lymphoma. New species of Helicobacter pylori are now being discovered, the Journal contains the entire field of Helicobacter research, which in order to increase communication among the fields: gastroenterology; microbiology; vaccine development; laboratory animal science. At the same time, Helicobacter will announce the results of a new discovery in molecular biology and clinical trials that provide greater room for patient care and treatment.

2.4.2 病毒性肝炎杂志

2.4.2 Journal of viral hepattis

主编（editor）：Graham Foster,US Editor: Nezam Afdhal, European Editors;Peter Karayiannis, Mark Thursz

2013IF（JCR 2014）:3.307

ISI JCR 学科排名（Discipline ranking）：

14/32（Virology）；

21/70（Infectious Diseases）；

22/74（Gastroenterology & Hepatology）

此刊是刊载病毒性肝炎领域评论、原始文献（全文论文）和短篇快讯的月刊。此刊汇集了诸多重要话题，文章来源于病毒学家、流行病学家、临床医生、病理学家、输血医学专家。

The Journal publishes reviews, original documents (full papers) and short rapid communications in the area of viral hepatitis. It brings together many important issues, including articles from epidemiologists, clinicians, pathologists, virologists, specialists in transfusion medicine.

2.5 心脏和心血管系统电子期刊

2.5 Cardiac & Cardiovascular Systems E-Journal

2.5.1 美国心脏病协会期刊

2.5.1 Journal of the american heart association

主编：Joseph Vita,MD

2013IF（JCR 2014）:2.882

ISI JCR 学科排名 47/125（Cardiac & Cardiovascular System）

该刊是同行评审期刊，出版心脏病及中风方面的高标准研究论文，同时出版发行了在线阅读，该刊为心脏病及中风发表提供了一个国际论坛。同时它也刊登基础的和临床的学术论文及最新研究成果。作为一个开放获取杂志，其内容更新迅速，提供免费阅读，能够有效加速科学理论到实践的转变。

The journal is a peer-reviewed journal, and publishes cardiopathy and paralytic stroke papers, it also publishes online reading. It provides an international forum for the publication of cardiopathy and paralytic stroke. It also publishes basic and clinical academic papers and the latest research results. As an open access journal, its contents update quickly, it provides free reading, which can effectively accelerate the transformation of scientific theories into practice.

2.5.2 心血管电生理学杂志

2.5.2 Journal of cardiovascular electrophysiology

主编：Eric N. Prystowsky

2013 IF（JCR 2014）:3.234

ISI JCRip tu rdjd qk :42/125（Cardiac & Cardiovascular System））JCE

读者在此期刊中能够了解心律失常疾病研究的最新发展，是专注于心脏电生理学研究的一流期刊。JCE 刊载经过同行评审的原创性临床研究论文和基础研究论文、评论、病例报告、Epltu 像和心律失常周期。其特色部分包括：分子观点、技术科学及临床评论。

Readers are able to understand the latest developments in the study of cardiac arrhythmias in this journal, and it is one of the leading journals in cardiac electrophysiology research. JCE publishes original peer-reviewed clinical research papers and basic research papers, reviews, case reports, Epltu images, and cardiac arrhythmias. Its features include molecular perspectives, technical science and clinical review.

2.5.3 心血管治疗学

2.5.3 Cardiovascular therapeutics

主编：Henry Krum, PhD and Chim C.Lang,MD

2013IF（JCR 2014）:2.536

ISI JCR 学科排名 56/125（Cardiac & Cardiovascular System））；109/254（Pharmacology &Pharmacy）

该刊有关心血管疾病治疗的评认和原创论文。该刊主要刊登心血管药理学、临床药理学和临床试验方面的论文；还刊登关于转化研究、药物基因组学和个体化用药、器械、基因和细胞治疗及药物流行病学的论文。

The journal focuses on the recognition of cardiovascular disease treatment and original papers. It mainly publishes the papers on cardiovascular pharmacology, clinical pharmacology and clinical trials. It also publishes the papers on translational research, pharmacogenomics and personalized medicine, instrumentation, gene and cell therapy, and epidemiology.

2.5.4 导管插入术与心血管介入

2.5.4 Catheterization and cardiovascular interventions

主编 :Steven R.Bailey

2013IF（JCR 2014）:2.396

ISI JCR 学科排名：58/125（Cardiac & Cardiovascular System））

这是一本国际期刊，涵盖心血管疾病的广泛领域。该期刊内容包括侵入性和介性冠状血管技术及有关的基础信息和临床信息。该期刊为直接服务病人的临床医师提供具有直接实用价值的材料。除了传统的原创研究、病例报告和综合评论外，该刊还刊载初级报告和研究进展论文，定期发布有关热门主题和技术发展的观点。

This is an international journal covering a wide range of cardiovascular diseases. The contents include the basic information and clinical information of invasive and intermediate coronary vascular techniques and related information. This journal provides a direct and practical material for clinicians who serve patients directly. In addition to traditional original research, case reports and comprehensive reviews, it also reports on the development of primary reports and research. Journals will also regularly publish views on popular themes and technological developments.

2.5.5 临床心脏病学

2.5.5 Clinical cardiology

主编 :A.J.Camm

2013IF（JCR 2014）:2.396

ISI JCR 学科排名：58/125（Cardiac & Cardiovascular System）

该刊刊载有关心血管药物和心血管手术中诊断和治疗问题的原创临床研究和简评，是美国预防心脏病学会的官方刊物。其内容有：临床研究、综述、自由评论、主编的每月评论、补充论文、专家小组讨论和临床评论。

The journal publishes original research and review on the clinical diagnosis and treatment of problems related to cardiovascular drugs and cardiovascular surgery. The journal is the official journal of the American Society for the prevention of heart disease. Its contents include clinical research, review, free review, editor's monthly review, supplementary articles, expert panel discussions and clinical reviews.

2.6 免疫学电子期刊

2.6 Immunology E-Journal

2.6.1 儿科变态反应和免疫学

2.6.1 Pediatic allergy and immunology

主编（editor）：Ulrich Wahn

2013IF（JCR 2014）:3.859

ISI JCR 学科排名（Discipline ranking）：5/21（Allergy）;5/118（Pediatrics）;44/144（Immunology）

此刊是目前世界上儿科变态反应的主要杂志，出版关于儿童免疫缺陷和变态反应、炎症和传染性疾病理解和治疗的原创文献和综合评论。其他关注的领域包括：特殊和附属免疫的发展；怀孕和哺乳期间母亲孩子之间的免疫相互作用；儿科变态反应和免疫对基础研究科学家和儿童研究的临

The journal is the world's leading journal of pediatric allergy, it publishes original documents and comprehensive reviews about understanding and treatment of child immunodeficiency and allergic reaction, inflammation and communicable disease. Other areas of interest in this journal include development of specific

床医生之间交流的促进。

and accessory immunity, immunity interactions between mothers and children during pregnancy and lactation, promoting the communication between clinicians of pediatric allergy and immunology of basic research scientists and research on children.

2.6.2 临床与实验免疫学

2.6.2 Clinical and experimental immunology (cei)

主编 M.Peakman

2013IF（JCR 2014）:3.278

ISI JCR 学科排名 :60/144（Immunology）

它提供了一个国际论坛，刊载关于临床免疫学和转化免疫学所有方面的原创研究，内容包括：传染性和寄生虫疾病的免疫发病机制；风湿、肾和内分泌症；其他器官系统的免疫症；恶性肿瘤和移植。

The journal provides an international forum, in which scholars can publish original research on all aspects of clinical immunology and transforming immunology, its contents include the pathogenesis of infectious and parasitic diseases, rheumatism, kidney and endocrine disease, immunity disease of other organ system, malignant tumor and transplantation.

2.7 药理学与药剂学电子期刊

2.7 Pharmacology & Pharmacy E-Journal

2.7.1 药物化学

2.7.1 Chemmedchem

主编 :Natalia Ort ú zar

2013IF（JCR2014）:3.046

ISI JCR 学科排名 :18/58（Chemistry Medicinal）; 75/256（Pharmacology & Pharmcy）

其创立于欧洲，刊载来自世界各地的原创和重要的二次与三次信息。该刊正在逐渐成为化学、生物学与医学交叉学科的主要期刊。其宗旨是实现药物与制药科学领域的整合，包括如下主题：从药物设计与发现到药物开发与传递，从分子建模到组合化学，从靶标验证到先导物衍化以及药物吸收、分布、代谢、排泄与毒性研究。

It is founded in Europe, and published the original papers, critical secondary and tertiary information from authors all over the world. It is becoming the main journal of chemistry, biology and medicine. Its mission is to integrate pharmaceutical and pharmaceutical Sciences, such as from drug design and discovery to drug development and delivery, from molecular modeling to combinatorial chemistry, from target validation to lead generation, and research on drug absorption, distribution, metabolism, excretion and toxicity.

2.7.2 药物科学杂志

2.7.2 Journal of pharmaceutical sciences

主编：Dr.Ronald T. Borchardt

2013IF（JCR 2014）:3.007

ISI JCR 学科排名：20/58（Chemistry Medicinal）;43/148（Chemistry Multidisciplinary）;77/256（Pharmacology & Pharmacy）

其刊载原创性研究论文、原创性研究纪要、特约专题评述（包括短篇评述）和评论和新闻。该刊关注基本药物科学方面的以及药物化学加工等话题，包括：药物技术和目标药物转运有关的结晶化、冻干、药物化学稳定性、药物动力学、生物药剂学、药效学、前体药物发展、生物活性剂、代谢配置、剂型设计、蛋白－肽化学和生物技术等。

This journal published original research papers, original research notes, invited topical reviews (including Minireviews) and editorial commentary and news. The journal focuses on the topics of basic pharmaceutical science and pharmacochemistry processing, including pharmaceutical technology and crystallization of target drug transporters, lyophilization, drug chemical stability, pharmacokinetics, biopharmaceutics, pharmacodynamics, pro–drug developments, biological active agent, metabolic disposition, dosage form design, protein–peptide chemistry and biotechnology.

2.7.3 临床药理学杂志

2.7.3 Journal of clinical pharmacology

主编 :Joseph S. Bertino,Jr.,Scenectady, NY

2013IF（JCR 2014）: 2.472

ISI JCR 学科排名：116/256（Pharmacology & Pharmacy）

它是美国临床药理学协会的同行评审的国际性月刊。自 1961 年创刊以来，它一直为读者提供原创论文、综述、评论和有关药品发展的各类案例报导。从 2013 年起，该刊只发布电子版。

It is a peer–reviewed international journal of the American Society of clinical pharmacology. Since its foundation in 1961, it has been providing readers with original articles, reviews and comments on the various types of cases and drug development report. Since 2013, the journal has only released the electronic version.

2.7.5 临床与实验药理学和生理学

2.7.5 Clinical and experimental pharmacology and physiology

主编：Prof Jun-Ping Liu

2013 IF（JCR 2014）:2.405

ISI JCR 学科排名：38/81（Physiology）;118/256（Pharmacology & Pharmacy）

它主要发表药理学与生理学临床与实验研究成果的原创性研究论文、短篇通讯文章、研究快报和理论文章（假说）。该期刊偶尔还会刊载特邀市政府文章。

它旨在为全世界范围内工作在这些相互关联学科领域的科学家之间的交流做出重大贡献。它已被澳大利亚高血压研究委员会（High Blood Pressure Research Council of Australia,HBPRCA）和澳大利亚临床与实验药理学家和毒理学家学会（Australasian Society of Clinical and Experimental Pharmacologists and Toxicologists,ASCEPT）所采用。

It mainly publishes original research papers, short communication articles, research letters and theoretical articles (hypothesis). The journal publishes articles occasionally invited municipal government.

It aims to make a significant contribution to the communication between scientists working in these interrelated disciplines all over the world. It has been adopted by High Blood Pressure in Research Council of Australia (HBPRCA) and Australasian Society of Clinical and Experimental Pharmacologists and Toxicologists (ASCEPT).

2.7.6 植物疗法研究

2.7.6 Phytotherapy research

主编（editor）：Elizabeth M.Williamson, lzzo,Sung Hoon–Kim,Rajan Radhakrishnan

2013 IF（JCR 2014）:2.397

ISI JCR 学科排名（Discipline ranking）：29/58（Chemistry Medicinal）；

119/254（Pharmacology& Pharmacy）

这是一本刊载有关药用植物研究的原创性研究论文，短讯、综述、读者来信的国际期刊，按月发行。该期刊涉及的重要领域为天然药物的药理学、毒理学及其在医学中的临床应用，涵盖从病例到完整的临床试验等内容，包括中草药与药物的交互作用与草药安全性其他方面的研究。此期刊尤其欢迎介绍包括商业产品在内的常见食品配料和标准化植物提取物效果的论文，以及分离出的天然产物的机理研究。

This is an international journal publishing full–length original research papers, short communications, reviews and letters on medicinal plant research, it issues monthly. The important areas it involves are the herbs and natural product's pharmacology, toxicology and their clinical applications in medicine. The journal's contents vary from case histories to full clinical trials,including Studying on the interaction between Chinese herbal medicine and medicine and other aspects of herbal safety. Papers concerned with the effects of common food ingredients and standardised plant extracts including commercial products are welcome as mechanistic studies on isolated natural products.

该刊不刊载农业、植物化学、结构解析、质量控制或者植物鉴定的论文，除非此类论文与当前使用的植物药物的药理学效应或者总体安全性直接有关。

It does not publish purely agricultural phytochemical structure elucidation and identification papers unless pertinent to the pharmacological effects or overall safety of plant based medicines currently in use.

2.7.7 基础与临床药理学和毒理学   2.7.7 Basic & clinical pharmacology

主编 :Kim Bresen

2013 IF（JCR 2014）:2.294

ISI JCR 学科排名：47/87（Toxicology）；

125/256（Pharmacology & Pharmacy）

它是一份独立的期刊，刊载毒理学、基础及临床药理学所有领域中的原创科学研究。这些领域包括：实验动物药理学和毒理学分子（遗传学）、生物化学及细胞药理学和毒理学；还包括临床药理学的所有方面：药代动力学、药效学、治疗药物监测、药物/药物相互作用、药物遗传学/基因组学、药物流行病学、药物经济学、随机对照临床试验和合理的药物治疗。对于研究中所用的所有化合物，应当知晓化学成分和组成，天然化合物也是如此。

It is an independent journal that publishes original scientific research in all areas of toxicology, basic and clinical pharmacology. These areas include experimental animal pharmacology and Toxicology (molecular genetics), pharmacology and toxicology of biochemistry and cell; it also includes all aspects of clinical pharmacology: pharmacokinetics, pharmacodynamics, therapeutic drug monitoring, drug / drug interactions, drug genetics / genomics, drug epidemiology, pharmacoeconomics, randomized controlled clinical test and rational drug therapy. For all compounds used in the study, chemical composition and composition should be known, So are natural compounds.

2.8 医学化学电子期刊

2.8 Medical Chemistry E-Journal

2.8.1 生物化学

2.8.1 Chembiochem

主编：Peter Gölitz

ISI JCR 学科排名 127/291(Biochemistry & Molecular Biology) ; 17/58(Chemistry, Medicinal)

它涵盖短篇通讯文章、全文论文、综述、小综述及热点概念的国际性期刊，是化学生物学、生物有机（无机）化学整个领域的重要原创和二次文献信息的主要来源，它的宗旨是实现这一重要领域的整合，包括如下主题：从复杂碳水化合物以及多肽 / 蛋白质到 DNA/RNA，从组合化学和生物学到信息传导，从催化抗体到蛋白质折叠，从生物信息学和结构生物学到药物设计。

The journal is the international journal of containing short papers, full text paper,review and hot topic concepts. It is the important resource of important primary and secondary information on the whole of chemical biology bio (in) organic chemistry and biochemistry. Its mission is to integrate this wide and flourishing field, including these topics: from complex carbohydrates through peptides/proteins to DNA/RNA, from combinatorial chemistry and biology to information transduction, from catalytic antibodies to protein folding, from bioinformatics and structural biology to drug design.

2.8.2 药物化学

2.8.2 Chemmedchem

主编：Natalia Ort ú zar

2013IF（JCR2014）:3.046

ISI JCR 学科排名 18/58（Chemistry Medicinal）; 75/256（Pharmacology & Pharmacy）

它创立于欧州，面向全世界，刊载来自于世界各地的原创以及重要的二次与三次信息。其正在逐渐面为化学、生物学与医学交叉学科的主要期刊。其宗旨是实现药物与制药科学领域的整合，包括如下主题：从药物设计与发现到药物开发与传递，从分子建模到组全化学，从靶标验证到先导物衍化以及药物吸收、分布、代谢、排泄与毒性研究。

The journal founded in Europe, and published Original papers, critical secondary and tertiary information from all over the world. It is gradually becoming the main journal of chemistry, biology and medicine. Its mission is to integrate the wide and flourishing field of medicinal and pharmaceutical sciences, including these topics: from drug design and discovery to drug development and delivery, from molecular modeling to combinatorial chemistry, from target validation to lead generation and ADMET studies.

2.8.3 化学生物学与药物研制

2.8.3 Chemical biology & drug design

主编：David Selwood

2013 IF（JCR 2014）:2.507

ISI JCR 学科排名：28/58（Chemistry; Medicinal）173/291（Biochemistry & Molecular Biology）

该刊是一本同行评审科学期刊，专注于发展创新科学、技术和医学，关注化学生物学和药物研制的跨学科领域。该刊的目标是捕捉突出化学生物学和药物研制领域中的新概念、观点和新发现的有意义的研究和药物发现。以下课题均属于该刊的关注范围：蛋白质、肽、类肽、核酸、脂质、碳水化合物和天然产物化学生物

The journal is a peer-reviewed scientific journal, it is dedicated to the advancement of innovative science, technology and medicine and focuses on on the multidisciplinary fields of chemical biology and drug design. Its aim is to catch new concepts, perspectives and new discoveries in the field of chemical biology and drug discovery, as well as meaningful

学和药物研制。

research and drug discovery. The following topics are of concern to the journal: proteins, peptides, peptides, nucleic acids, lipids, chemicobiology of carbohydrate and natural products, drug development.

注：本章所涉及的英文缩写 IF、JCR、ISI 的含义如下。

Note: the meaning of English abbreviations IF, JCR and ISI in this chapter is listed below.

IF：Impact Factor，影响因子，是国际上通用的期刊评价指标，是测度期刊有用性和学术水平的评价指标。

IF:Impact Factor, which is an international general journal evaluation index,and is a measure of the usefulness of the journal and academic level evaluation index.

JCR：Journal Citation Reports，期刊引证报告，是查询影响因子的官方网站。

JCR:Journal Citation Reports, which is the official website to query the impact factor.

ISI：Institute for Scientific Information，美国科学信息研究所，ISI 数据库包括了科学、社会科学、艺术和人文科学的 16000 多种国际期刊、书和各种文献集。

ISI:Institute for Scientific Information of America.the ISI database includes more than 16000 international journals of science, social sciences, arts and humanities.

第三章 会议文献
Chapter three　Conference Proceedings

会议文献是学术文献的重要组成部分，是在会议上交流的未公开发表的论文，具有学术前沿的性质。因此，在学习和研究过程中，会议论文是重要的参考文献。

The conference papers are an important part of the academic literature, and they are unpublished papers at the conference with the nature of the academic. Therefore, in the process of learning and research, conference papers are important references.

3.1 科技会议录索引

3.1 Index to Scientific & Technical Proceedings（ISTP）

国际上著名的会议论文索引《科技会议录索引》（ISTP），是国际三大文献索引之一。科技论文索引提供了国际会议论文文摘及参考文献索引等信息，收录的会议论文涉及自然科学和工程技术领域。从 2008 年 10 月 20 日起，ISTP 统一改成 CPCI（Conference Proceedings Citation Index 的简称）。CPCI 是 ISI 出版的会议索引数据库，美国 ISI 将 Conference Proceedings Citation Index – Science（科技会议

The index of the International Scientific *Conference Proceedings Index*（ISTP）is one of three international document indexings. ISTP provides international conference abstracts and reference index information. Conference papers coveres natural science and Engineering areas. From October 20, 2008, ISTP unified CPCI（Conference Proceedings Citation Index）. CPCI is the conference index database of ISI, and

录索引，CPCI-S）和 Conference Proceedings Citation Index -Social Science & Humanities（社会科学与人文会议录索引，CPCI-SSH）两大会议录索引集成为 ISI Proceedings。两大会议录共用一个检索平台 Web of Science Proceedings（WOSP）。

CPCI 会议出版物包括 IERI Press、SMSSI Press、Atlantis Press。

3.1.1 IERI Press 教育研究进展（刊号：2160-1070）

教育研究系列进展（AER）旨在出版教育领域理论和方法方面的会议，涉及教育、人文和社会科学。研究领域包括心理学、社会学、历史学、传播学、经济学、法学、政治学、教育与学习、环境研究、哲学、管理等。该会议录旨在出版国际会议上交流的原始论文。随着网络周转达时间加快和免费获取的特点，该系列会议录能迅速地将参与者的文章发表出去。

ISI integrated Conference Proceedings Citation Index – Science (CPCI–S) and Conference Proceedings Citation Index–Social Science & Humanities (CPCI–SSH) into ISI Proceedings, and this two proceedings share one search platform—Web of Science Proceedings (WOSP).

The Conference publications of CPCI include IERI Press、SMSSI Press and Atlantis Press.

3.1.1 Advances in education research（ISSN: 2160-1070）

The proceedings series Advances in Education Research (AER) aims at publishing proceedings from conferences on the theories and methods in fields of education,humanities and social sciences. Research areas include psychology, sociology, history, communication studies,economics, law, political science, education and e-learning, environmental studies and philosophy, management and so on.The proceedings publishes original proceedings from international conferences, with a fast turnaround time and free access on the Internet.

3.1.2 SMSSI Press 社会科学和行为科学进展（刊号：2339-5133）

从 2013 起，所接受的论文将被出版并且被 CPCI-SSH 索引，被索引的论文对所有读者都有价值。从 2015 年起，它所接受的论文主题包括：人文社会科学；信息、数据处理和网络；旅游文化；教育改革政策；教学技巧和方法；社会、文化和人文；IT 和人工智能；工业经济管理；材料工程与电气工程。

3.1.3 亚特兰蒂斯出版社

亚特兰蒂斯出版社正在建立知识库，知识库里的文章来自图书、期刊、会议、研讨会和专题讨论会。所有的文章提交索引并提供主要索引服务，包括索引 / EI、CPCI（*）、CPCI-SSH，学者谷歌等。亚特兰蒂斯出版社出版下列系列会议：智能系统研究进展；计算机科学研究进展；社会科学、教育与人文研究进展；工程研究进展；物理学进展；经济学、商业与

3.1.2 Advances in social and behavioral sciences（ISSN: 2339-5133）

All accepted papers will be published and submitted for indexing by CPCI-SSH. since 2013. The indexed papers are valuable for all the readers. Since 2015, all accepted papers' topics include humanities and social sciences; information, data processing and networking; tourism and culture; education reform and policy; teaching techniques and ethods; social, cultural and humanities; It and artificial intelligence; industrial and economic management; materials engineering and electrical engineering.

3.1.3 Atlantis press

Atlantis Press is building up a repository of articles from books, journals and conferences, workshops and symposia. All articles are fully interlinked and relevant proceedings are submitted for indexing to major indexing services, incl. Compendex/EI, CPCI（*）, CPCI-SSH, Scholar Google, etc.. Atlantis Press publishes proceedings in the following series: Advances in Intelligent Systems

管理研究进展；生物科学研究的进展。

要想自己的论文被 CPCI 索引，应该积极参加国际会议，这样可以扩大与同行间的信息交流，把握研究领域的学术前沿。美国 CPCI 收录的中国区来源论文，一般都源自国际级别的大型国际学术会议。国际上一些著名的学会、协会，如 IEEE、IEE、ASTM 等，每年都举办年会，其会议论文集被 CPCI 收录。

3.2 医学会议网站

3.2.1 医会通

医会通会议平台是专业医学会议服务平台，是国内外医学会议在线查询网站，提供免费的会议建站、会议报名、会议征文提交、会议资料分享等服务。

Research, Advances in Computer Science Research, Advances in Engineering Research, Advances in Physics Research, Advances in Economics, Business and Management Research, Advances in Biological Sciences Research.

In order to be indexed by CPCI, you should take an active part in the international conference, so as to expand the information exchange between the peers and master the academic frontier of the research field. U.S. CPCI collected the source papers in China, generally from the international level and large scale international academic conference. Some famous international societies and associations, such as IEEE, IEE, ASTM etc. hold the annual meeting every year, the conference papers are collected into CPCI.

3.2 Medical Conference Website

3.2.1 Yihuitong

Yihuitong conference platform is a professional medical conference service platform. It is a domestic and foreign medical conference online query website and provides such service: free site building, conference registration, conference papers submitted, marketing conference information sharing.

3.2.2 学术会议云

它是国内外学术会议在线检索的门户网站，在此网站上可以发布学术会议、参加学术会议、检索学术会议，可以在线对感兴趣的会议投稿。

3.2.2 Academic meeting cloud

It's domestic and international academic meeting online retrieval website. you can post academic conference, join academic conference, retrieve the academic meeting, you also can submit conference papers online to the meeting you are interested.

学术会议云

会议检索（学术会议名称）

| 首页 | 最新会议 | 学术会议 | 行业会议 | 论坛峰会 | 培训公开课 | 其他会议 |

当前位置：首页 >> 学术会议云-是国内外学术会议在线检索的门户网站-发布学术会议、参加学术会议、找学术会议就上学术会议云！热门标签：北

在线发布会

小贴士：当您完成
中英文会议活动所
览，三网联动宣传
费、投稿、审稿等
主办单位试用！

注册单

创建会

the 6th Pediatric Otolaryngology forum
第六届亚太小儿耳鼻喉年会

May 12. to 14, 2017 Beijing

2017中国国际骨科技术与成果展   2017-4-21 上海市

30+行业领袖演讲
30+Speeches
55+精品展台
55+Exhibitors
500+行业精英
500+Industry Leaders
6场专业分论坛
6 Fourms

中国国际骨科技术与成果展（ORTHO-CHINA）将于2017年4月21-22在上海
召开，ORTHO-CHINA立足骨科全产业链，致力于搭建产业链上下游资源
的合作与贸易平台，行业专业信息的集散平台和行业学术、技术的交流平台
ORTHO-CHINA将在全球范围内邀请参展企业与专业观众，为骨科领域产
医不同单位在不同发展阶段寻找最合适…………

会议征稿　会议注册　1人　3205　　查看详情

2017中国国际人工关节大会暨展览会   2017-4-21 上海市

目前全球人工关节需求迅猛增长，美国平均每年人工关节消费量超过100万
套，产值超过100亿美元。据测算，我国人工关节潜在需求量超过300万套
2014年实际消费量40余万套，目前仍保持年均15%-20%的高速增长，市
力巨大。与我国巨大的潜在市场极不相称的是，我国人工关节基础研究相
弱，在一些领域中甚至是空白。人工关节设计新理念、新材料…………

会议征稿　会议注册　0人　4095　　查看详情

3.2.3 中国学术会议网

中国学术会议网（conf.cnki.net）由 CNKI 主办，是为会议主办方、作者、参会者设计并开发的网络化学术会议服务平台。用户通过该网站可以检索到适合自己并感兴趣的网站，可以在线投稿，在线注册，可以通过网站获得所关注的会议最新通知，公告信息和稿件是否被录用的情况。

3.2.3 China academic conference network

"China academic conference network"（conf.cnki.net）sponsored by CNKI（Chinese National Knowledge Infrastructure）, it's a networked academic conference service platform, which is designed and devoloped for conference organizers, authors and attendees. Users can retrieve the meeting websites suitable and they are interested. Also users can be online submission, online registration, and get the information about the latest meeting notice and whether the paper submitted is employed.

3.2.4 医学会议网

该网站提供最新国内医学会议在线信息和国际医学会议查询时间，免费提供医学会议服务和中华医学会会议报名时间。

3.2.5 医学会议在线

医学会议在线是一个以医学会议信息发布，医学会议内容报道为主题的医学专业网站。医学会议在线包括：发布会议、最新会议、会议报道、会议课件、专家访谈、医学资讯、医药调研、会议管理等栏目。

该网站每天都有最新会议信息更新和发布，近三个月将要举办的会议会罗列出来，供读者参阅；该网站对会议的前期准备、开会期间和会后有不同形式的报道，并且在会后为读者提供会议期间交流的课件，读者可以下载或在线观看，了解专家的观点和行业学术动态；该网站还提供医学专业信息，在此平台上实现信息的一站式搜索。

3.2.4 Medical conference network

The site provides the latest domestic medical conference information online and international medical conference query time, and also provides free medical services and the meeting time signing up of Chinese medical association.

3.2.5 Medical meeting online

Medical Meeting Online is medical professional website, on which topics are medical conference information distribution and medical conference contents reports. This website includes these columns: conference release, the latest meeting, conference reports, conference courseware, expert interview, medical information, medical research and meeting management.

The website information is updated and the latest meeting information released every day.It will list the upcoming meeting's name nearly three months in order to be read by users. There are different forms of reports　before the meeting, during the meeting and after the meeting,and it provides meeting's coursewares communicated during and after the meeting for readers, where readers can download or watch online in order to know experts point of view and academic trends. The site also provides medical specialty information and realize the one-stop search of information.

第四章 MOOC 资源
Chapter four MOOC Resourses

4.1 关于 MOOC

4.1 On MOOC

4.1.1 MOOC 的含义

4.1.1 MOOC's meaning

MOOC 的全英文名称是 "Massive Open Online Courses"，即大规模的开放式的网络课程。

"M" 代表 Massive（大规模），指在这个教育平台上，参与的高校众多，学生数量庞大，与传统课程只有几十个或几百个学生不同，一门 MOOC 课程学生人数有时能达到上万人；在课程教学过程中，不是一个教师的教学活动，而是多个教师以团队的形式参与进来；在此平台上，有大量的网络课程可供师生自主选择，最重要的一点是 MOOC 的完成需要大量的人力、物力和财力的投入。

MOOC's full English name is "massive open online courses", which is a large-scale open network courses.

"M" represents Massive (mass), it means that in the education platform, there are many colleges and universities, the large number of students to participate in. MOOC is different from the traditional course,which has only dozens or hundreds of students, a kind of MOOC course's students can sometimes reach tens of thousands of people; in the process of curriculum, not a teacher in teaching activities, but many teachers to form a team to participate in. In this platform, there are a large number of web courses for students to choose, the most important point is that the completion of MOOC requires a lot of manpower, material and financial resources.

第二个字母"O"代表 Open（开放），指教育理念、教育内容、教育形式、教育对象的全面开放；开放还体现在课程的公开性，保证了其内容的高质量；同时开放性还体现在兴趣导向上，凡是想学习的，都可以进来学，不分国籍，只需要一个邮箱，就可注册参与。

The second letter "O " represents Open (open), it means the fully open of education idea, education content, education form, education object. The opening is also reflected in the open course, which ensures the high quality of its contents; and openness is also reflected in the interest oriented, those who want to learn, can come in learn, regardless of nationality. Only need a mailbox, you can register to participate in.

第三个字母"O"代表 Online（在线），在线学习通过网络完成，不受时空限制。

The third letters "O" represents "Online" (online). It means you can learn the course on the internet, not be limited by time and space.

第四个字母"C"代表 Course（课程）。在线学习课程是指课程上传者可以将教育资源随时随地传播到网络平台上，学习者在上网条件许可的情况下在任何时间，任何地点，以自己的学习方式和学习节奏学习。此平台对学习者的学习行为和过程适时记录，学习者能够及时得到学习反馈，最重要的一点就是在线学习不用付高额的学费，仅凭这一点，就会吸引更多的学习者利用此平台来学习。

The fourth letter "C" represents "Course" (course). The course on the network platform is uploaded anytime, and the learner can learn it at anytime,any place with their own learning style and learning rhythm.During learning,the platform can record the learner's learning behavior and process timely, the learners can get feedback in time. The most important thing is that the online learning can't pay the high tuition fees,which attract more learners use this platform to learn.

4.1.2 MOOC 的特点

MOOC 在课程组织方式、课程内容、课程学习方式和课程评价方式上发生了重大变革。MOOC 在组织方式上强调"翻转课堂"，即学习的决定权转移给学生，让学生的学习更加灵活、主动地参与到课程中来。"翻转课堂"颠覆了传统课堂教学结构与教学流程；在课程的内容上强调重组；学习方式上强调互动与回应，如小组合作等；MOOC 在评价方式上创新，使用客观的自动化的线上评量系统，如是随堂测验、考试等。

MOOC 的主要构成是课堂演讲视频。视频以简短、突出重要性为制作理念，长度限定在 8~12 分钟。为了测试学生对知识的掌握程度，视频可能有多次的暂停，如弹出一个小测试，或者写一些文字等，课程助教会在后台进行查看，通过系统自动给出反馈。整个课程都结束后，会有作业或考试，对学生的学习情况给出评价。

4.1.2 MOOC's characteristics

MOOC has undergone significant changes in the curriculum organization methods, curriculum content, curriculum learning methods and curriculum evaluation methods. On organization methods,MOOC emphasizes the "flipped classroom",which means the learning decision transfers to the students, so that students learn more flexible and active participation in the curriculum. "Flip the classroom" overturn the traditional classroom teaching structure and teaching process; MOOC emphasizes on restructuring in the curriculum content; learning methods emphasizes on interaction and response, such as group work; MOOC uses an objective and automated online evaluation system, such as the quizzes, exams and so on to innovate the evaluation methods.

MOOC's main composition is the classroom lecture video. The video's production concept is the brief and the highlighting importance. Video's length is limited in 8~12 minutes.In order to test students' mastery of the knowledge, the video should have many pause, such as popping up a small test, or writing some words and so on. Course assistants

4.1.3 MOOC 的分类

根据教学型模式的不同，MOOC 可以分 cMOOC、xMOOC 及 tMOOC 三大类。

（1）cMOOC

cMOOC 形式是 MOOC 最初出现的形式。2008 年，George Siemens 为了讨论和传播他的联通主义学习理论，在网上使用同步交流工具和异步交流工具，在网络上组织大规模讨论，影响颇大。在这种模式下，老师给定学习内容，提供资源并发起话题，学习者通过对话和社交媒体建构知识。cMOOC 特点是分散的，基于网络的，非线性的组织结构，强调探索和会话。

may view in the background through the automatic feedback system. After the end of the whole course, there will be assignments or exams, which evaluate students' learning situation.

4.1.3 Classification of MOOC

According to the different teaching mode, MOOCs can be divided into three categories : cMOOC, xMOOC and tMOOC.

（1）cMOOC

The cMOOC form is the first form of MOOC. In 2008, in order to discuss and disseminate his Connectivism study theory, George Siemens used simultaneous communication tools and asynchronous communication tools and organized large-scale discussion on the network, which bring great influence. Under this form, teachers give learning content, provide resources and create topics, learners construct knowledge through dialogue and social media, cMOOC's characteristics are decentralized, based on network,nonlinear organization structure. cMOOC emphasizes the exploration and conversation.

（2）xMOOC

xMOOC 被称为斯坦福模式，与 cMOOC 不同的是，该模式是高度集中的，基于内容的和线性的组织结构。xMOOC 更接近传统教学过程和理念，侧重知识传播和复制，强调视频、作业和测试等学习方式。

（3）tMOOC

tMOOC 是 2015 年 3 月 17 日由天津达内科技精品在线推出的一个学习平台，它致力于 IT 技能职业培训。此平台上的全部课程都是经过精挑细选的，具有实用价值的课程。tMOOC 平台是一个基于 O2O 学习模式的技术学习平台，使用者只要在平台上注册帐号就可以免费学习平台上的所有课程。tMOOC 采用线上线下相结合的 O2O 学习模式，保证了学生的学习质量。

（2）xMOOC

xMOOC is known as the Standford model, unlike cMOOC, xMOOC's characteristics are highly centralized, based on content and linear organizational structure. xMOOC is more close to the traditional teaching process and ideas, focusing on knowledge dissemination and replication, emphasizing on video, homework and test learning methods.

（3）tMOOC

tMOOC is a learning platform, which comes out by the Tianjin DaNei science and technology high quality online. It is committed to the IT occupation skill training. All the courses on this platform are carefully selected and have practical value. tMOOC platform is a technology learning platform based on O2O learning model, as long as the user registered on the platform, they can be free to learn all the courses on the platform. tMOOC uses O2O learning model, a combination of online and offline, to ensure students' learning quality.

4.2 MOOC 课程平台介绍

4.2.1 三大国际著名课程平台

（1）Cousera（https://www.coursera.org/）

Cousera 由美国加利福尼亚州斯坦福大学的计算机科学教师于 2012 年 4 月创立。到目前为止，它是全球用户最多的课程平台，汇集了 100 多所国外知名高校的 MOOC 课程，中国的清华大学、北京大学、上海交通大学、复旦大学等跟 Coursera 有合作。它是一个综合性平台，各种学科、各种语言的课程都有，一些英文课程还会提供中文字幕。

Coursera 与世界各地大学建立合作关系，这意味着它将不断扩展课程科目，增加不同语言的课程设置。这些语言包括中文、西班牙语、法语和意大利语等。

Coursera 大部分课程是提供证书的，有些不提供。课程视频一般可以免费观看，但是如果需要得到签名认

4.2 Introduction of MOOC Course Platform

4.2.1 Three famous international curriculum platforms

（1）Cousera (https://www.coursera. org/)

Cousera was founded by a California Stanford University computer science teacher in April 2012. So far, it is a platform with the largest global users. It brings more than 100 well-known foreign universities MOOC courses together all over the world. Many universities in China have established a cooperative relationship with Coursera, for example, Tsinghua University, Peking University, Shanghai Jiao Tong University, Fudan University, and so on. Cousera is a comprehensive platform, it has a variety of subjects, a variety of language courses, some English courses will also provide Chinese subtitles.

Coursera build partnerships with universities around the world,which means that it will continue to expand the curriculum and increase different language courses, including Spanish, French, Italian and Chinese, etc..

Most courses in Coursera provide certificates, some do not provide. General users can watch video courses for free,

证的证书需要交费。在这个平台上课，没有访问限制，可以直接上课。其部分功能较完善，如课程筛选功能、讨论交流功能、检索功能等。以前很多定期开的好课程现在不受时间限制，随时都可以开始学。

（2）EdX（https://www.edx.org/）

由美国哈佛大学和麻省理工学院（MIT）成立的 EdX，同样汇集了 100 多所名校课程，中国的清华大学、北京大学、香港科技大学是它的合作伙伴。EdX 已经将新增的 6 所国际大学，包括澳大利亚国立大学、荷兰代尔夫特理工大学加入了其组织的 X 大学联盟。

EdX 平台上的所有课程都是免费的，并且有自愿损款的选项。课程结束后，如果想得到签名认证的证书需要交费。此平台在访问时会受到访问限制，部分用户在上课时可能存在一定的问题。现在有了 APP，还把一些课搬到了国内网站——学堂在线上，解决了访问受限制的问题。

but if you need to take the signature certification, you should pay. In this platform, there is no access restrictions, you can directly go to have lessons. Some functions such as Course selection function, discussion and communication function, retrieval function are more perfect. Many regular courses are now free from time limit, you can start learning at any time.

（2）EdX（https://www.edx.org/）

EdX was established by Harvard University and Massachusetts Institute of Technology (MIT), its platform also have many courses from more than 100 famous universities, Tsinghua University, Peking University, The Hong Kong University of Science & Technology (HKUST) are its cooperative partners. EdX has added 6 new international universities into its university League, including Australian National University, Technische Universiteit Delft (TUD) of Holland.

All the courses on the EdX platform are free, and there are options for voluntary damage in this platform. After the end of the course, if you want to get the signature certification, fee is required. This platform will have access restrictions, some users may have some problems during class. Now with the emergence of APP, some

（3）Udacity（https://www.udacity.com）

2012 年，由大卫·史蒂芬斯（David Stavens）、塞巴斯蒂安·史朗（Sebastian Thrun）和迈克尔·索科尔斯基（Michael Sokolsky）共同创办的Udacity，拥有与计算机和网络相关的课程。

Udacity 的课程范围是数学和计算机科学，并且着重于实际应用。Udacity 与 Coursera 等不同之处体现在教师的选择上。Udacity 选择教师时，依据的是他们的教学水平，并非是他们的学术研究能力。此平台上的课程部分是免费的，有的在开课一周或两周后开始收费。

4.2.2 国外的其他 MOOC 网站

（1）iversity https://iversity.org/

德国 MOOC 平台，课程以德语为主，部分课程是英语。

courses are moved to our Chinese school website–SchoolOnline, which are solving the problem of restricted access.

（3）Udacity（https://www.udacity.com）

In 2012, David Stavens, Sebastian Thrun and Michael Sokolsky founded the MOOC platform—Udacity. Its courses most related to computer science and network.

The range of Udacity's curriculum is about mathematics and computer science, and they focuse on practical applications. The difference between Udacity and Coursera is reflected in the choice of teachers, Udacity choose teachers based on their teaching level, not their academic research ability. Part of the courses on this platform are free, some courses start charging a week or two weeks later.

4.2.2 Other MOOC sites abroad

（1）iversity https://iversity.org/

German MOOC platform, on which most courses are in German, some are in English.

（2）Massive Open Online English Course http://mooec.com/

面向学习英语的 MOOC 平台。

（3）open2study https://www.open2study.com/

澳大利亚 MOOC 平台。

（4）Open learning https://www.openlearning.com/

澳大利亚的 MOOC 平台，部分课程收费。

（5）NovoED venture lab https://novoed.com/

斯坦福大学社会化 MOOC，部分收费。

（6）https://class.stanford.edu/

它虽然使用 EdX 平台，但是却是一个独立网站，里面的课程都是斯坦福大学课程。

（7）Future Learn https://www.futurelearn.com/

英国 MOOC 平台，可参加考试获得高级证书。

（8）OpenupEd http://openuped.eu/

欧盟 MOOC 平台，包括 12 种语言近 170 门课程。

（2）Massive Open Online English Course http://mooec.com/

MOOC platform for learning English

（3）open2study https://www.open2study.com/

Australian MOOC platform

（4）Open learning https://www.openlearning.com/

Australian MOOC platform,some courses need to pay.

（5）NovoED venture lab https://novoed.com/

Stanford University social MOOC, part of courses need to pay.

（6）https://class.stanford.edu/

Although it uses the EdX platform, but it is an independent website,its curriculum are all Stanford University courses.

（7）Future Learn https://www.futurelearn.com/

British MOOC platform, you can participate in the examination to obtain advanced Certificate.

（8）OpenupEd http://openuped.eu/

EU MOOC platform, including nearly 170 courses in 12 languages.

（9）Alison http://alison.com/

早期 MOOC 平台，偏向职业培训课程。

（10）JANUX https://janux.ou.edu/landing/

Oklahoma University 的 MOOC 平台。

（11）P2PU https://p2pu.org/

协作式点对点的 MOOC 学习平台。

（12）Course Sites https://www.coursesites.com

Blackboard 公司创建的 MOOC 站。

（13）Academic Earth http://academicearth.org/

此平台拥有大学公开的课程链接和资源。

（14）Class2Go UWA

https://www.class2go.uwa.edu.au/ University of Western

（15）Schoo http://schoo.jp/

日本最大的 MOOC 平台，以日语为主，超过百门课程。

（16）FUN

https://www.france-universite-numerique-mooc.fr/

法国综合 MOOC 平台，以法语为主。

（9）Alison http://alison.com/

It's a early MOOC platform,it bias vocational training courses.

（10）JANUX https://janux.ou.edu/landing/

It is Oklahoma University's MOOC platform.

（11）P2PU https://p2pu.org/

Cooperative peer to peer learning platform based on MOOC

（12）Course Sites https://www.coursesites.com

Blackboard company created this MOOC station

（13）Academic Earth http://academicearth.org/

In this platform,there are university curriculum links and resources.

（14）Class2Go UWA

（15）Schoo http://schoo.jp/

The largest MOOC platform in Japan, it's mainly Japanese, there are more than 100 courses.

（16）FUN

https://www.france-universite-numerique-mooc.fr/

A comprehensive MOOC platform in France. It based on French.

（17）Miriada X https://www.
miriadax.net/

西班牙语综合 MOOC 平台。

（18）Open Classrooms http://
fr.openclassrooms.com/

法语 MOOC 网站。

（19）universarium http://
universarium.org/

俄罗斯的一个MOOC平台（俄语）。

（21）Redunx http://www.redunx.org/

西班牙语和葡萄牙语 MOOC 平台

（22）My Open Courses http://www.
myopencourses.com/

印度的大型 MOOC 平台，以英语
为主。

（23）Veduca http://www.veduca.
com.br/

巴西的 MOOC 平台，以葡萄牙语
为主。

（24）Jmoochttp://www.jmooc.jp/en/

日本的 MOOC 平台（日语）。

（25）MRUniversity http://
mruniversity.com/

经济学 MOOC 平台。

（17）Miriada X https://www.
miriadax.net/

A comprehensive MOOC platform
based on Spanish

（18）Open Classrooms http://
fr.openclassrooms.com/

A MOOC website based on French

（19）universarium http://
universarium.org/

A MOOC platform of Russia, based
on Russian.

（21）Redunx http://www.redunx.org/

A MOOC platform based on Spanish
and Portuguese

（22）My Open Courses http://www.
myopencourses.com/

A large MOOC platform in
India,based on English.

（23）Veduca http://www.veduca.
com.br/

Brazil's MOOC platform, mainly
language is Portuguese.

（24）Jmoochttp://www.jmooc.jp/en/

A MOOC platform in Japan, mainly
language is Japanese.

（25）MRUniversity http://
mruniversity.com/

Economics MOOC platform

（26）First business mooc

http://firstbusinessmooc.org/

商业 MOOC 平台。

（27）http://www.mooc-list.com/

MOOC 课程导航网站。

（28）http://www.mooctivity.com/

MOOC 课程导航网站。

（29）http://mooc.studentadvisor.com/

MOOC 课程导航网站。

4.2.3 中国主要的 MOOC 学习平台

（1）学堂在线 http://www.xuetangx.com/

学堂在线是中国第一个由清华大学发起的中文 MOOC 平台，合作高校有包括北京大学、浙江大学、南京大学、上海交通大学等部分 C9 联盟高校在内的国内知名高校。2014 年年初，学堂在线作为清华大学参股的公司开始独立运营，学堂在线获得 EdX 平台课程在中国的唯一官方授权。

（26）First business mooc

http://firstbusinessmooc.org/

business MOOC platform

（27）http://www.mooc-list.com/

MOOC course website navigation

（28）http://www.mooctivity.com/

MOOC course website navigation

（29）http://mooc.studentadvisor.com/

MOOC course website navigation

4.2.3 The main MOOC learning platform in China

（1）School online

School online is the first Chinese MOOC platform foundeded by Tsinghua University, Cooperative universities with it include some famous universities:Peking University. Zhejiang University, Nanjing University, Shanghai Jiao Tong University and other C9 Union Colleges in China. In early 2014, School online began to operate independently as a subsidiary of the company of Tsinghua University, and School online get the only official authorized to access to the EdX platform in China.

学堂在线是依托知名高校的盈利性质的在线教育公司，课程基本都是中文课程，并且提供的都是大学各专业的基础课程。各门课程的老师都能耐心、及时地与学生互动交流。用户每周学习时间不长。该平台学习人数较多，有专门的 QQ 群，有专门解答问题的管理人员，完成课程并且达到课程要求的学生会得到证书或推荐信。

The School online is a kind of online education company for-profit relying on famous universities. The courses language is Chinese,and all the courses are basic courses from universities. Teachers can patiently and timely interact with students.The users spend no long time studying online every week. There are many learners in this platform, and also there is a dedicated QQ group,a manager who specializes in solving problems. After completing the course and meeting the requirements of the course,the users will receive a certificate or a letter of recommendation.

（2）中国大学 MOOC

http://www.icourse163.org/

2014 年 5 月，爱课程网与云课堂联合推出"中国大学 MOOC"平台，它由教育出版公司与互联网公司联合非营利运营。该平台汇集了全国 39 所 985 高校的顶级课程，是国内最好的中文 MOOC 学习平台。同年，"中国大学 MOOC"平台上线 SPOC 功能，为校内教学提供服务，各高校可通过该平台进行 MOOC 建设和应用。

（2）Chinese University MOOC

In May 2014, icourse network and cloud classroom launched. The Chinese University MOOC,which is a non-profit platform, and operated by educational publishing company and Internet Co. The platform brings together top courses from 39 top universities in China,it is the best Chinese MOOC learning platform. In the same year, the Chinese University MOOC platform provides SPOC features, which provide services to the school teaching,

之所以该平台会成为国内最好的中文学习平台，主要原因在于"爱课程网"在承担国家精品开放课程项目时积累了良好的在线课程资源，与各高校有良好的合作基础。其课程内容涉及范围广泛，而且全部免费。学习方式以在线学习为主，线下有讨论会，课件可下载并且离线观看。每一位在这里学习的学生都可以学习到最优质的大学课程，学完还可获得免费电子认证证书。

every university can use the platform to finish MOOC's construction and application.

The reason why this platform is the best study platform for Chinese people is that "icourse network" has accumulated good online course resources during undertaking the national excellent open Courses,and it has a good foundation for cooperation between the colleges and universities.The course covers a wide range of activities, and all courses are free. The learning method is mainly online learning, there'll be a discussion under the line,the courseware can be downloaded and be viewed offline, every student who studies here can learn the best university courses. After learning,they can also get free electronic certificate.

（3）好大学在线

http://www.cnmooc.org/home/index.mooc

此平台是由部分中国高水平大学联盟并自愿组建的开放式合作教育平台。该平台与百度公司、上海交通大学合作，实现了知识导航、作业互评、翻转课堂、学分认定、证书认证等功能。

（3）Good University Online

http://www.cnmooc.org/home/index.mooc

This Open cooperative education platform is formed voluntarily by Chinese high level University Alliance, the platform cooperates with Baidu Inc. and Shanghai Jiao Tong University, and realize knowledge navigation, read the homework each other, flipped the classroom, credit identification, certificate authentication and other functions.

（4）慕课网

http://www.imooc.com/

它是国内最大的 IT 技能学习平台，是学习编程最简单的免费平台。慕课网提供了丰富的移动端开发、php 开发、web 前端、android 开发以及 html5 等视频教程资源公开课。

（4）IMOOC

http://www.imooc.com/

This website is the largest IT skills learning platform, and the most simple learning programming free platform. IMOOC provides richful video tutorial free open resources on mobile client development, PHP development, web front-end, android development and HTML5.

（5）智慧树网

http://www.zhihuishu.com/

2009 年 4 月，智慧树网开始研发启动，2012 年 12 月上线运营，2013 年 4 月东西部高校联盟成立。智慧树网以全球视野开启学习的绿色通道。智慧树已为超过 1000 万同学提供世界级水准的课程，并帮助其获得学分，提升个人能力。智慧树网上的学分课只对在智慧树选课的在校大学生开放。所有课程由学科名师与教育专家层层把关，不断优化课程内容，帮助学生更好地获取及提升运用知识能力。智慧树网满足了学习者与名校名师面对面互动、提问的需求。目前，超过 2000

（5）Wisdom Tree network

April 2009, the wisdom tree network began to start research and development, it began to operate on-line in December 2012. In April 2013,East and West University Alliance founded.Wisdom tree network opens a green channel to study at a global scale. Wisdom tree provides world-class standard courses to more than 10 million students, helping them get credit, improving their personal ability. The credit course in Wisdom tree web only opens to college students who has selected course on the Wisdom tree web.

所中国知名大学都选择了智慧树网。

All courses are taught by teachers and experts, they constantly optimize the course content to help students better access knowledge and enhance the ability to use knowledge. Wisdom tree network meets the needs of learners and teachers face to face interaction, and asking questions. At present, more than 2000 well-known universities in China have chosen the Wisdom tree network.

4.2.4 与医学相关的 MOOC 平台介绍

4.2.4 MOOC platform related to medicine

（1）临床试验基础

哈佛医学院的这门《临床试验基础》，教会你如何解读试验结果，怎样去设计试验。

（1）Fundamentals of Clinical Trials

The course "clinical trials foundation" given by Harvard Medical School teach you how to interpret the results of the test, how to design the test.

（2）临床研究数据管理

主要是教了 redcap 的一些基本功能，如创建和录入 EDC、survey 这些基本功能，对于临床试验 eCRF 的设计有些帮助。

（2）Data Management for Clinical Research

To teach some of the basic functions of redcap, such as EDC, survey, some help for the design of clinical trials eCRF.

（3）健康：临床与公共卫生研究的定量方法

（3）Health in Numbers: Quantitative Methods in Clinical & public health research

（4）科学写作

来自耶鲁大学医学院，教你写出一手专业不难懂的英文论文

（5）临床试验设计与解释

（6）卫生专业人员概述

（7）基于案例的统计学介绍

药学、制药方面的 MOOC：

（8）药学导论

（9）药物与大脑

（10）处方：处方药物滥用的科学背后

（11）疫苗试验：方法和最佳实践

内科方面的 MOOC：

（12）糖尿病——全球性挑战

（13）全球结核病（TB）临床管理与研究

医学影像方面的 MOOC

（14）生物医学影像导论

（15）fMRI 数据统计分析

神经科的 MOOC

（4）Writing in the Sciences

From the Yale University medical school, to teach you how to write a professional English paper.

（5）Design and Interpretation of Clinical Trials

（6）Understanding Research: An Overview for Health Professionals

（7）Case-Based Introduction to Biostatistics

Pharmaceutical & Pharmaceutical MOOC

（8）Introduction to Pharmacy

（9）Drugs and the Brain

（10）Generation Rx: The Science Behind Prescription Drug Abuse

（11）Vaccine Trials: Methods and Best Practices

Internal medicine MOOC

（12）Diabetes—a Global Challenge

（13）Global Tuberculosis (TB) Clinical Management and Research

Medical imaging MOOC

（14）Introduction to Biomedical Imaging

（15）Statistical Analysis of fMRI Data

neurology MOOC

（16）医药神经科学

（17）计算神经科学

（18）细胞神经科学

（19）认知神经科学

（20）神经科学基础：第一部分

（21）神经认知障碍

（22）神经元和大脑精神科方面的MOOC

（23）初级卫生保健

（24）公共卫生的社区变化

（25）人口中的抑郁症：公共卫生方法

（26）心理健康与疾病的社会背景

公共卫生方面的 MOOC

（27）流行病学：公共卫生基础科学

（28）公共卫生统计推理：估计、推理与解释

（29）肥胖经济学原理

（30）全球健康：案例研究从社会的视角

（31）一次拯救数百万人：全球疾病控制政策与计划

（16）Medical Neuroscience

（17）Computational Neuroscience

（18）Cellular neuroscience

（19）Cognitive neuroscience

（20）Fundamentals of Neuroscience, Part I

（21）Neurocognitive Disorders

（22）Synapses, Neurons and Brains Psychiatry MOOC

（23）Health for All Through Primary Health Care

（24）Community Change in Public Health

（25）Major Depression in the Population: A Public Health Approach

（26）The Social Context of Mental Health and Illness

Public health MOOC

（27）Epidemiology: The Basic Science of Public Health

（28）Statistical Reasoning for Public Health: Estimation, Inference, & Interpretation

（29）Principles of Obesity Economics

（30）Global Health: Case Studies from a Biosocial Perspective

（31）Saving Lives Millions at a Time: Global Disease Control Policies & Programs

医学人文、伦理、政策、教学方面的 MOOC

（32）美国卫生政策

（33）卫生职业教育教学方法

（34）神经伦理学

（35）豚鼠、英雄与绝望患者：人类研究的历史与伦理学

医疗创新、创业方面的 MOOC

（36）生物信息学的方法

（37）医疗创新与创业

（38）保健创新

（39）移动健康无国界

（40）云中的健康信息学

（41）希波克拉底的挑战

（42）跨专业医疗信息

4.3 MOOC 的产生及发展趋势

MOOC 被喻为教育史上的"一场海啸"或"一次教育风暴"，是 500 年来高等教育领域最为深刻的技术变革。它将网络技术、信息技术与优质教育结合在一起，将教育资源通过网络输送到世界各地，让学习者不出家门就可以获得免费的优质资源。

Medical Humanities & Ethics & Policy & Teaching MOOC

（32）United States Health Policy

（33）Instructional Methods in Health Professions Education

（34）Neuroethics

（35）Guinea Pigs, Heroes & Desperate Patients: The History & Ethics of Human Research

Medical innovation & Entrepreneurship MOOC

（36）Bioinformatic Methods

（37）Healthcare Innovation and Entrepreneurship

（38）Innovating in Health Care

（39）Mobile Health without Borders

（40）Health Informatics in the Cloud

（41）Hippocrates Challenge

（42）Interprofessional Healthcare Informatics

4.3 MOOC's Emergence and Development Trend

MOOC is regarded as the "tsunami" or "education storm" in the history of education, which is the most profound technological change in the field of higher education in the past 500 years. It combines network technology, information

2008 年，加拿大国家自由教育研究协会的研究员布兰恩·亚历山大（Bryan Alexander）和爱德华王子岛大学的戴夫·科米尔（Davecormier）提出了 MOOC 概念。至此，MOOC 开始在国内外的高校蔓延开来。第一个 MOOC 平台大约在 2011 年出现。美国斯坦福大学教授塞巴斯蒂安·史朗把他的课程放在了互联网上，吸引了来自 190 多个不同国家的 160000 名学生。2011 年 12 月，塞巴期蒂安·特伦、大卫·斯塔文斯与麦克·索科斯基开办了 Udacity 公司，同一时间开放两个在线课堂，《纽约时报》将 2012 年称为"MOOC 元年"。这一年，几个资金实力雄厚的投资商与顶尖大学合作，创造了包括 Coursera, Udacity, EdX 等在内的课程平台 MOOC。同年 9 月，谷歌发布了一个制作 MOOC 的工具，MOOC 相继大量出现，斯坦福大学建造了一个名 "Class2Go" 的网络课程平台。2013 年 2 月，新加坡国立大学与美国公司 Coursera 合作，加入大

technology and quality education together, pushing the education resources through the network to all over the world, so that learners can get free high-quality resources at home.

In 2008,Bryan Alexander, the researcher of the Free Education Research Association in Canada and Dave Cormier (Davecormier) from University of Prince Edward Island proposed the concept of MOOC.So far, MOOC began to spread in universities at home and abroad. The first MOOC platform appeared around 2011. Sebastian, a professor at Stanford University in the United States, has placed his course on the Internet, attracting 160000 students from more than 190 countries. In December 2011, Sebastian thuin. Trent, David Starr Vince and Mike Suokesiji Starr launched Udacity company, at the same time opened two online cources. *New York Times* called 2012 as "the first year of MOOC". This year, a number of financial strength of the investors and the top universities to create the curriculum platform MOOC,including Coursera, Udacity, EdX. In September of the same year, Google released a tool

型开放式网络课程平台。2014年5月，爱课程网和网易合作推出了拥有中国自主知识产权的 MOOC 平台——中国大学 MOOC。

虽然大量公开免费线上教学课程是 2000 年之后才发展起来的，但是其理论基础最远可追溯至 20 世纪 60 年代。具有代表性的是一次演讲和一个纲领的提出。1961 年 4 月 22 日巴克敏斯特·富勒发表的一个演讲，此演讲内容主要是针对教育科技的工业化。1962 年，美国发明家道格拉斯·恩格尔巴特向史丹福研究中心提出一个研究"扩大人类智力之概念纲领"。在此纲领里，他提出了使用计算机辅助学习的可能性。恩格尔巴特提倡计算机个人化、个人计算机与网络的配合将产生巨大的学习力量。

for the production of MOOC, MOOC has emerged in large numbers, Stanford University has built a name Class2Go network course platform. In February 2013, National University of Singapore and the United States Coursera company join a large open online course platform. In May 2014, icourse network and Netease launched a MOOC platform with China's own intellectual property rights—Chinese University MOOC.

Although a large number of open free online courses are developed in 2000, its theoretical basis can be traced back to 1960s. The representation is a presentation and a program. On April 22, 1961 Buckminster Fuller made a speech, the speech content is mainly for education in science and technology industrialization. In 1962, American inventor Douglas Engelbart proposed a research "to expand the concept of human intelligence program" to Shi Danfu research center, in which, he raised the possibility of computer assisted-learning, he advocated with personal computer, and the combination of personal computers and the Internet will generate tremendous learning power.

2012 年，美国发布的《2012 地平线报告》（高等教育出版社），在此报告中提及了 MOOC。2013 年，在其发布的《2013 地平线报告》从全世界的角度对 2013 — 2018 年未来 5 年影响高等教育发展的六大趋势及将要面临的六大挑战作了展望，而 MOOC 作为六大趋势之首，被放在了突出的地位。世界知名大学为了不在这场 MOOC 淘汰赛中退出历史舞台，纷纷加入 MOOC 并开办自己的 MOOC 平台。

虽然开放课程在制作过程中需要制作费，但是还有更多的国内外顶尖大学愿意通过网络提供免费资源。北欧国家建立了免费高等教育制度，美国俨然已成为免费开放课程的开创先锋。为了让更多不同语言国家的学生学习课程，Coursera 新增中文、法文、西班牙文和意大利文四种授课语言。两家提供网上课程的机构宣布，将与加拿大、墨西哥、欧洲、中国、新加坡、日本和澳大利亚的顶尖大学合作，同时还会跟更多美国学府签约。

In 2012,the "2012 horizon report" (Higher Education Edition) was published in America, in which mentioned the MOOC. In 2013, the "2013 horizon report" was published,in which it made prospect from world perspective on six trends of higher education development and six challenges to be faced in the next 5 years from 2013 to 2018,and MOOC was placed in a prominent position as the six major trends of the first. In order not to quit the stage of history, the world famous universities have joined MOOC and set up their own MOOC platform to eliminate the MOOC stage.

Although open courses need production cost to be made, but there are more domestic and foreign universities which are willing to provide free resources through the network. The Nordic countries have established a free higher education system, the United States seems to have become a pioneer in free open courses. In order to let more different language students learn courses, Coursera added four language courses: Chinese, French, Spanish and Italian. The two companies that offer online courses have announced that they will work with top universities in Canada, Mexico, Europe, China, Singapore, Japan and Australia, as well as with more American colleges and Universities

随着清华大学、北京大学等高校加入 MOOC 阵营以来，中国也掀起了一场 MOOC 热潮。清华大学、北京大学先后推出学堂在线和北京大学视频公开课 MOOC 平台，清华大学、北京大学牵头的 C9 联盟、上海交通大学带领的 C20 联盟推出自己的 MOOC 平台好大学在线，国内三大网络巨头 BAT（百度、阿里巴巴、腾讯）也都纷纷开始探索 MOOC 模式的在线教育，并有了一定的实践。腾讯的腾讯课堂、百度投资的传课网、阿里巴巴的淘宝同学等。虽然目前这些都不是成型的 MOOC 模式，但都在向着 MOOC 模式发展。

With Tsinghua University, Peking University and other universities joining into MOOC camp, it has set off a MOOC boom in China. Tsinghua University has launched MOOC platform--School online; Peking University has launched online video open class;C9 alliance led by Tsinghua University and Peking University and C20 alliance led by Shanghai Jiao Tong University have launched their MOOC platform——Good University Online; three network giant in China BAT（Baidu, Alibaba, Tencent）also have started online education exploration of MOOC mode, and have a certain practical. Tencent's Tencent classroom、Baidu's investment in the course network, Alibaba's Taobao Classmates,etc. Although these are not the formation of the MOOC model, but they are in the development of MOOC model.

4.4 MOOC 资源的获取

这里以"中国大学 MOOC"为例来介绍如何获取和使用 MOOC 资源。

4.4 MOOC Resources Access

Now，let's use "Chinese University MOOC" as an example, and introduce how to access and use MOOC resources.

4.4.1 MOOC 注册

利用百度搜索"中国大学MOOC"官方网站，点击搜索到的地址进入"中国大学 MOOC"官方网站。

4.4.1 MOOC registration

Use Baidu to search "Chinese University MOOC" official website, click on the address searched to enter "Chinese University MOOC" official website.

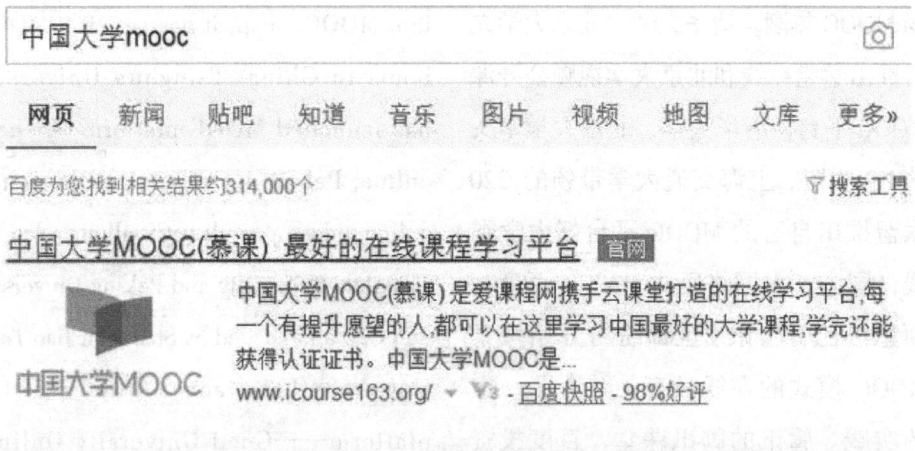

点击官网右上角的"注册"字样，即可注册。

Click on the upper right corner of the official website "注册", you can register.

"中国大学 MOOC"平台注册有三种方式：网易通行证、爱课程网帐号、使用第三方帐号快速登录。用户可以选择任一种注册方式进行注册。

There are three ways to register on "Chinese University MOOC" platform: NetEase pass, icourse network account, quick login using third party accounts. You can choose either registration to register.

4.4.2 使用 MOOC

登录帐号后点击最上方的头像，在下拉菜单中选择"设置"按钮，输入个人的详细信息，在帐号设置中可以修改密码和绑定邮箱。个人信息要真实，因为用户学完课程要申请认证证书。

4.4.2 Using MOOC

After logining account, click on the the top of the head, in the drop-down menu, select the "设置"button, enter personal details, in the account settings,you can modify the password and bind e-mail. Personal information must be true, because you want to apply for a certificate after finishing the course.

点击最上方的"学校"字样，可以看到 MOOC 中的所有学校。点击图标，就可以进入喜欢的大学，学习喜欢的课程；或者点击最上方的"课

Click on the top of the button "学校", you can see all the school in MOOC, click on the icon you can enter the university you like and learn the course; or click on

程"字样，页面上就会列出全部的课程。左边的一栏显示的是课程详尽的分类，下方还有搜索课程的搜索栏，看课程的详细情况。

the top of the "课程", then all the courses listed on the page,the left column shows the course detailed classification, there is a search bar below to search the course,then see details of the course.

选好课程后，在此课程下方桔色框中点击"立即参加"就可以开始学习了。例如，选择的是武汉大学的《急救常识》。

After the course is selected, click on the "立即参加" in the orange bar below to start learning. For example, choose the course of Wuhan University "急救常识".

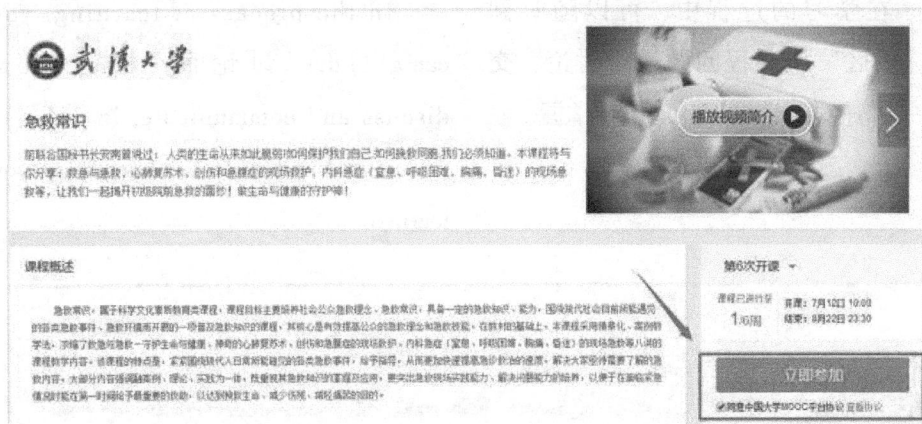

如果想知道都选了哪些课程，这些课程的状态都是怎样的，可以点击个人的帐户名进入"我的课程"界面。"正在进行""即将开始""已结束"三种状态表达了课程学习情况。

If you want to know what courses you have chosen, what are the status of these courses, you can click on your account name into the interface "我的课程"。"正在进行""即将开始""已结束"three states can express your course learning condition.

在学习的过程中，可以随时到"讨论区"就课程问题进行讨论、交流，加速对所学知识的理解和掌握。

In the process of learning, you can go to the "讨论区" at any time to discuss and communicate, in order to understand and grasp the knowledge you learned.

在学习过程中，要想知道用户自己对所学知识的掌握情况，可以点击"测试与作业"，了解自己的学习情况。

In the learning process, in order to know what you have learned, you can click on the button "测试与作业" to understand your learning.

学习结束后，可以点击"考试"来检验学习情况。

After finishing the course, you can click on the button "考试" to test your learning.

考试结束后，看看评分标准和细则，对用户自己的学习情况有一个客观的了解。

After the exam, take a look at the scoring criteria and rules, and have an objective understanding on your learning situation.

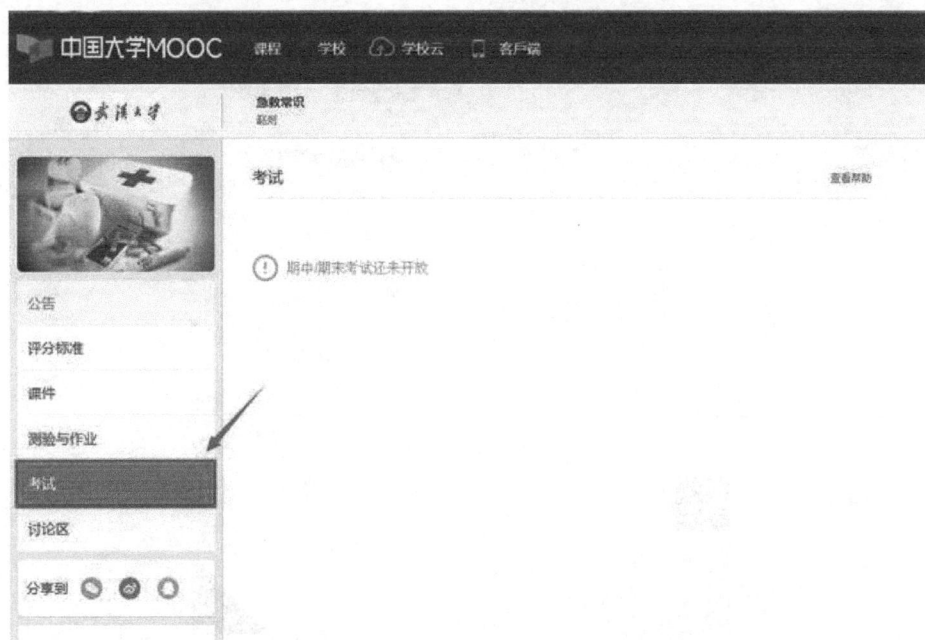

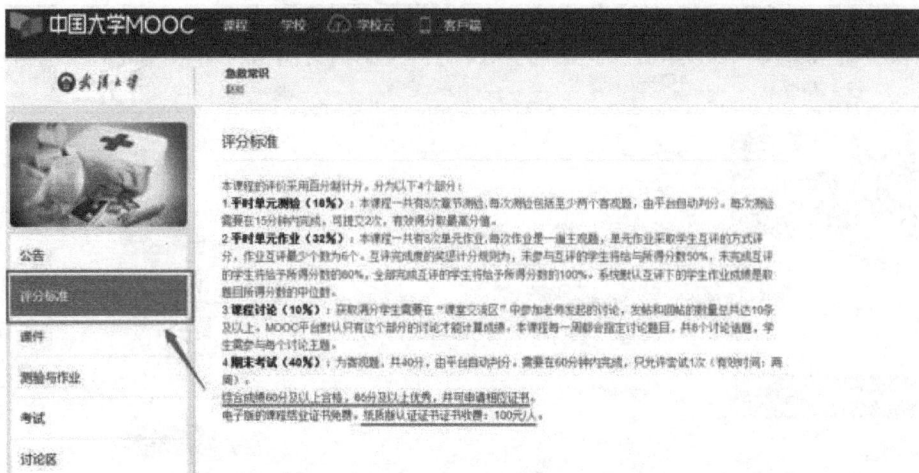

下图是这门课的结课证明。　　　　　　The following figure is the lesson of the course certificate.

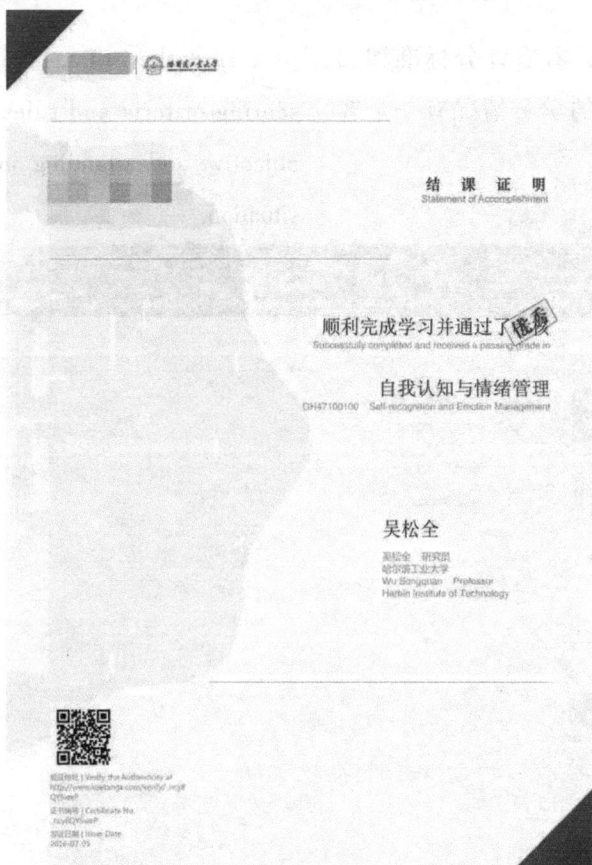

4.4.3 MOOC 平台使用的注意事项

（1）MOOC 平台使用前，要先注册获得帐号，用获得的帐号登录后，再去选课。

（2）一般情况下，课程结束前都可以进去上课。如果错过了开课时间，可以看已经发布的授课视频。在学习过程中，应该按时交作业。

（3）如果课程已经结束，可耐心等待下一次课程。有些 MOOC 平台支持课程订阅。

在 MOOC 平台上只有按时听课，完成作业并通过考试才能拿到证书。

根据自己的兴趣、爱好和时间，有计划地选课，这样才能很好地完成网上课程。

4.4.3 Notes on the use of MOOC platform

Before using MOOC platform, you must first register to get the account, with the account login, and then go to class.

In general, before the end of the course, you can go to have a lesson. If you miss the start time, you can see the videos released. In the process of learning, you should hand in homework on time.

If the course is over, you should be patient and wait for the next course. Some MOOC platforms support course subscription.

In the MOOC platform, you can't get a certificate until you have lessons,do homework and complete the exam on time.

According to your own interests, hobbies and time to plan to have lessons, so as to be able to complete the online course.

第五章　视频资料
Chapter five　Video Materials

视频资料是声像型文献的一种，主要用来表现和传递那些难以用文字来描述的信息。图文并茂是其突出的特点，受到使用者的青睐，特别适合现代用户的阅读方式。本章列举了一些获得医学视频的网址，供大家学习使用。

Video materials is a kind of audio-visual document, which is mainly used to express and transmit information that is difficult to describe with words. Illustrated is the prominent characteristics, users like this document. It especially is suitable for the modern user's way of reading. This chapter lists a number of websites to access to medical video for everyone to learn to use.

5.1 医学视频类网址 /Medical video URL

临床体格检查 /Clinical physical examination

http://mc.xjtu.edu.cn/film/linchuangchati512M.asf

中医学 /Chinese Medicine

http://mc.xjtu.edu.cn/down/zhongyi.rar

外科学 /Surgery

http://mc.xjtu.edu.cn/down/waike.rar

http://www.so138.com/so/so138.aspx?id=2197%20

http://www.so138.com/so/so138.aspx?id=1112%20

诊断学 /Diagnostics

http://mc.xjtu.edu.cn/down/zhenduan.rar

心理学 /Psychology

http://mc.xjtu.edu.cn/down/xinli.rar

影像学 /Imaging

http://mc.xjtu.edu.cn/down/yingxiang.rar

医学伦理学 /Medical ethics

http://mc.xjtu.edu.cn/down/lunli.rar

生理学 /Physiology

http://www.sdutcm.edu.cn/vod/shengli.MPG

大量医学视频下载 /Medical video

http://www.2728.cn/Soft/List_59.shtml

妇产科学（中山大学）/Obstetrics and gynecology (Zhongshan University)

http://www.so138.com/so/so138.aspx?id=2190%20

妇科手术视频录象 /Gynecological surgery video

http://www.so138.com/so/so138.aspx?id=712%20

外科手术教学视频下载 /Surgical teaching video download

ttp://www.so138.com/so/so138.aspx?id=581%20

医学视频——人体各器官解剖 /Anatomy of human organs

http://www.so138.com/so/so138.aspx?id=1879%20

中国针灸学（经典）/Chinese acupuncture (Classics)

http://www.so138.com/so/so138.aspx?id=2071%20

解剖学（山东大学）/Anatomy (Shandong University)

http://www.so138.com/so/so138.aspx?id=2192%20

辽宁医学视频 /Liaoning medical videos

http://www.so138.com/so/so138.aspx?id=1878%20

执业医师体格检查（视频下载）/Physician physical examination

http://www.so138.com/so/so138.aspx?id=1886%20

人体解剖学（中山大学）/Human anatomy (Zhongshan University)

http://www.so138.com/so/so138.aspx?id=2180%20

诊断学（山东大学）/Diagnostics (Shandong University)

http://www.so138.com/so/so138.aspx?id=2199%20

医学免疫学 /Medical Immunology

http://www.so138.com/so/so138.aspx?id=2227%20

病理学（中山大学）/Pathology (Zhongshan University)

http://www.so138.com/so/so138.aspx?id=2179%20

传染病学（中山大学）/Infectious diseases (Zhongshan University)

http://www.so138.com/so/so138.aspx?id=2189%20

医学视频——病理生理学 /Pathophysiology

http://www.so138.com/so/so138.aspx?id=730%20

心脏听诊 /Cardiac auscultation

http://www.so138.com/so/so138.aspx?id=1461%20

护理学—药理学（吉林大学）/Nursing Pharmacology (Jilin University)

http://www.so138.com/so/so138.aspx?id=1380%20

预防医学（山东大学）/Preventive medicine (Shandong University)

http://www.so138.com/so/so138.aspx?id=2228%20

医学视频资料——基本操作 /Medicine basic operations

http://www.so138.com/so/so138.aspx?id=1113%20

精神病学（中山大学）/Psychiatry (Zhongshan University)

http://www.so138.com/so/so138.aspx?id=2193%20

内科学视频（94 集）/Medicine, (94 set)

http://219.218.115.63/courseware/zy/lcyx/nkx/

外科学视频（70 讲）/Surgery videos (70 Lectures)

http://219.218.115.63/courseware/zy/lcyx/wkx/

儿科学（40 讲）/Pediatrics (40 Lectures)

http://219.218.115.63/courseware/zy/lcyx/ekx/

妇产科学（40 讲）/Obstetrics and gynecology (40 Lectures)

http://219.218.115.63/courseware/zy/lcyx/fckx

5.2 医学视频网站

5.2.1 医学视频网

　　医学视频网设置了内科视频、外科视频、儿科视频、医学保健、中医视频、医学考试、基础医学、专题等栏目。读者可根据自己需要选择栏目学习。

5.2 Medical Video Website

5.2.1 Medical video network

　　Medical video network sets up medical video, surgical video, pediatric video, medical care, Chinese medicine video, medical examination, basic medicine, special topics and other columns. Readers can choose the column according to their own needs to learn.

5.2.2 医学多媒体资源网

5.2.2 Medical multimedia resources network

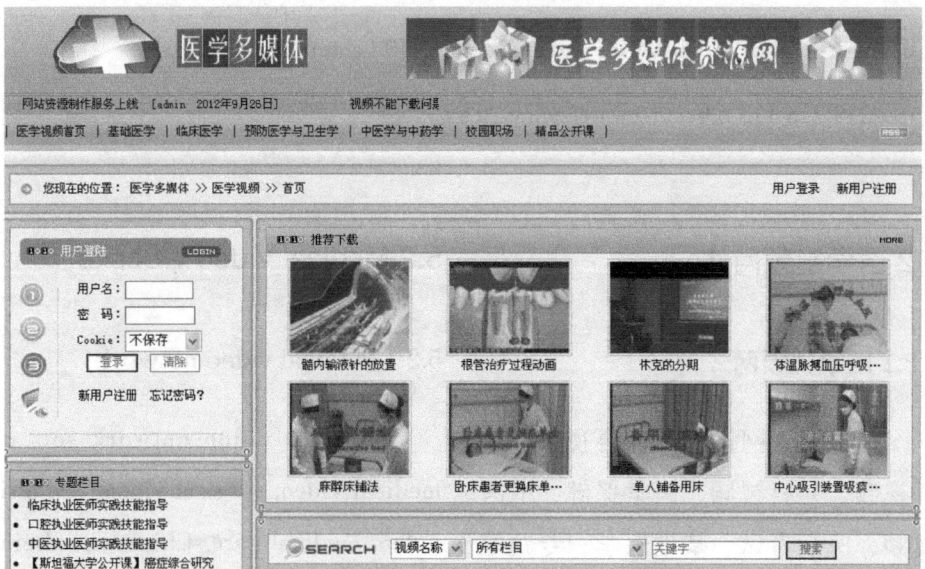

医学多媒体资源网由南京医科大学现代教育技术中心创设，按医学专题进行分类：基础医学、临床医

Medical multimedia resources is created by modern educational technology center of Nanjing Medical University,

学、预防医学与卫生学、中医学与中药学、精品公开课、校园职场等。多媒体包括医学文摘、医学图片、医学动画、医学视频、医学课件、网络课程、医学电子书、医学考试等。视频按照专题分类，使用者根据自己的需求搜索所需要的专题视频。

and classified according to medical topics: basic medicine, clinical medicine, preventive medicine and hygienics, traditional Chinese medicine and Chinese materia medica, boutique open courses, career in campus, and so on. Multimedia resources contain medical abstracts, medical multimedia pictures, medical animation, medical video, medical courseware, network course,medical e-books, medical examination etc..Video is classified according to the subjects, users can search the required video according to their needs.

5.2.3 丁香园

5.2.3 dingxiangyuan

这是一个专业性强的医学门户，所有的医学信息专业性较强，主要面向中高级的医学专业人员。

5.2.4 爱爱医

This is a professional medical portal, all medical information is more professional, it is mainly for senior medical professionals.

5.2.4 Aiaiyi

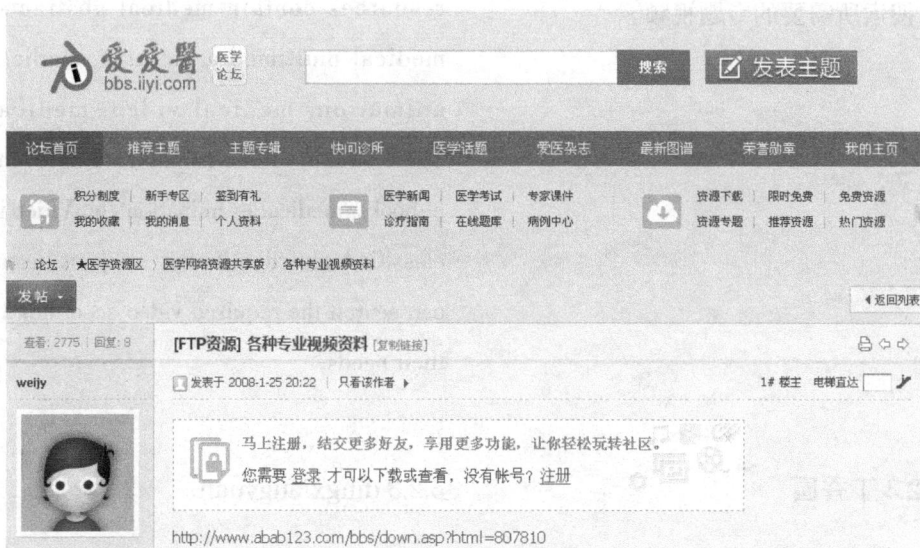

网站上的医学信息适合于初中级医务工作者。

5.2.5 好医生

这是一个收费类医学继续教育平台，较系统、较专业。"好医生"是一家为中国医务人员提供全方位服务平台的企业，目前主要服务领域包括：教育培训、医学信息和信息技术和其他医学和信息技术相结合的衍生服务。

Medical information on the site is suitable for junior medical workers.

5.2.5 Haoyisheng

This is a charging platform for continuing medical education, it is more systematic, more professional. "Good doctor" is an enterprises of full-service platform for Chinese medical staff, its main service areas are: education and training, medical information and information technology and derivative services of other combination of medicine and information technology.

5.3 国外医学网址 /Foreign Medical URL

医学检索 /medical retrieval

http://www.medmatrix.org/index.asp ;http://www.healthatoz.com;

http://www.medexplorer.com/m–publi.htm;

http://www.healtheon.com/;

http://www.biomedcentral.com/;

http://www.medbioworld.com/index.html;

医学资料数据库 /Medicine Database

http://www.nlm.nih.gov ;

http://www.nlm.nih.gov/databases/medline.html ;

http://vh.radiology.uiowa.edu ;

http://www.mayohealth.org ;

http://www.medscape.com ;

健康信息检索 /Health information retrieval

http://www.healthfinder.org ;

http://www.noah.cuny.edu ;

http://www.hon.ch ;

http://www.healthy.net/ ;

http://www.healthexplorer.com ;

http://www.medicinenet.com ;

http://www.social.com/health ;

http://www.reutershealth.com ;

老年病 /Senile disease

http://www.medicare.gov/NHCompare/Home.asp ;

http://www.seniorpro.com/ ;

牙科 /Dentistry

http://www.4smile.com/ ;

http://dentalinks.com/search.html ;

http://www.dds4u.com/ ;

http://www.dental−resources.com/ ;

http://www.smilefinder.com/ ;

心血管 /Cardiovascular

http://www.cardioguide.com/cardio/ ;

眼科 /Ophthalmology

http://www.lasikdocshop.com/ ;

http://www.lensprice.com/ ;

http://www.ophthoguide.com/ophthalmology/ ;

http://www.optisearch.com/ ;

耳鼻喉 /Otorhinolaryngology

http://www.bcm.tmc.edu/oto/others.html

药物 /Pharmaceutical

http://1st-spot.net/topic_pharmacy.html ;

http://www.drugdiscoveryonline.c ... t.asp?

http://mtdesk.com/mfg.shtml ;

http://www.farma.com/secciones/noticias.asp ;

http://web.quipo.it/box/ ;

http://www.pharmaceuticalonline. ... t.asp?

http://www.pharmweb.net/ ;

http://www.rxlist.com/ ;

http://www.vabpharmacy.com/ ;

艾滋病 /AIDS

http://planetq.com/aidsvl/ ;

http://www.aids-info.com/ ;

http://www.cdcnac.org ;

http://www.teleport.com/~celinec/aids.shtml ;

http://www.thebody.com ;

过敏 /Allergies

http://www.cs.unc.edu/~kupstas/FAQ.html ;

http://www.immune.com/allergy/allabc.html ;

http://www.pslgroup.com/allergies.htm ;

解剖学 /Anatomy

http://www.innerbody.com/ ;

http://www.rad.washington.edu/ ;

http://www1.biostr.washington.edu/ ;

痤疮与湿疹 /Acne & Eczema

http://freenet.uchsc.edu/2000/adolescent/acne.html ;

http://victorvalley.com/health%261aw/hlaw−apr/skin.htm ;

血液图谱 /Atlas of Hematology

http://www.md.huji.ac.il/mirrors/pathy/Pictures/atoras.html ;

http://www.ppfa.org/ppfa/lev2bc.html

哮喘网址 /Asthma URL

http://www.healthtouch.com/level1/hi−toc−htm ;

http://www.aetnaushc.com/topics/index.html ;

http://www.mednet.de/asthma/index.html ;

哮喘诊治指南 /Asthma treatment guidelines

http://www.nhlbi.nih.gov/nhlbi/lung/asthma/ ;

http://www.ginasthma.com ;

关节炎 /Arthritis

http://www.arthritis.org ;

http://www.pslgroup.com/arthritis.htm ;

麻醉学 /Anesthesiology

http://gasnet.med.yale.edu/ ;

http://www.usyd.edu.au/su/anaes/VAT/VAT.html ;

http://www.invivo.net/bg/index2.html ;

癌症与肿瘤 /Cancer & Oncology

http://cancer.med.upenn.edu/ ;

http://www.cancerguide.org ;

http://www.gretmar.com/webdoctor/oncology.html ;

http://www.icic.nci.nih.gov/ ;

http://www.oncolink.upenn.edu ;

乳腺瘤 /Breast Cancer

http://nysernet.org/bcic/ ;

http://www.nabco.org/ ;

http://www.breastcancer.net ;

脑肿瘤 /Brain Tumors

http://www.oncolink.upenn.edu/disease/brain/ ;

结肠炎 /Crohn's Disease & Colitis

http://www.ccfc.ca ;

儿童健康 /Children's Health

http://www.kidshealth.org ;

疲劳综合征 /Chronic Fatigue Syndrome

http://www.cais.com/cfs-news/ ;

http://www.uab.edu/pedinfo ;

儿童精神健康 /Children's Mental Health

http://www.aacap.org/web/aacap/factsFam ;

皮肤病 /Dermatology

http://biomed.nus.sg/nsc/skin.html ;

http://www.rrze.uni-erlangen.de/docs/FAU/fakultaet/ ;

http://www.dermguide.com/ ;

口腔学 /Dentistry

http://www.dental-resources.com/ ;

http://www.smiledoc.com/ ;
囊状纤维症 /Cystic Fibrosis

http://www.ai.mit.edu/people/mernst/cf/ ;

http://www.ccff.ca/~cfwww/ ;

糖尿病 /American Diabetes Association

http://www.diabetes.org ;

http://www.diabetes.com ;

http://www.castleweb.com/diabetes ;

http://www.cdc.gov/nccdphp/ddt ;

http://www.cis.ohio-state.edu/hypertext/ ;
faq/usenet/diabetes/top.html

http://www.niddk.nih.gov/DiabetesDictionary/ ;
DiaDictindex.html

http://www.pslgroup.com/diabetes.html ;

理疗 /Medicine Physics

http://www.sum.org ;

http://www.mbnet.mb.ca/~jwiens/chiro.html ;

http://www.panix.com/~tonto1/dc.html ;

http://www.li.uib.no/~kjartan/backrubfaq/ ;

http://www.concentric.net/~Ericdo ;

http://www.rolf.org ;

http://www.teleport.com/~amrta/rolfing.html ;

http://www.doubleclickd.com/shiatsu.html ;

http://www1.tip.nl/users/t283083/e_index.htm ;

子宫内膜炎 /Endometriosis

http://cmhc.com/factsfam/endo.htm ;

http://www.ivf.com/endoassn.html ;

http://www.ivf.com/endohtml.html ;

免疫学 /Immunology

http://rehd.med.upenn.edu:1025 ;

http://www.scienceXchange.com/aai ;

癫痫 /Epilepsy

http://www.efa.org ;

不孕 /Infertility

http://www.ihr.com/infertility/ ;

法医学 /Forensic Medicine

http://users.bart.nl/~geradts/forensic.html ;

急救医学 /Emergency Medicine

http://gema.library.ucsf.edu:8081/ ;

http://www.embbs.com ;

医学教育资源 /Medicine Education

http://www.med.virginia.edu/med–ed/otherMedEd.html ;

http://dpalm2.med.uth.tmc.edu/ ;

医学图书 /Medicine Libraries

http://www.arcade.uiowa.edu/hardin–www/hslibs.html

http://www.kumc.edu/mla/resource.html ;

医学书店 /Medicine bookstore

http://www.lww.com ;

http://www.hk.super.net/~wwap ;

按摩 /Massage

http://www.crpht.lu/FAQ/backrubs/archive/archive.html ;

医学院校学生用资源 /Medical Students

http://www.ama–assn.org/mem–data/special/ ;

ama–mss/ama–mss.htm

http://www.special/ama–mss/ama–mss.htm ;

http://www.amsa.org ;

http://www.s2smed.com ;

过敏与传染病 /Allergies and infectious diseases

http://www.niaid.nih.gov ;

医学资源 /Medicine Resources

http://www–med.stanford.edu/medworld/home/ ;

http://www.nim.nih.gov ;

精神健康 /Mental Health

http://www.cmhc.com ;

医学软件 /Medical Software

http://www.pilot.infi.net/~cksmith/medstu/ ;

http://cac.psu.edu/~sxb41/Med/med_soft.html ;

器官移植 /Organ Transplants

http://www.cis.ohio–state.edu/hypertext/faq/usenet/ ;

medicine/transplant–faq/top.html

http://www.gen.emory.edu/medweb/medweb.transplant.html ;

http://www.infi.net/~donation/ ;

放射学与影像 /Radiology & Imaging

http://members.aol.com/ricter/private/ ;

home/med.rad.home.html

http://www.radserv.med−rz.uni−sb.de/en.index.html ;

http://www.rana.org ;

药学 /Pharmacy

http://pharminfo.com/drg_mnu.html ;

http://www.cpb.uokhsc.edu/pharmacy/pharmint.html ;

http://www.ns.net/~ryan/ ;

http://www.pharmacytimes.com ;

护理学 /Nursing

http://www.ajn.org ;

http://www.kencomp.com/internurse ;

http://www.rapidnet.com/~csurgtech/Nurses/ ;

远程医疗 /Telemedicine

http://www.telemed.org

网上医学信息 /Webdocto   r

http://www.gretmar.com/webdoctor ;

http://www.acupuncture.com ;

http://www.rhemamed.com/tcm.htm ;

香味疗法 /Aromatherapy

http://www.halcyon.com/kway ;

http://www.healthy.net/clinic/therapy/aroma ;

紧张 /Stress

http://www.fitnesslink.com/mind/stress.htm ;

http://www.soton.ac.uk/~ktakeda/massage/stress.html ;

气功 /Mind & Imagery Therapy

http://www.electriciti.com/atlantis ;

音乐疗法 /Music Therapy

http://falcon.cc.ukans.edu/~memt/mt.html ;

http://www.namt.com/namt ;

放松压力 /Relaxation Techniques

http://web1.french.wsu.edu/cs/cs_1.htm ;

http://www.gasou.edu/psychweb/mtsite/smpage.html ;

http://www.shsu.edu/~counsel/relaxation.html ;

http://www.shsu.edu/~counsel/shortr.html ;

解除抑郁 /Relieve Depression

http://www.execpc.com/~corbeau ;

美国健康网络 /American Health Network

http://www.ahn.com ;[/hide]

矫正口吃 /Correct a Stammer

http://www.mankato.msus.edu/dept/comdis/ ;

kuster/stutter.html

http://www.asfnet.org ;

戒烟 /Smoking Addiction

http://www.rampages.onramp.net/~nica ;

世界卫生组织 /World Health Organization

http://www.who.ch ;

蛇咬处理 /Snakebites

http://patc.simplenet.com/snakbite.html ;

新英格兰医学杂志 /New England Journal of Medicine

http://www.nejm.org ;

妇女健康 /Women's Health

http://www.femina.com/femina/HealthandWellness ;

男性健康 /Men's Health

http://www.malehealthcenter.com ;

http://www.menshealth.com ;

下 篇
Part two

国际执业医师考试资源
Resources on International Medical Licensing Examination

第六章 美国执业医师考试
Chapter six USMLE

6.1 关于 USMLE

6.1.1 什么是 USMLE

USMLE 的全称是美国医师执照考试，在美国它是一个由国家医学委员会联合会主办（FSMB）和国家医学考试委员会（NBME）发起的，三级医学执照考试。

FSMB 是一个非营利组织，代表着美国及其领土的 70 个州级医学与骨科委员会。FSMB 对执业医生和病人的投诉负责，FSMB 的责任是规范医生的行为并解决患者的投诉。FSMB 提供国家评估程序、便利的证书文件和工具，赞助建立跟踪纪律处分数据库，在许可证发放和实践方面具有权威性。

6.1 on USMLE

6.1.1 What's USMLE?

USMLE's full name is United States Medical Licensing Examination, it is a three-step examination for medical licensure in the United States and is sponsored by the Federation of State Medical Boards (FSMB) and the National Board of Medical Examiners (NBME).

FSMB is a non-profit organization that represents the 70 state medical and department of orthopedics Committee of the United States. FSMB is responsible for the practice of doctors and patients complaints, it is illegal for doctors to regulate. FSMB provides the national assessment process, the convenience of the certificate documents and tools, the sponsorship of the establishment of tracking disciplinary database, it has authority in licensing and practice.

NBME 是一个非营利组织，通过健康专家的评估，为公众提供服务。它约有 80 名成员，委员会包括来自全美的专家代表，他们对考试的设计提出意见和观点。还有一些组织包括：美国医学院协会（AAMC），代表美国医学专业委员会（ABMS）；美国医学协会（AMA），AMA 的居民和研究员；美国医学生协会（AMSA）；美国医学专业委员会（CMSS）；外国医学毕业生教育委员会（ECFMG）；FSMB；学生国家医学协会（SNMA）。NBME 开发一些用于医学教育、执照、认证的评估程序，旨在促进医学教育和科学评估。

美国医师执照考试评估医生应用知识、概念和原则的能力，并要求展示基本的以病人为中心的能力，这在健康和疾病中很重要。USMLE 三级考试中的每一级都是对其他级别的补充，没有任何一级在医疗执照准备评估中独立存在。

NBME is a non-profit organization that provides services to the public through the assessment of health professionals. It has about 80 members of the Committee including experts from across the country on behalf of design for the examination opinions and views. There are some organizations including the association of American Medical Institute (AAMC), on behalf of the American Medical Specialized Committee (ABMS), the American Medical Association (AMA), the residents and fellows of AMA, American Medical Student Association (AMSA), American Medical Specialized Committee (CMSS), the Educational Commission for foreign medical graduates (ECFMG), FSMB, the student National Medical Association (SNMA) . NBME develops programs for medical education, licensing, and certification to promote medical education and scientific assessment.

The USMLE assesses a physician's ability to apply knowledge, concepts, and principles, and to demonstrate fundamental patient-centered skills, that are important in health and disease. Each of the three Steps of the USMLE complements the others, no step can stand alone in the assessment of readiness for medical licensure.

在美国，各个司法管辖区的个人医疗许可机构（"国家医疗委员会"）授予行医执照。每个医疗许可权限设定自己的规则和条例，并且要求通过能够证明其执业资格的考试。通过了USMLE考试，就可以获得医疗许可机构授予的执业资格。

In the United States, the individual medical licensing authorities ("state medical boards") of the various jurisdictions grant a license to practice medicine. Each medical licensing authority sets its own rules and regulations and required to pass the examination to prove their qualifications. Through the USMLE exam, you can get granted by the medical licensing authority.

USMLE由一个委员会管理，包括来自ECFMG、FSMB、NBME成员和公众的成员。该委员会负责整个计划的方向，识别和批准的程序得分和确定通过/失败的标准，以及所有重要的政策和程序。USMLE考试委员会的成员包括生物医学科学家、教育工作者和来自美国的每一个地区的临床医生。几乎所有的医学教育联络委员会认可的美国医学院校已在USMLE考试委员会代表。USMLE考试委员会成员代表"国家医学院"医学院校的州医学委员会和临床实践设置在美国。

USMLE is managed by a committee comprising members from the ECFMG, FSMB, NBME and members of the public. The committee is responsible for the overall direction of the program, the identification and approval of the program score and the determination of the pass / fail criteria, as well as all important policies and procedures. The members of the USMLE Examination Committee include biomedical scientists, educators, and clinicians from every region of the United states. Almost all of the medical education liaison committees recognized by the American medical schools have been represented on the USMLE examination board. Members of the USMLE examinations Committee represent the national medical school, the medical school of the state medical board and the clinical practice setting in the United states.

USMLE 的目标和使命是：向授权机关提供评估医生的有意义的信息，包括医生的医疗知识，技能，价值观和态度，这些信息对于安全有效的病人护理具有重要性；对于设计开发评估体系有重要作用，这些评估对象主要是医学教育者及其机构、授权机构成员、执业医生；通过最高的专业测试标准确保医生选拔的公平和公正；USMLE 可以完善对执业医生更准确、更全面的评估。

USMLE's goals and mission: provide meaningful assessment information of doctors to the authorities, including the doctor's medical knowledge, skills, values and attitudes, which are important to the provision of safe and effective patient care; there is an important role for the design and development of the evaluation system, the evaluation object is mainly on medical educators and their institutions, authority members, practicing doctors; ensure the fairness and justice on doctor selection through the highest professional testing standards; USMLE can improve the assessment of practitioners more accurate and comprehensive.

6.1.2 USMLE 考前准备

USMLE 考试分三级：阶段 1、阶段 2、阶段 3。根据美国外国医学毕业生教育委员会（ECFMG）规定，有资格参加阶段 1、阶段 2 考试的美国及加拿大境外的学生，可以查询其所毕业的

6.1.2 Preparations for USMLE

USMLE examination is divided into three stages: step 1, Step 2, step 3. According to the Education Commission for foreign medical graduates（ECFMG）, students who are eligible to participate in

医学院校是否被列入了国际医学教育名录（IMED），资格查询可以登录：http://www.wdoms.org/，确认了具备考试资格后，登录 ECFMG 官方网站查阅对于考试资格的说明。中国 171 所医科院校可在 ECFMG 官方网站查询到，即承认该校学生有资格参加 USMLE。

一般情况下，申请人必须在医学院完成至少两年的学业，即考生必须完成基础医学科学部分的课程。临床医学专业本科学历的在校生或毕业生，都能参加 USMLE 考试。如果本科是中西医、中医、医学影像、麻醉、儿科、预防医学等专业，学习内容与临床医学相近。如果学校出具的学位证书是 Bachelor of Medicine，需要通过 ECFMG 个案审查。如果在本科阶段学的专业不是临床医学，但研究生是临床医学专业，不能报考 USMLE。在校学生只要没毕业，都可以以学生身份报名，研究生不能以学生身份报名，应当按毕业生报名。

the step 1 and Step 2 examinations outside of the United States and Canada can check whether the medical schools you have graduated from are listed in the International Medical Education Directory（IMED）.You can login the web address for qualification query: http://www.wdoms.org/, after confirming the qualification examination, login ECFMG official website for examination qualification description. 171 Chinese medical institutions in the ECFMG official website can be found,students graduated from these colleges are admitted to participate in USMLE.

In general,the applicant must complete the courses at least two years in medical school, that is, candidates must complete basic medical science courses. Clinical medicine undergraduate degree students or graduates, can participate in the USMLE exam. If your specialty is the Chinese and Western Medicine, Chinese medicine, medical imaging, anesthesia, pediatrics, preventive medicine professional, or other professional,which learning content is similar to clinical medicine, the degree certificate you got is Bachelor of Medicine, you need to be

如果想参加阶段 3 阶段的考试，必须拥有以下资格：通过了阶段 1、阶段 2 考试，并取得 ECFMG 的证书；取得医学博士学位（MD）或骨科医师（OD）证书。

阶段 1、阶段 2 考试申请流程可以按照 ECFMG 网站上的说明填写申请表并提交给 ECFMG，考生在 8~10 周可以收到 ECFMG 的注册许可证明——Scheduling Permit，考生按照注册许可证明指导完成注册，并提交上去。Step 3 阶段考试的申请可以浏览 FSMB（美国联邦医学理事会）网站，该网站接受申请 step 3 的注册，按照申请 step 3 的资格要求及申请程序和申请说明，填写申请表并提交给医学执照权威机构或 FSMB 的指定机构。

accepted ECFMG case review. As long as the students do not graduate, students can apply for identity, graduate students can not be registered as a student, should be registered by the graduates.

If you want to participate in the Step 3 exam, you must have the following qualifications: passed the step 1, Step 2 exam and obtained ECFMG certificate; To obtain a doctor's degree in medicine (MD) or a certificate in Department of orthopedics (OD).

Step1, Step2 examination application process can be completed in accordance with the instructions on the ECFMG website and submit the application form to ECFMG, Candidates can receive ECFMG registration license—Scheduling Permit in 8–10 weeks. Candidates complete the registration in accordance with the registration permit guidance, and submit it. Application for Step 3 examination can browse FSMB (US Federal Medical Board) website, the website accepts the application for Step 3 registration, in accordance with the eligibility requirements of the application Step 3, application procedures and application notes, fill in the application form and submit to the medical licensing authority or the designated body of FSMB.

6.1.3 如何备考 USMLE

USMLE 是一种专业的考试。在美国，如果想成为一个医生，必须通过考试。准备 USMLE 是一个伤脑筋的过程。大多数人可能认为，如果得到60分，将通过考试，但这是错误的。即使得了60分，也不是每个人都能通过考试的。例如，如果得到61分，但最低的分数是62分，即使通过了考试的分数，但不能通过。USMLE 分数将大大反映考生投入学习和对考试的态度。因此，制订学习计划表是非常重要的。

（1）尽早制定 USMLE 的学习计划

制定 USMLE 的学习计划没有捷径可走。有些学生在上大学之前可能有成为美国医生的想法，有些学生在完成基础医学课程学习后会有一些想法，也有很多人在医院工作过。所以很难说什么时候应该开始为 USMLE 学习。本书认为，考生开始得越早，会得到更好的分数。考生应该根据自己

6.1.3 How to prepare for the USMLE

USMLE is a kind of professional exam. In America, if you want to be a doctor, you must pass through the exam. Preparing for USMLE is a nerve-wracking experience. Most people perhaps think that if they get 60 scores, they will pass the exam, but it's wrong. Not everybody can get through the exam even if you get 60 scores. For example, if you get 61 scores,but the lowest score is 62 scores, even if you passed the exam's scores, but you can't get through. Your scores on the USMLE will greatly reflect the attitude you put into studying and the exam. So it's important to schedule your plan to study on USMLE.

（1）Make USMLE learning plan as soon as possible

There's no simple way to answer it. Some students perhaps have ideas to be an American doctor before they go to colleges, some students have ideas after they finish studying the basic medical courses. Also there are many people who have worked in hospitals. So it's hard to say when you begin studying for the USMLE. But I

的实际情况安排学习时间。选择适当的学习方式学习。

（2）知道如何选择材料

有数以百计的复习书籍可以帮助考生准备这次考试。虽然这些书的内容可能都有点重复，但是资料和资料间还是有很大的不同的。好的复习书的选择是购买一些契合自己学习风格和 USMLE 考试形式的书籍。有时面前的书越多，就感觉越混乱，学习效率越低。换句话说，过度的资源最终会成为学习的障碍。最有效的应试者是随着时间的推移来巩固学习材料的学生。开始学习的时候选择一本最新版本的 *First Aid for the USMLE Step* 1。如果第一次参加 USMLE 的考试，这将是第一本很重要的资源。考生可以在网上购买这种书。这本书是大纲，然后可以参考（推荐）书背后的书。买相应的书，看书的内容加上这本书。可以把这本书作为一个总的学习大纲。

think, the earlier you start, the better score you'll get. You should arrange your time to study according to your actual condition. You should choose the appropriate study style to learn.

（2）Know how to choose the materials

There are hundreds of review books available to help you prepare for this exam. While the content in these books may overlap quite a bit, the way that material is presented can vary drastically from resource to resource. The trick to select good review books is to purchase a few that mesh well with your learning style and the actual format of the USMLE. The more books you have in front of you, the greater potential for confusion and the less productive you will feel. In other words, an over abundance of resources eventually will become an impediment to your studying. The most efficient test takers are the students who consolidate their study materials as time goes by. Start with a fresh copy of the newest edition of First Aid for the USMLE Step 1, this will be your primary resource for the USMLE. If you are the first time to join the exam, you can buy a FA step 1 on the line, the book as an outline, You can refer to (recommend) the books behind the book. You can buy the corresponding book, and see the contents of the book to add to this book. You can regard the book as a toal outline.

When your entire knowledge system has been over, you should buy USMLE Q & A. Now you begin to do the simulation test, you can buy the latest book. I don't think you are right that you read USMLE Q&A in the beginning. After you have understood all the basic knowledge, you will find that this book is a real God book.

（3）Set up a study schedule as early as possible

Determine when you will begin studying, how much time you will dedicate to the exam each week or month.Keep in mind that you will need the last few weeks before exams to review all of the content that you have studied. Make a flexible study schedule, especially early in your preparations. Give yourself some free time every day to enjoy other activities and relax your mind.This will increase the productivity of your study time.

When you go over the USMLE,You should aim high and keep your chin up. Don't give up.

当整个知识体系已经结束，应该买 USMLE Q&A。从现在开始做模拟试题，买最新的书。如果一开始就阅读 USMLE Q&A 是不对的。当了解了所有的基本知识后，考生会发现这本书是真正的神书。

（3）尽早制订学习进度表

确定什么时候开始学习，每周或每个月会花多少时间参加考试，记住需要在考试前的最后几周复习你学习过的所有内容。制订灵活的学习计划，尤其是在准备工作中。每天给自己一些空闲时间做其他的活动，放松思维，这会提高学习效率。在复习过程中，应该有信心，别放弃。

6.2 USMLE Step 1 考试

USMLE 共分有阶段 1、阶段 2 Clinical Knowledge、阶段 2 Clinical Skill 和阶段 3 的三个步骤、四个考试。美国医学院学生在毕业之前会通过阶段 1 和阶段 2，然后进入住院医培训阶段，并在期间完成阶段 3，最终取得在美国独立行医资格。在美国以外获得医学学位的国际医学毕业生（International Medical Graduate, IMG），如果希望在美国获得行医资格，也需要通过 USMLE 考试。对于 IMG 来说，在学生阶段或毕业之后均可以参加 USMLE 各步考试。

6.2.1 USMLE 阶段 1 考试内容

USMLE 阶段 1 是基础医学考试，涵盖解剖、组织和胚胎、微生物和免疫、生化和遗传、生理、药理、病理及行为医学等内容，相对应于中国医学教育中的基础医学阶段。第一阶段的试题一般来说是测验考生解读图表的能力，以及如何将基础医学知识应用到临床问题上。这项考试的分数非常具有竞争性且对任何一位想要在美

6.2 USMLE Step 1 Exam

USMLE has a total of Step 1, Step 2 Clinical Knowledge, Step 2 Clinical Skill and Step 3 in three steps, four examinations. American medical students will pass Step1 and Step 2 before graduation, and then enter the residency training stage, finish Step 3 exam, and ultimately achieve independent medical practice in the United states. International medical graduates (International Medical Graduate, IMG) of outside the United States, if they want to get medical practice in the United States, they need to pass the USMLE exam. IMG can take part in the USMLE test in the student stage or after graduation.

6.2.1 USMLE Step 1 exam contents

USMLE Step 1 is a basic medical examination, including anatomy, tissue and embryo, microbiology and immunology, biochemistry and genetics, physiology, pharmacology, pathology and behavioral medicine etc., corresponding to the basic stage of medical China in medical education. In general, The questions of step1 test candidates' ability on

国当医生的人非常重要，主要原因在于几乎所有的医院都以此考试作为录取住院医生的其中一个主要标准。

阶段1考试试题由考试委员会编写的多项选择题组成，考试委员会由本领域知名的学者、教师、临床工作者和许可机关的人员组成。阶段1的考试时间是1天，共8个小时，考试形式是7个部分，每个部分1小时的答题时间。每个部分的考试题目数量是不同的，但是不能超过40道，7个版块的题目数量不超过280道。

阶段1考试目标是测试考生对基本知识的掌握情况，一些试题是对考生的信息量进行测试，但是多数题目要求考生对图形和表格资料进行解释，找出微观病理和正常标本，通过基本理论运用来解决实际问题。

interpreting charts and how to apply basic medical knowledge to clinical problems. The scores of step1 are very competitive and are very important to anyone who want to be a physician in America, The reason is that almost all hospitals take this test as one of the main criteria for admission to a residency.

Step 1 examination questions are composed of a number of multiple topics written by the examination committee. The examination committee are selected by the field of well-known scholars, teachers, clinical workers and licensing agencies. Step 1 examination time is one day, a total of eight hours. The examination form has seven sections, and each piece has an hour's time. Each section of the test subject number is different, but not more than 40. The number of the topics of the seven sections are no more than 280.

Step 1 goal is to test the examinee's basic knowledge. Some of the questions test the examinee's fund of information, but most questions are asked by examinees to explain the graphical and tabular data, to find out the microscopic pathological and normal specimens, to solve practical problems by using the basic theory.

阶段 1 考试内容包括以下传统的医学学科：解剖、行为科学、生物化学、生物统计学、流行病学、微生物学、药理、生理、病理。除此之外，它还涵盖了以下相关学科领域的内容：衰老、遗传学、免疫学、分子与细胞生物学、营养学。

并不是所有在大纲中列出的条目都会在考试中出现。大多数器官系统划分为正常流程和异常流程，包括特定的疾病类别的过程。在多数的病案中，通过考生对病程发生的背景或特定病理的理解来考查其在课程中所学到的知识。

USMLE 阶段 1 测试的详细系统和流程

阶段 1 的各系统和流程的测试所占百分比是变化的，在执业医师考试大纲中，这些问题包括一般性原则，生物统计学/循证医学或者社会科学。更详细的信息请看 USMLE 网站（http://www.usmle.org）

Step 1 test includes the following traditional medical disciplines: anatomy, behavioral science, biochemistry, biostatistics, epidemiology, microbiology, pharmacology, physiology and pathology. In addition, it covers the following subjects: aging, genetics, immunology, molecular and cellular biology, nutrition.

Not all of the topics listed in the outline will appear in the exam. Most organ systems are divided into normal and abnormal processes, including the process of a specific disease category. In most cases, the knowledge of the normal course of the examinee is assessed by understanding the context of a disease process or a particular pathology.

USMLE step 1 test detailed system and process

The percentage of Step1 tests systems and processes can change at any time. These issues include the general principles, Biostatistics / evidence-based medicine, or social science in the medical licensing examination outline. For more details, access the USMLE website (http://www.usmle.org)

System	Range
General Principles of Foundational Science**	15%～20%
Organ System • Immune System • Blood and Lymphoreticular System • Behavioral Health • Nervous System & Special Senses • Skin & Subcutaneous Tissue • Musculoskeletal System • Cardiovascular System • Respiratory System • Gastrointestinal System • Renal & Urinary System • Pregnancy, Childbirth, & the Puerperium • Female Reproductive & Breast • Male Reproductive • Endocrine System	60%～70%
Multisystem Processes & Disorders Biostatistics & Epidemiology/Population Health Social Sciences	15%～20%

Process	Range
Normal Processes†	10%～15%
Abnormal Processes	55%～60%
Principles of Therapeutics	15%～20%
Other‡	10%～15%

医生的任务/能力的考察内容如下表。

The contents of the doctor's tasks / abilities are as follows.

Competency	Range
Medical Knowledge/Scientific Concepts	55%～65%
Patient Care: Diagnosis • History/Physical Examination • Laboratory/Diagnostic Studies • Diagnosis • Prognosis/Outcome	20%～30%
Patient Care: Management** • Health Maintenance/Disease Prevention • Pharmacotherapy	7%～12%
Communication Professionalism	2%～5%
Practice-based Learning and Improvement	4%～8%

百分比是随时可以变化的。阶段 1 包括仅在本表中列出的类别的管理问题。它不包括与临床干预、混合管理或疾病复发监测有关的问题。

Percentage can change at any time. The Step 1 examination includes management questions in only the categories listed in this table. It does not include questions related to clinical interventions, mixed management, or surveillance for disease recurrence.

6.3 USMLE 阶段 2 考试内容

USMLE 阶段 2 考试包括阶段 2 CK 和阶段 2 CS 两部分，主要是测试医学生的应用医学知识和临床技术的能力。美国医学生在 4 年级的时候会报考该考试。

6.3.1 USMLE 阶段 2 CK 考试

第二阶段的临床医学考试阶段 2 CK，评估考生医学知识应用能力和技能，了解临床科学为病人提供护理的认识。它的考试分 8 个板块，每个板块不超过 45 个问题，总题数在 340~355 之间，考试时间是 1 天，9 个小时在计算机上完成。每个板块不论题目多少，都需要 1 小时完成。

6.3 USMLE Step 2 Exam Contents

USMLE Step 2 exam includes two parts: Step 2 CK and step 2 CS, they mainly test the application of medical knowledge and clinical skills of medical students. Medical students in the United States will apply for the exams in grade 4.

6.3.1 USMLE Step 2 CK exam

The second step of the clinical examination Step 2 CK (Clinical Knowledge), focuses on evaluation of examinees' ability and skills in medical knowledge, understanding of clinical science to provide care for patients. The exam is divided into 8 blocks, each block is not more than 45 questions, the total number of questions are 340~355, the examination time is a nine-hour single-day computer-based test. No matter how many questions each block has, each block is one hour long.

在考试开始有 15 分钟的熟悉软件使用的教程，如果应试者对这方面比较熟悉，可以选择跳过，这样可以增加休息时间。一天的考试过程中有 45 分钟时间是休息时间。如果考生在 1 小时期限之前完成了该板块所有题目可以提交，将剩余的时间增加到休息时间里。

阶段 2 CK 考试内容包括：内科、产科学、妇科医学、小儿科、预防药品、精神医学、外科及其他提供医疗照顾之相关领域。专题着重于考生对临床情况的描述、提供诊断和预后，健康维持和预防措施等。

阶段 2 CK 的考试题综合了医学领域的各方面问题，它经常需要考生对一些问题解释，如表格、实验室数据、影像资料、解剖图、显微图像及其他一些诊断资料。

There is a 15-minute tutorial at the beginning of the exam, which the test-taker can choose to skip if he or she is familiar with it, and has time to add to the break time. There are 45 minutes for breaks in total for the whole day. If the test-taker finishes any block before the allotted 1 hour time limit, the remainder of the time is added to break time.

Step 2 CK examination includes: internal medicine, obstetrics, gynecology, pediatrics, preventive medicine, psychiatry, surgery and other related field of medical care. The questions focus on examinees' description of the clinical situation, providing diagnosis and prognosis, health maintenance and preventive measures.

Step 2 CK exam comprehensive all aspects of the problem in the field of medicine, it often requires test-takers to explain for some problems, such as the explaination for form, laboratory data, image data, anatomy, microscopic images and other diagnostic studies.

阶段 2 CK 考试形式有两种：第一种是单问题考题形式，即在叙述完 1 个病案后，给出一个问题，有相应的 4 或 5 个选项，选出正确的 1 个；第二种是序贯问题考题形式，即在叙述完 1 个病案后，有 2~3 个连续提出，每个问题测试点不同，每个问题要选 出一个最佳答案。问题之间在设计上是有顺序的。考生必须单击"转到下一个项目"来查看设置中的下一个项目；一旦单击此按钮，将无法添加或更改显示的（上一个）项目的答案。

There are three types of Step 2 CK questions the first type is single items, that is, a single patient-centered vignette is associated with one question followed by four or more response options (ie,A,B,C,D,E), choose the best one answer to the question; the second type is sequential item sets, that is, a single patient-centered vignette may be associated with two or three consecutive questions about the information presented. Each question is associated with the initial patient vignette but is testing a different point. You are required to select the ONE BEST answer to each question, questions are designed to be answered in sequential order. You must click "Proceed to Next Item" to view the next item in the set ; once you click on this button,you will not be able to add or change an answer to the displayed (previous) item.

阶段 2 CK 测试项目主要是从两个维度展开，一个是疾病种类，另一个是医生的任务和职责。

Step2 CK test project is mainly from two dimensions, one is the disease type, and the other is the doctor's duties and responsibilities.

Step 2 CK 考试内容

System	Range
General Principles of Foundational Science**	1%~3%
Immune System Blood & Lymphoreticular Systems Behavioral Health Nervous System & Special Senses Skin & Subcutaneous Tissue Musculoskeletal System Cardiovascular System Respiratory System Gastrointestinal System Renal & Urinary Systems Pregnancy, Childbirth, & the Puerperium Female Reproductive System & Breast Male Reproductive System Endocrine System Multisystem Processes & Disorders	85%~95%
Biostatistics & Epidemiology/Population Health Interpretation of the Medical Literature	1%~5%

上表显示了阶段 2 CK 考试的内容和百分比，百分比随时变化，详情请参照 USMLE 网站最新消息。（ http://www.usmle.org ）。

阶段 2 CK 考试的一般原则包括正常流程的测试项目而不限于特殊器官系统。各个器官系统的类别包括有关系统正常和异常过程的测试项目。

Table shows the contents and percentage of the Step 2 CK exam, percentage changes at any time. For more information, please browse the latest news on the USMLE website. (http://www.usmle.org)

The general principles of the Step 2 CK test include the normal test items and not limited to the special organ system. The categories of each organ system include test items about the system's normal and abnormal processes.

通过上表，可以看出考试内容所占百分比情况，其中基础科学的一般性原则所占比例为 1%~3%；各个系统和器官内容占 80%~85%；生物统计学和流行病学和人口健康和医学文献解读，社会科学所占比例为 14%~18%。

We can see the percentage of the content of the examination from table, on which the proportion of the general principle of the scientific basis is 1%–3%; each system and organ contents is 80%–85%; biostatistics and epidemiology and population health and medical literature, social sciences is 14%–18%.

医生的任务和能力

Competency	Range
Medical Knowledge/Scientific Concepts	10%~15%
Patient Care: Diagnosis • History/Physical Examination • Laboratory/Diagnostic Studies • Diagnosis • Prognosis/Outcome	40%~50%
Patient Care: Management • Health Maintenance/Disease Prevention • Pharmacotherapy • Clinical Interventions • Mixed Management • Surveillance for Disease Recurrence	30%~35%
Communication Professionalism Systems-based Practice/Patient Safety Practice-based Learning	3%~7%

阶段 2 CK 考试内容的另一个维度是医生的任务和能力。上表是关于医生的任务和能力的考试内容和百分比，百分比随时变化，详情参照

Another dimension of the Step 2 CK exam content is the doctor's task and ability. Table is about physicians' task and competency and its percentage. The

USMLE 网站最新消息。

考试题目的设置重点评估考生对病人诊断的管理。在考试内容的百分比中，中医学知识掌握能力占 10%~15%，考生对病人诊断能力（病史采集、体检、实验资料的理解、诊断和预后）占 40%~50%，考生对病人的处理能力（健康维持、疾病预防、药物治疗、临床干预、疾病复发的监测）占 30%~35%，考生的交流能力，专业能力，病人安全和实践学习能力占 3%~7%。

阶段 2 CK 得分报告是一个 3 位数的分数。大部分考生得分在 140~260 之间，美国和加拿大范围内的考生得分在 220~230 之间，标准偏差一般约 28。

percentage changes at any time, details refer to the latest news on USMLE.

examination questions focus on the evaluation of examinees for patient diagnosis and management. In the percentage of test content, the percentage of competency to master and apply medical knowledge is 10%~15%, the percentage of diagnosis competency (history collection, physical examination, laboratory data studies, diagnosis and prognosis) is 40%~50%, the percentage of management competency for the patient (monitoring and health maintenance, disease prevention, drug treatment, clinical intervention, disease recurrence) is 30%~35%, the percentage of examinee's communicate, professional skills, patient safety and practice-based learning is 3%~7%.

The Step 2 CK score is a 3 digit scores. Most of the examinees' scores are between 140 and 260, the examinees' scores in United States and Canada are between 220~230, and the standard deviation is about 28.

6.3.2 USMLE 阶段 2 CS 考试

美国医师执照考试第二阶段的临床诊断能力的考察是由 NBME 和 FSMB 共同发起的。从 1997 年 7 月 1 日起，USMLE 阶段 2 增加了临床诊断能力的测验，其测验目的主要是测验考生临床诊断能力与英语会话能力。考生须在现场用英语帮病人正确诊断；评估考生运用医疗知识的能力、技能和对临床科学的理解；测试考生对病人的医疗管理水平技能；阶段 2 CS 强调健康促进和疾病预防；确保临床科学原理及以病人为核心的服务得到应有重视，这为安全有效的医学实践奠定了基础。

阶段 2 CS 考试使用模拟病人（SPs），他们是通过培训来模拟各种有临床问题的人，这种评估方法称为标准化患者考试。这种方法已至少创立 35 年，其程序已在美国和国际上进行了测试和验证。当进行阶段 2 CS 考试时，考生就有了与其他考生相同的机会来评估自己的临床技能水平。考试是标准化的，所以当标准化病人被问

6.3.2 USMLE Step 2 CS exam

The clinical diagnosis ability of the second step on USMLE is sponsored by NBME and FSMB.From July 1, 1997, USMLE Step 2 added to the clinical diagnosis ability test, which purpose is to test the examinees' clinical diagnosis ability and Spoken English ability. The test-taker should give correct diagnosis in English. It assesses the examinees' ability of applying medical knowledge, clinical skills and understanding clinical science. It tests examinees' medical management skills for patients; Step 2 CS emphasizes on health promotion and disease prevention. It ensures clinical scientific principle and clinical patient- centered services are valued, all of these lay the foundation for safe and effective medical practice.

The Step 2 CS exam uses simulated patients（SPs）, who are trained to simulate a variety of clinical problems, and this evaluation method is called standardized patient testing. This method has been established for at least 35 years and has been tested and verified in the United States and internationally. When you take the Step 2 CS exam, you have the

及相同或相似的问题时，考生们得到的信息是相同的。考试过程采用直播与录音监控的方式来管理，以保证考试的公平与公正。在考试过程中，考生会看到 12 个 SPs，他们的年龄、性别、种族、组织器官系统疾病不同。

执业医师与教师参与了病例的开发与审查，以保证它们是准确与恰当的。这些病例代表了美国医疗实践中通常遇见的病人与问题。病案中的病人的类型都是在见习期间遇到过的，有内科学、外科学、妇产科、儿科学、精神病学、家庭医学、急诊医学。考生不与儿童接触，而是由 SPs 模拟儿科病人的父母来叙述病人的病史，这种情况下不要求体检。

same opportunities as other examinees to evaluate your clinical skills. The tests are standardized, so when SPs are asked the same or similar questions, the information they receive is the same. In the course of examination, live and recording monitoring is adopted to ensure the fairness and justice of examination. During the examination, test-takers will see 12 SPs, who are mixed in terms of age, gender, ethnicity, organ system and discipline.

Practitioners and teachers are involved in the development and review of cases to ensure that they are accurate and appropriate. These cases represent patients and problems commonly encountered in American medical practice. Patient problems in the case are typically encountered during core clerkships in the curricula of accredited US medical schools as follows: Internal medicine; Surgery; Obstetrics and Gynecology; Pediatrics; Psychiatry; Family medicine; Emergency medicine. Examinees do not interact with children during pediatric encounters. Insread, SPs assuming the role of pediatric patients' parents recount patients' histories, and no physical exam is required under such circumstances.

有意参加该考试者还可参照 USMLE 网站（www.usmle.org）提供的培训视频。有关资格、注册与日程的信息参见 USMLE 网站的信息通告。国际考生必须同时留意 ECFMG 网站（www.ecfmg.org）的信息通告，在此记录的信息及其他材料同样适用于 USMLE 网站。USMLE 网站还会发布考试变化的信息，考生必须明确理解 USMLE 的最新政策。

在考生进入房间看标准化病人前，将有机会得到病人的一些初步信息。这些信息都张贴在房间的门上，其主要内容是病人特征（姓名、年龄、性别），主诉和生命体征（体温、脉搏、血压），考生对每一个病例有 15 分钟的处理时间，包括阅读门上的信息，进入房间介绍自己，获得适当的病史，进行集中体检，建立鉴别诊断和规划诊断检查。考生可能需要回答 SP 提出的任何关于诊断的问题，讨论病案。考生还要给出病人健康建议

Those who are interested in participating in the examination may also refer to the training video provided by USMLE website (www.usmle.org), on which there are information for qualifications, registration, and schedule. International examinees outside U.S and Canada must also pay attention to the bulliton on ECFMG website (www.ecfmg.org). The information and other materials on ECFMG website also are applied on USMLE website. USMLE site will also release information on the change in the exam, you must clearly understand the latest USMLE policy.

Before entering a room to interact with a SP, you will be given an opportunity to review some preliminary information, which is posted on the door of each room. Its main content is the patient characteristics (name, age and gender), and chief complaint and vitals (temperature, pulse, blood pressure), the examinees will be given 15 minutes to per-form the clinical encounter, which includes reading the doorway information, entering the room introducing yourself,

及定期复查计划。离开房间后，考生将有 10 分钟输入病案报告。

在 12 个病案中，有 10 个病案是记分的，另外两个病案是测试标准化病人和考官医生的。标准化病人要根据考生采集病史、体检、交流能力给出评估，医生评估考生的病案报告。

阶段 2 CS 的分数由三部分组成：综合临床知识（ICE）得分，这个分数将反映考生的数据采集和解释能力；沟通和人际交往能力（CIS）得分；英语口语熟练程度（SEP）得分。阶段 2 CS 没有具体的分数，其成绩是"及格"或"不及格"。

obtaining an appropriate history,conducing focused physical exam,formulating a differential diagnosis,and planning a diagnostic workup. Test-takers need to answer any questions raised by SP about the diagnosis, examinees should give the patient's health advice and follow-up plans. After leaving the room, you will have 10 minutes to type a patient note.

Of the 12 patient encounters, 10 will be scored, and the other two will score each encounter: the SP and a physician. The SP will evaluate test-taker's ability for history, physical examination and communication. The physician will evalute the PN (patient note), which examinees write after each encounter.

The score of Step 2 CS is composed of three parts: intergrated Clinical Encounter （ICE）score, which will reflect your data-gathering and interpretation skills; Communication and Interpersonal skills （CIS）score; Spoken English Proficiency （SEP）score. Step 2 CS has no specific score,the grade on the Step 2 CS will be either a "Pass" or a "fail".

在准备 Step 2 CS 考试的过程中，考生要具有某些基本的、关键的临床技能，这些技能保证其能通过考试。这些技能包括：以专业的和善解人意的方式和病人打交道的能力，良好的病史采集能力，适当的并且重要的体检能力，咨询和传播信息能力，输入有逻辑的组织良好的病案能力，病案包括合理的鉴别诊断。

In preparing for the Step 2 CS exam, examinees are required to have some fundamental and critical clinical skills that will enable you to pass the exam. These skills include: the ability to interact with patients in a professional and empathetic manner, the ability to take a good medical history, the ability to perform an appropriate and focused physical exam, the ability of information consultation and dissemination, the ability to type a logical and organized PN that includes a reasoned differential diagnosis.

6.4 USMLE 阶段 3 考试内容

6.4.1 阶段 3 的考试时间与形式

Step 3 的考试形式包括多项选择题（MCQ）和按照内容说明分配的计算机病例模拟（CCS），考试材料由代表医学界的考试委员会提供。Step 3 是为期两天的考试。第一天的测试包括 6 个模块 256 个多项选择题，每个模块 38~40 项题目，每个模块测试时间为 1 小时。第一天的考试时间大约 7 个小时，其中包括 45 分钟的休息时间，5 分钟计算机软件使用教程。第二天的

6.4 USMLE Step 3 Exam Contents

6.4.1 Step 3 exam time and formates

The form of Step 3 examination consists of multiple choice questions (MCQ) and Computer-based Case Simulation (CCS) in accordance with the description of contents. The examination materials are provided by the Examination Committee on behalf of the medical profession. Step 3 is a two-day exam. The first day of the test consists of 233 multiple-choice questions divided into 6 blocks, each

测试时间大约9个小时，包括7分钟计算机软件使用教程，后面跟着198个多项选择题，分属6个模块，33个考题，每个模块需要45分钟完成。其次是13个病例模拟，其中每一个病例分配最多10或20分钟的时间，休息时间最少45分钟。第二天最后还有一个可选的调查问卷，如果时间允许可以完成。测试项目通常从病人的角度详细说明临床情况，也可以用一个或多个图形、音频、视频来辅助说明。通过病人所处的环境和家庭来评估一个病人的情况是许多阶段3考试题的重要因素。

block has 38~40 questions, each block test time is one hour. The first day of the test time is about 7 hours, including a 45-minute break, a 5-minute tutorial. The second day of testing time is about 9 hours, including a 5-minute tutorial, followed by 180 multiple-choice questions, which are divided into 6 blocks, 30 items. The amount of time allocated to each block is 45 minutes, you should finish all the items of each block within 45 minutes. The second day also includes a 7-minute CCS tutorial, followed by a total of 13 cases, each of which is allocated for a maximum of 10 or 20 minutes, with a minimum of 45 minutes of rest. On the second day, there is an optional survey that can be completed if time permits. Test items are usually described in detail from the patient's clinical situation, you can also use one or more graphics, audio, video to help illustrate. Assessing the condition of a patient through the patient's environment and family is an important factor in many Step 3 exams.

阶段 3 考试致力于评估医生的知识和技能的重要性，评估医生为病人提供一般医疗服务的独立能力和责任。考试的第一天被称为独立的实践基础（FIP），第二天被称为高级临床医学（ACM）。

第一天考试重点是评估基本医疗知识和有效保健所必需的科学原则。它所涵盖的内容包括基础科学的应用、生物统计学和流行病学和人口健康的理解、医学文献的解读、社会科学的应用包括沟通和人际交往能力、医学伦理学、系统实践和病人安全。其内容还包括内容评估诊断和管理的知识，特别侧重于病史和身体检查、诊断和诊断研究的知识。

The Step 3 devotes to assess the importance of physician knowledge and skills and to assess the independent ability and responsibility of physicians who provide general medical services to patients. The first day of the exam is called Foundations of Independent Practice (FIP), the second day is called Advanced Clinical Medicine (ACM).

Day 1 focuses on assessment of knowledge of basic medical and scientific principles essential for effective health care. It covers the application of basic science, biostatistics and epidemiology and population health, understanding, interpretation and application of the medical literature, social sciences, including communication and interpersonal skills, medical ethics, practice and patient safety system. It also includes knowledge of content evaluation, diagnosis, and management, with a particular focus on knowledge of medical history and physical examination, diagnosis and diagnostic studies.

第一天的测试只包括多项选择题和一些新的题型，如那些基于科学文摘和药品广告的题型。

第二天的考试重点是评估医生在病人管理方面的运用健康和疾病综合医学知识的能力。它所涵盖的内容包括评估医生的诊断和管理的知识，特别侧重于预后和结果，健康维护和筛查，治疗和医疗决策，病史和身体检查，诊断和诊断研究的使用知识也被评估。

考试内容包括相关药学广告或科学文摘，每一个药品广告或科学摘要将显示为2~3个。考生将在考试中看到不超过5个的这些项目。每个模块在退出之前考生可以修改答案，一旦退出该模块，考生就没有机会检查和更改答案了。

The first day of testing includes only multiple-choice questions and some new questions, such as those based on scientific abstracts and drug advertising.

The second day test focuses on assessing the ability of physicians to apply health and disease integrated medical knowledge in patient management. The topics cover an assessment to the knowledge of the physician's diagnosis and management, with a particular focus on prognosis and outcomes, health maintenance and screening, treatment, and medical decision making. Knowledge of medical history and physical examination, diagnostic and diagnostic studies were also assessed.

The content of the exam will include the relevant pharmaceutical advertisements or scientific abstracts, each of which will be displayed as 2 or 3, and you will see no more than 5 items in the exam. Each block can be changed before you exit. Once you exit the block, you will not have

在网站上练习多项选择题，能让考生熟悉考试的计算机界面和对考试时间的把握。考试时会给考生提供一个正常的实验室数值表，包括国际标准转换表，这个表可以做为在线参考。选择按钮和复选框是用来推进时钟，改变病人的位置，审查先前显示的信息，并获得更新的病人资料。在每一个病例开始时，考生将看到临床设置、模拟病例时间和病人信息介绍，不会提供照片和声音。每个报告将提供正常或参考实验室值，一些试验还伴随临床解释。使用原始的 CCS 软件管理患者，最重要的是考生要完成 USMLE 网站提供的教程和样本。

the opportunity to check and change the answer.

The practice of multiple-choice questions on the USMLE website allows you to familiarize yourself with the computer interface and the timing of the test. The test will provide you with a normal laboratory numerical table, including the international standard conversion table, this table can be used as an online reference. The selection button and check box are used to advance the clock, change the patient's position, review previously displayed information, and obtain updated patient information. At the beginning of each case, you will see the clinical settings, simulated case time and patient information presentation, there are no photos and sound provided. Each report will provide normal or reference laboratory values, some of which are also subject to clinical interpretation. During using the original CCS software to manage patients, the most important thing is that you have to complete the tutorials and samples provided by the USMLE website.

在考生参加完 USMLE 考试后的 3~4 周就可查到成绩。分数是三位数。最低合格分数是 190 分，近年来第一参加考试的考生平均分在 215~235 之间，标准分差 20 分。

The USMLE typically reports scores three to four weeks after the examinee's test date. Scoring is reported in 3 digit scores.A minium score of 190 is required for passing. The mean score for first-time test takers rangers from 215 to 235 with a standard deviation of approxmate 20.

6.4.2 阶段 3 考试内容规范

6.4.2 Step 3 test content specifications

MCQ Test Content Specifications

System	Range
General Principles of Foundational Science**	1%~3%
Immune System Blood & Lymphoreticular System Behavioral Health Nervous System & Special Senses Skin & Subcutaneous Tissue Musculoskeletal System Cardiovascular System Respiratory System Gastrointestinal System Renal & Urinary System Pregnancy, Childbirth, & the Puerperium Female Reproductive System & Breast Male Reproductive System Endocrine System Multisystem Processes & Disorders	80%~85%
Biostatistics & Epidemiology/Population Health, & Interpretation of the Medical Literature Social Sciences	14%~18%

上表是多项选择题涉及的内容和所占百分比。百分比是随时变化的。考生可以看 USMLE 的网站（http://www.usmle.org）的最新信息了解其变化情况，并根据一般原则和个别器官系统组织内容。测试问题分为 18 个主要领域，取决于他们是否专注于概念和原则，重要的是跨器官系统或个别器官系统。针对个别器官系统的部分被细分为正常和异常的过程，包括治疗的原则。

基础科学的一般性原则所占比例为 1%~3%；各个系统和器官内容占 80%~85%；生物统计学和流行病学和人口健康和医学文献解读，社会科学所占比例为 14%~18%。

Table above is the content and percentage of the multiple-choice questions. Percentage is always changing. You can see the latest information on the USMLE website（http://www.usmle.org）to understand the changes. According to the general principles and individual organ systems, the test questions are divided into 18 main areas, depending on whether they are focused on the concepts and principles that are important across organ systems or in single organ systems. The part of the individual organ system is subdivided into normal and abnormal processes, including the principles of treatment.

The proportion of the general principle of the scientific basis is 1%~3%; each system and organ contents is 80%~85%; biostatistics and epidemiology and population health and medical literature, social sciences is 14%~18%.

Step 3 MCQ physicak tasks/Competencies specification

Competency	Step 3 Foundations of Independent Practice	Step 3 Advanced Clinical Medicine
Medical Knowledge/Scientific Concepts	18%~22%	
Patient Care: Diagnosis 　　History/Physical Exam 　　Laboratory/Diagnostic Studies 　　Diagnosis	40%~45%	
Prognosis/Outcome		20%~25%
Patient Care: Management 　　Health Maintenance/Disease Prevention 　　Pharmacotherapy 　　Clinical Interventions 　　Mixed Management		75%~80%
Communication and Professionalism	8%~12%	
Systems-based Practice/Patient Safety and 　　Practice-based Learning	22%~27%	

　　这是一个测试医生任务 / 能力的项目，更多信息可在 USMLE 的网站上看到。这一项目重点是要评估医生的以下能力。医学知识 / 科学概念：应用基础科学概念；病人护理：诊断；病人护理：管理；沟通和人际交往能力；专业精神，包括法律和道德问题；基于系统的实践，包括病人安全；基于实践的学习，包括生物统计学和流行病学。

　　This is an item to test physician tasks/competencies, more information about the physician tasks and competencies outline is available at the USMLE website（http://www.usmle.org/pdfs/tcom.pdf）. Items are constructed to focus on assessing one of the following competencies:Medical knowledge/scientific concepts: Applying foundational science concepts; Patient care: Diagnosis; Patient care: Management; Communication and interpersonal skills; Professionalism, including legal and ethical issues; Systems−based practice, including patient safety; Practice−based learning, including biostatistics and epidemiology.

在 FIP 测试中，考生医疗知识 / 科学概念占 18%~22%；病人诊断、病史采集、体检、诊断研究占 40%~45%；交流能力与专业评估占 8%~12%；考生医学系统内的实践能力、病人安全和实践能力学习方面的内容占 22%~27%。

In the FIP test, the proportion of the examinee's medical knowledge / science concepts is 18%~22%; patients' diagnosis, history, physical examination, diagnostic research is 40%~45%; communication skills and professional assessment is 8%~12%; the practice of medical candidates within the system, patient safety and practical ability of learning content is 22%~27%.

在 ACM 测试中，预后方面的内容占 20%~25%；对病人的处理（病人护理、健康维持 / 疾病维护，药物治疗，临床干预等）占 75%~80%。

In the ACM test, the proportion of prognosis contents is 20%~25%; patients treatment (patient care, health maintenance/ disease maintenance, drug treatment, clinical intervention, etc.) is 75%~80%.

MCQ 例子（MCQ example）：

例子关注以下能力和话题，这些能力和话题来自大纲中列出的不同领域。能力：医学知识 / 科学概念、应用基础科学概念。内容：中枢神经系统。

Example of MCQ:

The example concerns the following abilities and topics, which come from different areas listed in the outline. Ability: medical knowledge / scientific concept, applied basic science concept. Content: central nervous system.

一个 27 岁的男子因为不能走路被他的室友带到急诊室。2 天前他开始注意到他的平衡有些问题，从那时起，他走路变得越来越差。3 年前他有一只右眼视神经炎发作。他身高 157 厘

A 27-year-old man is brought to the emergency department by his roommates because of an inability to walk. He began to notice some problems with his balance 2 days ago, and his walking has become

米（5英尺2英寸），体重55千克（121磅）；BMI为22千克/M2。他的体温是37° C（华氏98.6度），脉搏55次/分，呼吸10/分钟，血压为110/70毫米汞柱。检查显示下肢痉挛，四肢无力，左下肢屈肌比伸肌更突出。上肢深部肌腱反射正常，下肢，尤指左下肢活动过度。左踝阵挛。左下肢，对振动的本体感受和知觉没有，右下肢下降到臀部的水平。肋缘及下方对疼痛和温度的感觉降低，最明显在右边。

下列哪种类型的细胞是最受病人的病情影响的？

（A）星形胶质细胞；（B）室管膜细胞；（C）神经元；（D）突胶质细胞；（E）Schwann细胞。

答案为：D

progressively worse since then. He had an episode of optic neuritis in the right eye 3 years ago. He is 157 cm（5 ft 2 in）tall and weighs 55 kg（121 lb）；BMI is 22 kg/m2 . His temperature is 37° C（98.6° F），pulse is 55/min, respirations are 10/min, and blood pressure is 110/70 mm Hg. Examination shows spastic lower extremities and moderate weakness of the left lower extremity, more prominently in the flexor than in the extensor muscles. Deep tendon reflexes are normal in the upper extremities but hyperactive in the lower extremities, especially on the left. There is clonus at the left ankle. Proprioception and sensation to vibration are absent over the left lower extremity and decreased over the right lower extremity to the level of the hip. Sensation to pain and temperature is decreased at the lower costal margin and below, most pronounced on the right.

Which of the following cell types is most affected by this patient's condition?

(A) Astrocytes, (B) Ependymal cells, (C) Neurons, (D) Oligodendrocytes, (E) Schwann cells.

Answer: D

6.4.3 Step 3 CCS 考试内容规范

CCS 全称：Computer-based Case Simulations（CCS），每一个病例设计都是对病人看护状态的动态的，交互式的模拟，目的是为了评估考生的临床管理和医学知识应用的方法，包括诊断、治疗和监测。

阶段 3 考试 CCS 部分中使用的病例都是按照考试形式要求而设的，考试形式主要集中在表现症状和呈现地点的检查形式。表现症状与美国医师执照考试大纲内容相关，包括但不限于，循环、消化、泌尿、内分泌 / 代谢、行为、情感、呼吸和生殖系统的问题。呈现地点包括门诊办公室、急诊科、住院病房、ICU、病人的家。

关于阶段 3 CCS 考试内容，见下表。

6.4.3 Step 3 CCS test contents specification

The full name of CCS is Computer-based Case Simulations (CCS). Each case is designed to be a dynamic, interactive simulation of the patient's care status, with the aim of evaluating your clinical management and application of medical knowledge, including diagnosis, treatment, and monitoring.

All the cases used in the part of CCS are accordance with the requirements of the examination formates. The examination form is mainly concentrated in the performance of the symptoms and the location of the inspection form. The symptoms are related to the syllabus of the American Medical Licensing Examination, including, but not limited to, circulation, digestion, urinary, endocrine / metabolic, behavioral, emotional, respiratory and reproductive problems. The presentation site includes outpatient office, emergency department, inpatient ward, ICU, patient's home.

The contents of the Step 5 CCS examination are shown in Table:

Step 3 CCS 内容

System
General Principles of Foundational Science
Immune System
Blood & Lymphoreticular System
Behavioral Health
Nervous System & Special Senses
Skin & Subcutaneous Tissue
Musculoskeletal System
Cardiovascular System
Respiratory System
Gastrointestinal System
Renal & Urinary System
Pregnancy, Childbirth, & the Puerperium
Female Reproductive System & Breast
Male Reproductive System
Endocrine System
Multisystem Processes & Disorders
Biostatistics & Epidemiology/Population Health, & Interpretation of the Medical Literature
Social Sciences

在阶段 3 CCS 部分，对医师任务 / 能力要求主要包括：医学知识 / 科学概念（应用基础科学概念）；病人护理（诊断与管理）；沟通和人际关系技巧；专业，包括法律和伦理问题；基于系统的实践，包括病人安全；基于实践的学习，包括生物统计学和流行病学

In the Step 3 CCS section, the physician task / competency requirements includes: Medical knowledge/scientific concepts (Applying foundational science Concepts); Patient care (diagnosis and management); Communication and interpersonal skills; Professionalism, including legal and ethical issues; Systems-based practice, including patient safety; Practice-based learning, including biostatistics and epidemiology

任务要求见下表。

The task requirements are shown in the table：

医生任务要求 (The physician task requirements)

Obtaining history and performing physical examination	● Objectives focus on interpreting the patient's history, knowing pertinent factors in the patient's history, and interpreting the history in terms of risk factors for the patient. ● Objectives focus on the physical examination, such as recognizing and interpreting pertinent physical findings and knowing required techniques in the physical examination.
Using laboratory and diagnostic studies	● Objectives focus on selecting the appropriate routine, initial, invasive, special, or follow-up studies; interpreting the results of laboratory or diagnostic tests; knowing the value of and indications for screening tests; and predicting the most likely test result.
Formulating the most likely diagnosis	● Objectives focus on selecting the most likely diagnosis in light of history, physical, or diagnostic test findings. Includes interpreting pictorial material and establishing a diagnosis.
Evaluating severity of patient's problems	● Objectives focus on interpreting the vignette, evaluating the severity of the patient's condition, and making judgment on the current status or prognosis of the patient as to the need for further action.

Managing the patient	● *Health maintenance* objectives focus on identifying risk factors, knowing incidence within patient groups at risk, knowing preliminary steps to ensure effectiveness of intended therapy, and selecting appropriate preventive therapeutic agents or techniques. ● *Clinical intervention* objectives focus on knowing priorities in emergency management, knowing present and long-term management of selected conditions, and knowing appropriate surgical treatment, including pre- and post-surgical events. They also include knowing pre- and post-procedural management and the appropriate follow-up schedule or monitoring approach. ● *Clinical therapeutics* objectives focus on selecting the appropriate pharmacotherapy, recognizing actions of drugs as applied to patient management, and knowing the importance of educating patients about effects of drugs and drug-drug interactions. ● *Legal/ethical and health care systems* objectives focus on issues such as patient autonomy, physician/patient relationships, use of unorthodox or experimental therapies, end-of-life considerations, treatment of minors, and physician error versus negligence.
Applying scientific concepts	● Objectives focus on identifying the underlying processes or pathways responsible for a given condition, recognizing associated disease conditions and complications, and recognizing and evaluating clinical findings or diagnostic studies to identify the underlying factors (eg, anatomic structure). ● Objectives focus on interpreting results of experimental or biometric data, including knowing design features of clinical studies, understanding issues regarding validity of research protocols, knowing sensitivity and specificity of selected tests, and recognizing potential bias in clinical studies.

能力要求见下表。

The competency requirements are

shown in the table

医生能力要求 (The physician competency requirements)

Competency
Medical Knowledge/Scientific Concepts
Patient Care: Diagnosis 　**History/Physical Exam** 　**Laboratory/Diagnostic Studies** 　**Diagnosis** 　**Prognosis/Outcome**
Patient Care: Management 　**Health Maintenance/Disease Prevention** 　**Pharmacotherapy** 　**Clinical Interventions** 　**Mixed Management**
Communication and Professionalism
Systems-based Practice/Patient Safety and Practice-based Learning

6.4.4 阶段 3 临床场景　　　　　6.4.4 Step 3 clinical setting

临床场景 clinical setting

INITIAL WORK-UP	CONTINUING CARE	URGENT INTERVENTION
1	2	3
Patient encounters characterized by initial assessment and management of clinical problems among patients seen principally in ambulatory settings for the first time. These encounters may also include new problems arising in patients for whom a history is available.	Patient encounters characterized by continuing management of previously diagnosed clinical problems among patients known to the physician and seen principally in ambulatory settings. Encounters focused on health maintenance are located in this frame. Also included are patient encounters characterized by acute exacerbations or complications, principally of chronic, progressive conditions among patients known to the physician. These encounters may occur in inpatient settings.	Patient encounters characterized by prompt assessment and management of life-threatening and organ-threatening emergencies, usually occurring in emergency department settings. Occasionally, these encounters may occur in the context of a hospitalized patient.
Clinical problems include ill-defined signs and symptoms; behavioral-emotional; acute limited; initial manifestation and presentation of chronic illness.	Clinical problems include frequently-occurring chronic diseases and behavioral-emotional problems. Periodic health evaluations of established patients are included here.	Clinical problems include severe life-threatening and organ-threatening conditions and exacerbations of chronic illness.
Physician tasks emphasized include data gathering and initial clinical intervention. Assessment of patients may lead to urgent intervention.	Physician tasks emphasized include recognition of new problems in an existing condition, assessment of severity, establishing prognosis, monitoring therapy, and long-term management.	Physician tasks emphasized include rapid assessment of complex presentations, assessment of patients' deteriorating condition, and prompt decision making.

（1）初诊处理

其特点是对于第一次到门诊的病人进行初步的临床问题的评估与处理。

（2）随访

其特点是医生对病人的不间断管理，这些病人在门诊看过病，医生对其以前被诊断出来的临床问题了解。

（3）紧急干预

其特点是及时评估管理遇到危及生命和危及器官的突发事件，通常发生在急诊科室。

6.4.5 考题类型

阶段 3 所有考题都是基于病案的。考题类型分为三种：第一种是单问题考题形式，即在叙述完 1 个病案后，有 1 个问题给出，相应的有 4 或 5 个选项，选出正确的 1 个；多问题的考题形式，即在叙述完 1 个病案后，有 2~3 个连续的不相关的考题，考题内容都是与所提供的小短文相关

（1）Initial workup

This is characterized by initial assessment and management of clinical problems among patients seen principally in ambulatory settings for the first time.

（2）Continuing care

Patient encounters characterized by continuing management of previously diagnosed clinical problems among patients known to the physician and seen principally in ambulato settings.

（3）Urgent intervention

Patient encounters characterized by prompt assessment management of life-threatening and organ-threatening emergencies, usually occurring in emergency department settings.

6.4.5 Type of questions

All questions in step3 are based on case. There are three types of questions are three: the first type is single items, that is, a single patient-centered vignette is associated with one question followed by four or more response options, choose the best one answer to the question; the

连，但是根据短文信息所提供的 2~3
个问题之间的内容都是独立的，不相
关的；第三种是序贯问题考题形式，
即在叙述完 1 个病案后，有 2~3 个连
续提出，每个问题测试点不同，每个
问题要选出一个最佳答案。问题之间
在设计上是有顺序的。考生必须单击
"转到下一个项目"来查看设置中的下
一个项目；一旦考生单击此按钮，将
无法添加或更改显示的（上一个）项
目的答案。

second type is multiple items sets, that is, a single patient-centered vignette may be associated with two or three consecutive questions about the information presented, each question within these sets is associated with the patient vignette and is independent of the other questions in the set. The items within this type are designed to be answered in any order; the third type is sequential item sets, that is, a single patient-centered vignette may be associated with two or three consecutive questions about the information presented. Each question is associated with the initial patient vignette but is testing a different point. You are required to select the ONE BEST answer to each question, questions are designed to be answered in sequential order. You must click "Proceed to Next Item" to view the next item in the set. Once you click on this button, you will not be able to add or change an answer to the displayed（previous）item.

6.5 USMLE 的网站

6.5.1 USMLE（http://www.usmle.org/）

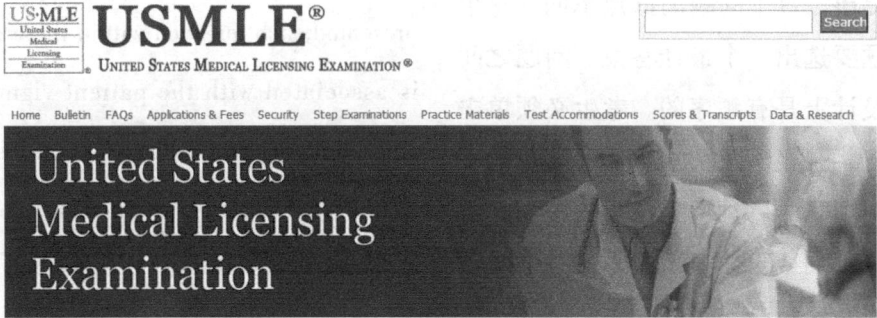

这是 USMLE 的官方网站，在此主页上，可以看到如下栏目：公告栏、常见问题解答、考试申请及费用、安全性、step 考试、USMLE 考试资料、测试设备、分数和成绩、数据研究等。这些栏目的设置可以解答你在 USMLE 考试过程中遇到的问题。

（1）公告栏

公告栏包括了 USMLE 考试过程中各方面的信息，如考试资格的要求、考试日期、考试内容改革与更新等，考试分数。特别是在申请 USMLE 阶段 1、阶段 2（CK 和 CS）、阶段 3 考试时，考生要认真阅读公告栏里的信息。

6.5 Websites On USMLE

6.5.1 USMLE（http://www.usmle.org/）

This is the official website of USMLE, on this homepage you can see the following sections: bulletin board, FAQ, application and examination fees, security, step test, USMLE test data, test equipment, scores and results, data research etc..

（1）Bulletin

The bulletin board includes information on all aspects of the USMLE examination process, such as examination eligibility requirements, test date, test content reform and update, etc.. Especially in the application of USMLE Step 1, Step 2 (CK and CS), Step 3 examination, examinees should read the bulletin board information seriously.

（2）常见问题解答

（2）FAQs

Examination

What is USMLE?

The **United States Medical Licensing Examination ®** (USMLE®) is a three-step examination for medical licensure in the United States and is sponsored by the Federation of State Medical Boards (FSMB) and the National Board of Medical Examiners® (NBME®).

The USMLE assesses a physician's ability to apply knowledge, concepts, and principles, and to demonstrate fundamental patient-centered skills, that are important in health and disease and that constitute the basis of safe and effective patient care. Each of the three Steps of the USMLE complements the others; no Step can stand alone in the assessment of readiness for medical licensure.

Who is USMLE?

Find out more about the USMLE »

ANNOUNCEMENTS

Enhanced security policies at Prometric test centers

USMLE Bulletin of Information

The **Bulletin** includes information on all aspects of USMLE, such as eligibility requirements, scheduling test dates, testing, and score reporting. **You must review** and become familiar with the Bulletin before completing your application for USMLE Step 1, Step 2 (CK and CS), or Step 3. Start reading the Bulletin of Information »

Download the PDF version of the 2017 Bulletin »
Download the PDF version of the 2016 Bulletin »

Upcoming Changes to USMLE

A summary of planned changes over the next few years is available. [Updated!]

The Composite Committee of the USMLE initiated a process to undertake a comprehensive review of the USMLE program in 2004. The Composite Committee establishes policy for the USMLE and is composed of representatives of the Federation of State Medical Boards (FSMB), National Board of Medical Examiners (NBME), the Educational Commission for Foreign

此页面信息能够回答经常遇到的一些问题。如如何申请，如何制定时间，考试费用问题，如何准备考试，如何获得关于 USMLE 的相关信息等。

Information on this homepage can answer some of the questions that can often be encountered, such as how to apply, how to develop time, examination fees, how to prepare for the exam, how to obtain information on the USMLE, etc.

（3）申请与费用

参加 USMLE 考试的考生必须在网站上申请并提交信息。该页面提供了阶段 1、阶段 2CK、阶段 2 CS 的申请信息。美国或加拿大考生与美国、加拿大以外考生的申请界面不同。在申请前，要仔细看清楚应该使用哪一个界面。美国或加拿大考生通过 NBME

（3）Applications & Fees

Examinees who take the USMLE examination must apply and submit information on the website. This homepage provides Step 1, Step 2 CK, Step 2 CS application page. Examinees in the United States or Canada, and the examinees outside the United States and Canada have

网 站 上 的 NLES（NBME Licensing Examination）申请，美国和加拿大以外的考生通过 ECFMG 网站上的 IWA（Interactive Web Applications）申请。阶段 3 考试申请是在阶段 1、阶段 2 CK、阶段 2 CS 都通过了以后，通过 FSMB 网站上的医学执业考试页面申请。

different application interface. Before application, you should carefully look at which interface to use. Examinees in the United States or Canada apply and submit information through the NLES (NBME Licensing Examination) on the NBME website, the examinees outside the United States and Canada apply and submit information through IWA (Interactive Web Applications) on ECFMG website. Step 3 exam application is through the FSMB site on the medical practice examination page application after Step 1, Step 2 CK, Step 2 CS exams have been passed.

（4）step 考试

（4）step examination

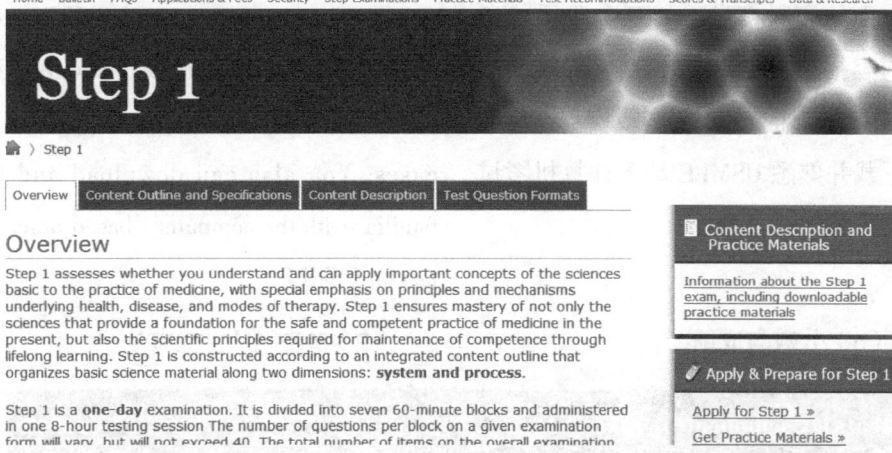

Step examination 页面提供了 USMLE 三个阶段考试的内容、大纲、考试形式，提供可免费下载的一些资料，同时还提供考试过程中出现的一些新情况、新信息。

Step examination homepage provides three stages information on USMLE, for example, USMLE's contents, outline, examination form,and it also provides free information download, and some new situations, new information in the examination process.

（5）考试资料

（5）practice materials

本页面提供了 USMLE 三个阶段考试方面的资料信息，如三个阶段的考试内容描述、考试样本、考试软件的使用说明、Step 3 CCS 实践病例。考生可下载并熟悉 USMLE 基于计算机考试的实践部分。

This page provides information of the three stages examination on USMLE, such as content description, test samples, the use of test software, Step 3 CCS practice cases. You also can download and be familiar with the computer –based practice test on USMLE.

（6）分数与成绩

（6）score & transcripts

Step(s)/Component(s) Taken	Recipient of Transcript	Contact
One or more USMLE Steps	Medical licensing authority	FSMB
All three USMLE Steps; or Step 1 and Step 2 CK and CS (if required), only when registered for or after taking Step 3	Any recipient	FSMB
Step 1 and/or Step 2 CK and/or CS only, registered by ECFMG	Any recipient other than a medical licensing authority	ECFMG
Step 1 and/or Step 2 CK and/or CS only, registered by NBME	Any recipient other than a medical licensing authority	NLES

Bulletin: Official Transcripts

每年 NBME 都会发布分数与成绩信息。这些数据将被第三方用来做研究，如果考生不希望自己的分数用于研究，就必须向 USMLE 提交书面申请。在此页面上，考生可以看到三个阶段的考试最低录取分数。要想获取成绩单，应该联系 ECFMG、FSMB 或者 NBME，支付相关费用，并注明成绩

Every year, it will release score & transcripts information on NBME website. These data will be used to do research by the third party, if you don't want your score for the study, you must submit a written application to USMLE. On this page, you can see the minimum admission score of

单的邮寄地址。

three stages. In order to obtain your transcript, you should contact ECFMG, FSMB, or NBME and pay the relevant fees, and indicate where your transcript should be sent.

6.5.2 NBME（http://www.nbme.org/）

NBME 的 全 称 是 National Board of Medical Examiners，国家医学考试委员会成立于 1915 年，是一个独立的、不以营利为目的的组织，通过其高质量的医疗保健专业人员的评估为公众提供服务。NBME 开发和管理 USMLE，个人许可委员会授予通过 USMLE 考试的人员行医执照，确保医生的医疗水平。NBME 和 FSMB（the Federation of State Medical Boards，国家医学委员会联合会）是 USMLE 的发起人，外国医学毕业生教育委员会（ECFMG）是 USMLE 的第三个合作者。

6.5.2 NBME（http://www.nbme.org/）

The full name of NBME is National Board of Medical Examiners, it is the national medical examination committee, and it was established in 1915. It is an independent, not-for-profit organization, which serves the public through its high- quality assessments of healthcare professionals. NBME develops and manages USMLE, the individual licensing boards grant the license to practice medicine, all medical boards in the US accept a passing score on the USMLE as evidence that an applicant demonstrates the core competencies to practice medicine. NBME and FSMB（the Federation State Medical Boards, the National Federation of medical committees）is the initiator of USMLE, the Foreign Medical Graduates Education Council（ECFMG）is the third partner of USMLE.

（1）学生及居民　　　　　　　　　　　（1）Students & Residents

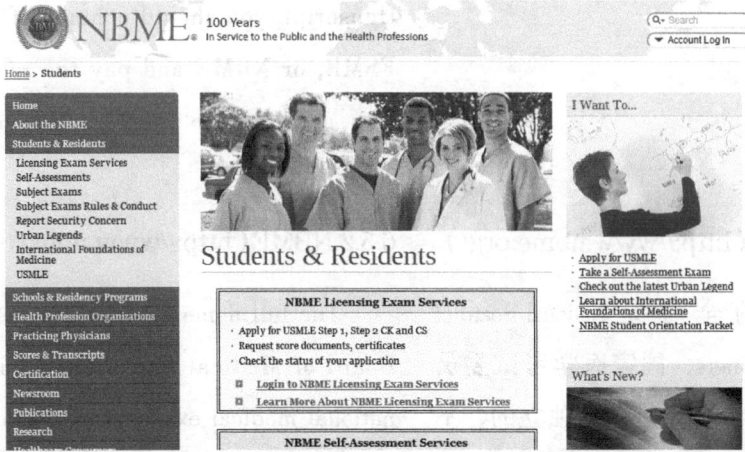

这个页面的信息包括：执照考试服务、自我评估、学科考试、科目考试规则与行为、报告安全问题、都市传说、国际医学基础、USMLE。详细的说明请查阅网站：http://www.nbme.org/Students/sas/sas.html.

The information on this page includes: licensing examination services; self assessment; subject examination; subject rule and behavior; reporting security issues; urban legends; international medical foundation; USMLE. Please refer to the website for more details: http://www.nbme.org/Students/sas/sas.html

（2）USMLE

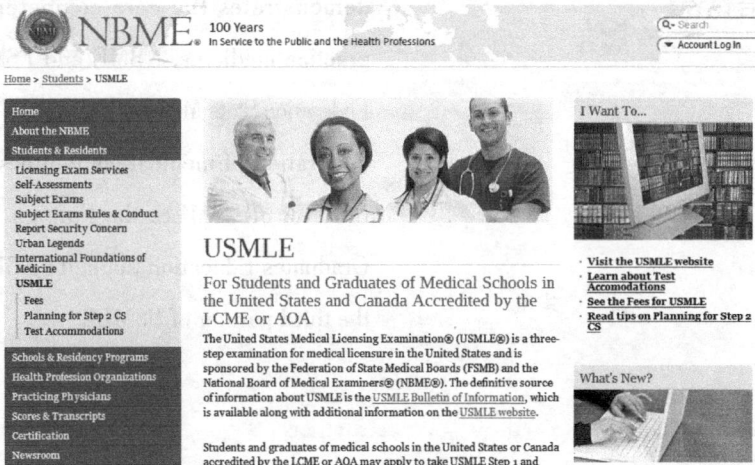

在 NBME 网页上可以了解关于 USMLE 的相关信息，如访问 USMLE 网站，考试申请方面的信息，USMLE 的费用信息，学习关于考试调整方面的信息，关于申请 Step 2 CS 的重要信息等，执照考试方面的服务等。

On the NBME page you can browse the relevant information about USMLE, such as visiting the USMLE website, the examination application information, the fees of USMLE information, learning about the examination adjustment information on the application of Step 2 CS and other important information, services on license test etc.

（3）分数与成绩

（3）Scores and Transcripts

NBME 100 Years
In Service to the Public and the Health Professions

Search
Account Log In

Home > Certification and Transcripts > Scores & Transcripts

Home
About the NBME
Students & Residents
Schools & Residency Programs
Health Profession Organizations
Practicing Physicians
Scores & Transcripts
　Obtaining a Transcript
Certification
Newsroom
Publications
Research
Healthcare Consumers
New Initiatives

Date Updated: June 22, 2015

Contact

Contact the NBME

Scores and Transcripts

Scores

For Steps 1, 2 CK, and 3, a score report includes a pass/fail designation, numerical scores, and graphical performance profiles summarizing areas of strength and weakness to aid in self-assessment. These profiles are developed solely for the benefit of examinees, and will not be reported or verified to any third party.

Performance on Step 2 CS is reported as pass or fail. Score reports include performance profiles, which reflect the relative strengths and weaknesses of an examinees' performance across the subcomponents of Step 2 CS.

Once the exam results are released, the score report will remain available online for approximately 120 days

在这个网页上，考生可以获得如下信息：从哪能里获得自己的成绩单，如何申请获得，获取成绩单的费用。

From this page, you can get the following information: where can I get my transcript, how to apply for it, the fee getting the transcript.

6.5.3 FSMB（https://www.fsmb.org/）

州医疗委员会联合会（FSMB）是一个全美的非营利性质的、代表美国及其领土 70 个医学委员会与骨科的委员会。自成立以来，FSMB 提供了从评估工具到政策性文件，从认证到纪律提醒服务，其最终的目的是在医疗实践、许可证发放和医疗规范方面做得更优越。国家医学委员会基金会联合举办教育和科研项目，旨在扩大公众对医学专业知识和挑战的影响，以及公众对医疗保健和卫生保健法规的认识。

6.5.3 FSMB（https://www.fsmb.org/）

The Federation of state medical boards（FSMB）is a national non-profit organization representing the United States and its territories, 70 medical committees and the Department of orthopedics committee. Since its inception, FSMB has provided from assessment tool to the policy document, from certification to disciplinary alert service, and its ultimate goal is to do better in terms of medical practice, license issuance and medical norms. The National Medical Council Foundation jointly organized educational and research projects to expand the understanding of public and medical expertise and the impact of challenges on health care and health care regulations.

FSMB and state medical boards working together to protect the public through licensure and regulation.

Licensure
Resources for Medical Professionals
» USMLE
» FCVS
» Uniform Application
» SPEX

Policy and Education
Resources for Consumers and State Medical Boards
» Advocacy & Policy
» Education & Meetings
» Consumer Resources

Credentialing
Resources for Credentialers
» Physician Data Center
» Entity Connect
» Residency Records

在 FSMB 网站上可以看到关于 USMLE 的相关信息，详细的情况请看网站：https://portal.fsmb.org/MyFsmb/。

On the FSMB site you can see the relevant information on the USMLE, a detailed look at the website: https://portal.fsmb.org/MyFsmb/.

6.5.4 kaplan Qbank（https://www.kaptest.com/）

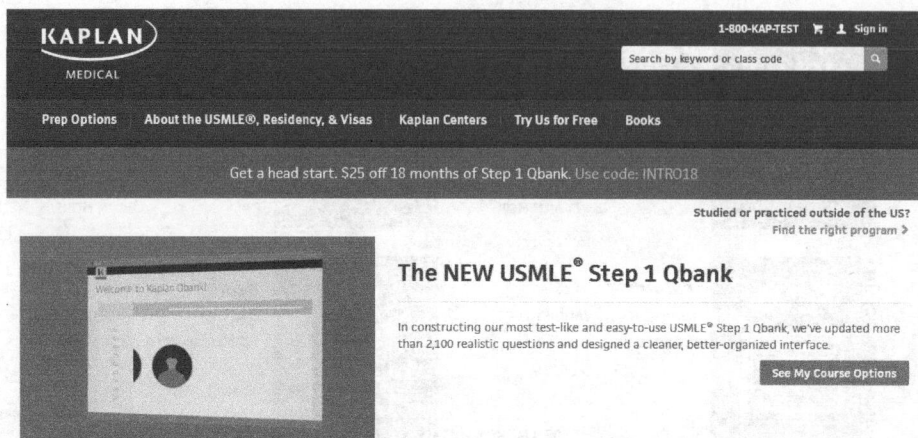

KaplanQbank 网站提供了 Prep Options、About the USMLE、Residency、Visas、Try us for free，book 等栏目。在使用这个网站时，这些栏目能提供所需要的信息。

6.5.4 kaplan Qbank（https://www.kaptest.com/）

KaplanQbank site provides Prep Options, About the USMLE, Residency, Visas, Try us for free, Books and other columns. When you use this site, these columns can provide you with the information you need.

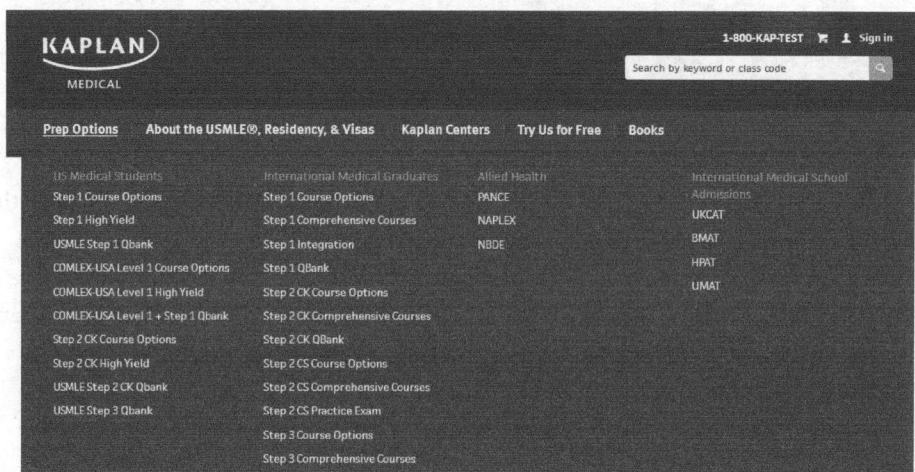

Ultimate USMLE Prep Giveaway. One winner, prep for every step. Up to $22,800 value. Enter thru 2/28.

Master the most challenging USMLE exam with content and strategies that Kaplan has perfected over 40 years.
Join the thousands of students who have aced Step 1 with the support of our expert faculty and matched into residency.

Live	Live Online	In Center	On Demand
Starting at	Starting at	Starting at	Starting at
$3999	$3999	$4099	$1999
or 3 installments of $1333.00	or 3 installments of $1333.00	or 3 installments of $1366.33	or 3 installments of $666.33
Attend live lectures by the most distinguished medical faculty in the industry at our full-service centers	Attend scheduled live and online lectures from anywhere you have internet access	Review Kaplan's world-class video lectures at your own pace at our full-service centers	Access our full Step 1 video library featuring over 200 hours of lectures delivered by expert faculty
Learn More	Learn More	Learn More	Learn More

（1）课程选择

该栏目为美国医学生和国际医学生提供了课程选择及各阶段考试题库，考生可根据自身情况选择适合自己的信息。课程选择有四种方式：参加现场讲座、在线讲座、视频讲座、点播。视频讲座是根据自身情况看视频学习，点播是在视频库里选择适合自己的课程。视频库拥有超过 200 小时的由专家教授的讲座。

（1）Prep Options

The column provides the courses selection and Qbanks of various steps of USMLE for U.S medical students and international medical students. Examinees can choose information according to their own conditions. There are four ways to choose the course: to participate in live lectures, online lectures, video lectures, on-demand. The video lectures is according to your own situation to watch the video, on demand learning is that you can select the courses in the video library, which has more than 200 hours of lectures by experts and professors.

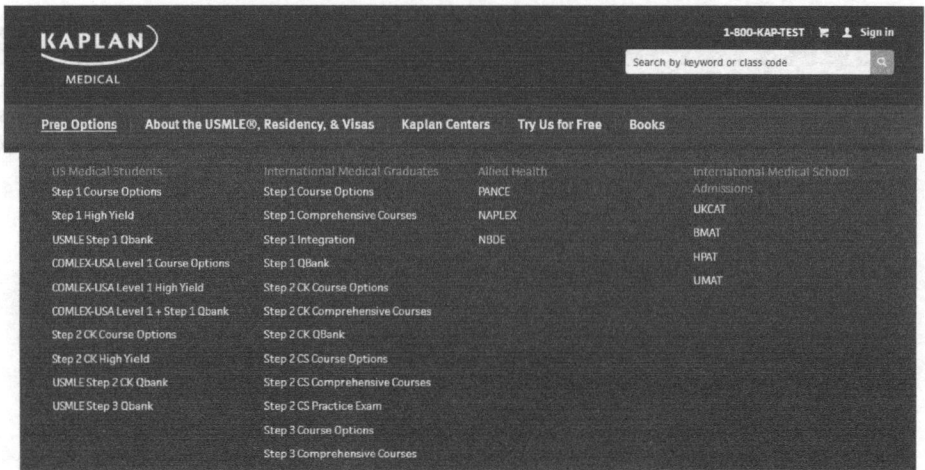

（2）USMLE 居留与签证

该栏目介绍了 USMLE、Residency、Visar 的情况。在 USMLE 的介绍中，主要介绍了三个考试阶段的基本信息。Residency 提供了在住院实习医师匹配项目准备过程中应该掌握哪些信息，详细地介绍了在住院医师计划，匹配过程，面谈准备，专业选择方面应该怎么做。Visa 介绍了一个国际医学生要想在美国准备 USMLE 考试，应该知道哪些事，如何申请，在这里都有详细的介绍。

（2）About the USMLE, Residency, & Visas

The column describes the situation of USMLE, Residency, Visar. In the introduction of USMLE, it introduces the basic information of the three examination steps, and residency column provides the information that should be grasped during the process of matching the residency. It introduced in detail how to do in the residency program, matching process, interview preparation, medical specialty choice. Visa column introduced how to prepare for the USMLE exam in the United States for an international medical students, and you should know some important information of application, there is a detailed introduction in the wensite.

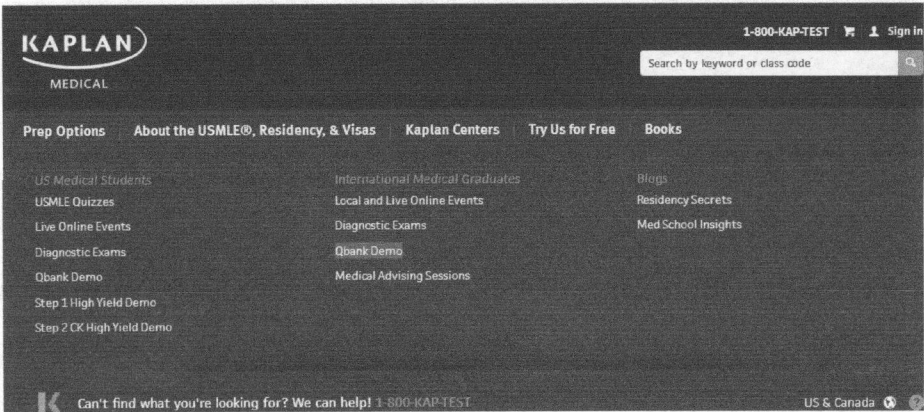

（3）免费使用

此栏目为国际医学生提供了免费的本地和在线的活动、诊断考试、Qbank 演示、医疗咨询会议、Residency Secrets 和 Med School Insights 两个博客。

（3）Try us for free

For international medical students,this column provides free Local and Live Online Events, Diagnostic Exams, QBank Demo,Medical Advising Sessions, as well as two blogs: Residency Secrets and Med School Insights.

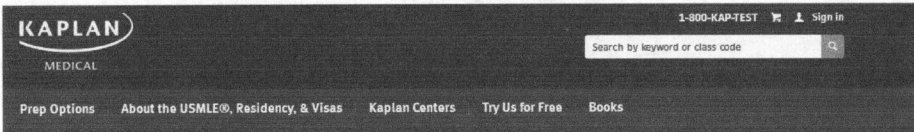

USMLE® Books

USMLE Step 1 Lecture Notes

Get the newest edition of the only *official *Kaplan lecture notes for USMLE Step 1 available for sale—complete with comprehensive information you need to ace this section of the boards and match into the residency of your choice.

Purchase On Amazon

Features:

（4）图书

提供了由 Kaplan 出版的 USMLE 专用图书，考生可以在线购买。

（4）Books

It provides USMLE dedicated books published by Kaplan, examinees can purchase online.

UWorld
YOUR WORLD OF LEARNING

MENU ☰

🛒 Cart ❓ Help 📶 Forums ⏻ Login

[USMLE]
The one-stop source for all your USMLE needs. The #1 question bank for Step 1, Step 2 & Step 3. Written by practicing physicians who excelled in the USMLE exams.

[BOARD CERTIFICATION]
The most comprehensive question bank for ABIM and ABFM certifications. These challenging questions are evidence-based and written by board-certified experts.

[NURSING]
An exam-specific, clinically based question bank that tests your critical thinking ability. Designed for NCLEX by experienced academic nurse educators.

6.5.5 USMLE WORLD（http://www.uworld.com/）

从这个网站上可以获得一站式的 USMLE 资源。这些资源适合 USMLE 所有阶段的考试。

（1）USMLE 阶段 1 题库

由 2400 多个非常好的、最博学的、专门的执业医生编写的选择题。题目是概念性的并且是热门话题，每道题需要多步骤地批判性思考，每个问题都有详细的解释与生动的插图和图表，易于理解和记忆，软件界面模拟真正考试。

（2）USMLE 阶段 2 CK 题库

由 2200 多个非常好的、最博学的、专门的执业医生编写的选择题。题目是概念性的并且是热门话题，每道题需要多步骤地批判性思考，每个问题都有详细的解释与生动的插图和

6.5.5 USMLE WORLD（http://www.uworld.com/）

From this website，you can obtain one-stop USMLE resource. These resources are suitable for all steps of USMLE examination.

（1）USMLE Step 1 Qbank

There are more than 2400 very good multiple-choice questions, written by the most knowledgeable and specialized practitioners, the questions are conceptual topics, each question requires multiple steps of critical thinking, every problem has a detailed explanation and vivid illustrations and diagrams, easy to understand and remember, software interface simulates the real exam.

（2）USMLE Step 2 CK Qbank

There are more than 2200 very good multiple-choice questions, written by the most knowledgeable and specialized practitioners, the questions are conceptual topics, each question requires multiple

图表，易于理解和记忆，软件界面模拟真正考试。

（3）USMLE 阶段 2 CS 题库

本题库中有 70 多个优秀的临床病例，让考生一次性完整地完成实践考试。该试题提供详细的病史采集和身体检查技术与视频，为实践案例输入模拟病人的病案笔记，病人咨询和如何应对病人的挑战性问题，考试成功的秘诀等。

（4）USMLE 阶段 3 题库

CCS 部分提供了唯一真正互动的临床病例模拟软件，51 例可互动的阶段 3 CCS 病案，41 个案例管理材料，按照官方的 CCS 软件关键词更新，对交互式案例管理、评分和时钟管理有详细解释。如下图。

steps of critical thinking, every problem has a detailed explanation and vivid illustrations and diagrams, easy to understand and remember, and software interface simulates the real exam.

（3）USMLE Step 2 CS Qbank

There are more than 70 excellent clinical cases, which allow you to finish a one-time complete practice exam. The test provides detailed medical history and physical examination techniques and videos, inputing a simulated patient's case notes for a practice case, patient consultation and how to respond to the challenges of the patient, the secrets of success, and so on.

（4）USMLE Step 3 Qbank

CCS: provides the only truly interactive clinical case simulation software, 51 cases of interactive Step 3 CCS cases, 41 cases management materials, in accordance with the official update of the CCS keyword. There are detailed explanation of interactive case management, scoring, and clock management. Following figure is listed below.

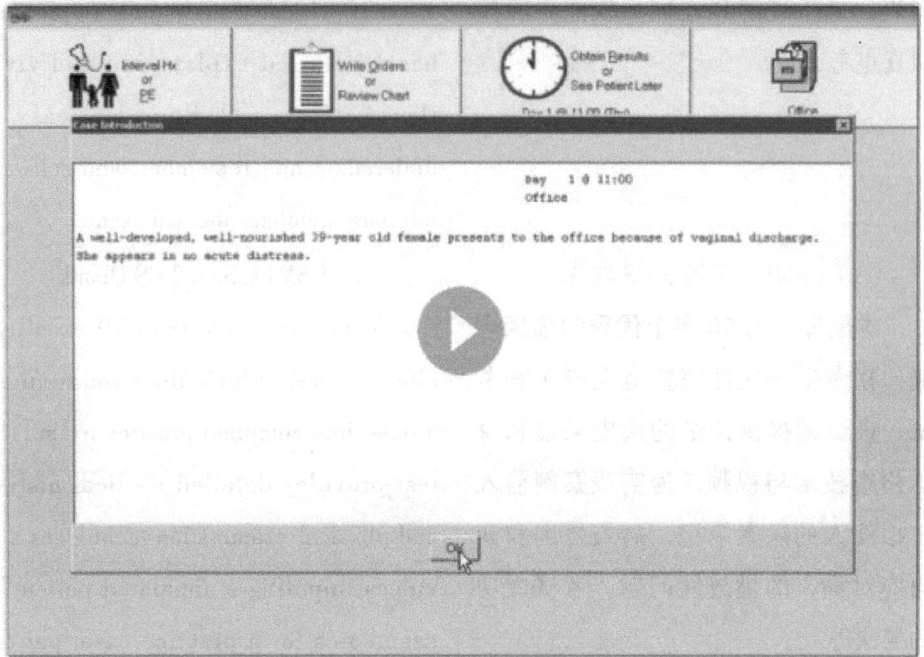

6.5.6 USMLE Consult（http://www.usmleconsult.com/）

USMLE Consult 是一个强大的 USMLE 考试准备和仿真工具。它是著名的 Elsevier 出版集团的旗舰产品 "The 'Consult' series" 之一，其内容出自于顶级 Elsevier 的作家 Edward Goljan 博士和 John Pelley 博士。他们根据 NBME 考试大纲要求设计了难度水平不同的问题。这些问题都是当下的热门话题，与 USMLE 的真题非常接近，因此在做题时不要关注题考试形式，要关注问题的答案。考生会发现题库中的问题都是现实模拟，有考试结果分析、定制和问题组合。在做每一个阶

6.5.6 USMLE Consult（http://www.usmleconsult.com/）

USMLE Consult is a powerful USMLE exam preparation and simulation tool. It is one of the famous Elsevier Publishing Group's flagship product "The 'Consult' series", which comes from one of the top Elsevier writers Drs. Edward and John Pelley Goljan. According to the requirements of the NBME outline, questions of different difficulty levels are designed.These questions are the hot topic of the moment, and are very close to the USMLE real exam, so don't concern the examination form in the title, you should

段的问题时可以选择一个计划，如 30 天、60 天、90 天。

pay attention to the answer to the question. You will find that the questions are a realistic simulation, there are the results of the examination analysis, customization and problem combination in the QBank. Before you do these questions of different steps, you can choose a plan, such as 30 days, 60 days, 90 days.

（1）USMLE Consult 阶段 1

它包括 2500 多道问题，这些问题由顶级 Elsevier 的作家之一 Edward Goljan 博士和 John Pelley 编写。这些问题难易程度不同，反映了 NBME 的考试大纲要求。在做题时，可参照 Elsevier 的知名资源，如 Netter、Gray's Anatomy、Rapid Review series、Robbins Pathology、Secrets series。

（1）USMLER Consult Step1

It includes more than 2500 questions, written by one of the top Elsevier writers, Dr. Goljan Edward and John Pelley. These questions are difficult to differ in degree, reflecting the NBME outline requirements. The well-known resources in the title can refer to Elsevier resources, such as Netter, Gray's, Anatomy, Rapid Review series, Robbins Pathology, Secrets series.

USMLE Consult's Robbins Pathology Question Bank 专注于由专家指导和分析的所有重要的病理学科，这些都是专门为 USMLE Consult 写的。

USMLE Consult Step 1 Premium Review 包括 Step 1 Question bank、Robbins Pathology Question Bank、Scorrelator、一本学生用电子图书 Rapid Review Physiology.

USMLE Consult's Pathology Question Bank focuses on expert guidance and analysis of all the important pathological disciplines, these are specifically written for USMLE Consult.

USMLE Consult Step 1 Premium Review includes Step1 Question bank, Robbins Pathology Bank Question, Scorrelator, an e-book for students Rapid Review Physiology.

详细的情况和说明请看网站：

http://www.usmleconsult.com/index.cfm

If you want to get more details of the situation and instructions, please access the website: http://www.usmleconsult.com/index.cfm

（2）USMLERx 阶段 2 多选题

USMLE Consult's 阶段 2 CK Question Bank 包括：由 Linda Costanzo 博士和 George Brenner 博士 编写的 2300 多道题。这些问题的难易程度不同，但都反映了 NBME 的考试大纲要求。在做题过程中，可参照 Netter、Gray's Anatomy、Ferri、Brochert、Rapid Review series、Secrets series 等 Elsevie 公司出版的知名资源。

USMLE Consult's Robbins Pathology Question Bank 专注于由专家指导和分析的所有重要的病理学科，这些都是专门为 USMLE Consult 写的。有 500 多例新的病理实践问题。

USMLE Consult's Step 2 Premium Review 包　括 Step 2 CK Question bank、Robbins Pathology Question Bank、Scorrelator、一本学生用电子图书 access to Rapid Review USMLE Step 2。有 3300 多个实践问题为考试做准备。

Rapid Review USMLE Step 2 简要概括了 USMLE 阶段 2 考试所涉及的资料。它强调介绍、诊断和治疗。每一

（2）USMLERx step2 Qmax

USMLE Consult's 2 CK Question Bank includes: more than 2300 questions written by Drs Linda Costanzo and George. The difficulty of these problems is different, but all of which reflect the requirements of the NBME outline. In the process of doing these questions, you can refer to Netter Gray's, Anatomy, Ferri, Brochert, Rapid Review series, Secrets series and other well-known resources which Elsevie company published.

USMLE Consult's Pathology Question Bank focuses on expert guidance and analysis of all the important pathological disciplines, these are specifically written for USMLE Consult. There are more than 500 new pathological practice questions.

USMLE Consult's Step 2 Review includes Step 2 CK bank Question bank, Robbins Question Bank, Scorrelator, a student with e-books access to Review USMLE Pathology Step,, Rapid. There are more than 3300 practical questions to prepare for the exam.

Rapid Review USMLE Step 2 provides a brief overview of the information involved in the USMLE Step 2 exam, which

种疾病都有总结性介绍，100 多个样题有详细的解释。详细的情况说明请参照网站：http://www.usmleconsult.com/usmle-step-two/usmle-step-two.cfm。

highlights the presentation, diagnosis and treatment. Every disease has a summary introduction, more than 100 questions are explained in detail. For detailed information, please refer to the website: http://www.usmleconsult.com/usmle-step-two/usmle-step-two.cfm.

（3）USMLERx 阶段 3 多选题

USMLE Consult's Step 3 CCS Case Bank 包括 100 例模拟案例，与 NBME CCS 病例有所不同，根据专业、临床场景或话题选择案例能最大限度地帮助考生提高考试准备时间。每一个病例都有详细的结果分析。USMLE Consult's Step 3 还包括 1500 个同行评审的实践问题，这些实践问题有不同的难度。

（3）USMLERx Step 3 Qmax

USMLE Consult's Step 3 CCS Case Bank includes 100 simulation cases, which are different from the NBME CCS case. Cases are selected according to the professional, clinical scene or topic to help you improve your exam preparation time. Each case has detailed results analysis. USMLE Consult's Step 3 also includes 1500 peer-review practice questions that have different difficulties in practice.

USMLE Consult's Step 3 Premium Review 能让考生得到全方位的网上学习材料以确保 USMLE 取得成功。这些资料包括：Step 3 CCS Bank. Step 3 Question bank. Scorrelator 和一本电子图书：access to Rapid Review USMLE Step 3。这些资料能为考生提供 3300 多个实践问题。

在网上考生可以获得一本由 Elsevier 作者 David Rolston 和 Craig Nielson 编写的 Rapid Review USMLE Step 3，它是一本快捷、高效、全面的功能强大的复习工具，知识面广，并且有关于问题的详细解释。详细的情况说明请参照网站 http://www.usmleconsult.com/usmle-step-three/usmle-step-three.cfm。

6.5.7 USMLERx（https://www.usmle-rx.com/）

在研究阶段 1 考试过程中最大的挑战就是哪些信息值得记住。USMLE-Rx 是唯一一个结合 First Aid 而开发的完整的学习系统。

USMLE Consult's Step 3 Premium Review allows you to get a full range of online learning materials to ensure the success of USMLE. These include: Step 3 CCS Bank, Step 3 Question bank, Scorrelator, and an e-book: access to Review USMLE Step 3, these information can provide you with more than 3300 practice questions.

On the Internet you can get a book *Rapid Review USMLE Step 3* written by David Rolston and Craig Nielson from Elsevier. It is a fast, efficient and comprehensive review tool, knowledge widely covered, and detailed explanation about question. For detailed information, please refer to the website http://www.usmleconsult.com/usmle-step-three/usmle-step-three.cfm.

6.5.7 USMLERx（https://www.usmle-rx.com/）

The biggest challenge in studying the Step 1 exam is what information is worth remembering. USMLE-Rx is the only complete learning system combination of First Aid .

（1）USMLERx 360 阶段 1　　　　　　（1）USMLERx 360 Step 1

USMLERx 360 阶段 1 与 First Aid for the USMLE Step 1 完全集成而形成的唯一数字产品，它可以帮助考生学习医学方面和各科课程。这套产品包括如下部分。

阶段 1 Qmax（2300 多道高质量的带有解释的问题，免费的自我评估试题，根据难易水平定制测试，便于预测实际的水平）。

USMLERx 360 Step 1 and First Aid for the USMLE Step 1 fully integrated into the only digital product, it can help you learn medical courses. This product includes:

Step 1 Qmax: there are more than 2300 high quality questions with interpretation, free self-assessment questions, according to the different difficulty level to custom testing, easy to predict the actual level.

First Aid Step 1 Flash Facts（10000 多张抽认卡，可以随时随地学习，3500 多张基于病案的抽认卡，根据自己的实际情况建立抽认卡，并且可以搜索、浏览、注释和标志急救主题）。

First Aid Step1 Flash Facts: there are more than 10000 flash cards, more than 3500 case-based cards to learn whenever and wherever possible, the flash cards. You can set up flash cards based on the actual situation, and you can search, browse, comment and sign for emergency theme.

First Aid Step 1 Express Videos（近 80 小时的高质量视频辅以一个 200 多页工作簿，600 多个额外的图像和多媒体剪辑）

First Aid Step 1 Express Videos: there are high quality video with nearly 80 hours and a workbook with more than 200 pages, more than 600 additional images and multimedia clips.

（2）USMLERx 阶段 2 Qmax

阶段 2 Qmax 对 Step 2 CK 考试产详细解释帮助考生了解应用临床知识的要点。Step 2 Qmax 包括 2100 多道 USMLE 类型题，NBMEFast Random Enquiry Display 快速随机询问显示界面。根据考试模式、题材和试题难度定制题。

（2）USMLERx Step 2 Qmax

Step 2 Qmax explains in detail for Step 2 CK test products to help you understand the key points of the application of clinical knowledge. Step 2 Qmax includes more than 2100 USMLE type questions, NBME Fast Random Enquiry Display interface. Custom questions are made according to the examination mode, subject matter, the difficulty of the test questions.

usmle
from the authors of FIRST AID

PRODUCTS　　AUTHORS　　SUPPORT　　FIRST AID TEAM BLOG　　SCHOLAR RX

Step 2 Qmax

Ace the Step 2 CK exam with detailed explanations and performance feedback that help you understand the finer points of applying clinical knowledge.

✓ 2,100+ top-rated USMLE-style questions
✓ NBME FRED-style interface
✓ Customize by test mode, subject matter, question difficulty

Subscribe　　　　Take a Tour

（3）USMLERx 阶段 3 Qmax

（3）USMLERx Step 3 Qmax

阶段 3 Qmax 包括 2100 多道 USMLE 类型题，NBMEFast Random Enquiry Display 快速随机询问显示界面。根据考试模式、题材、试题难度定制题。

Step 3 Qmax includes more than 2100 USMLE type questions, NBME Fast Random Enquiry Display interface. Custom questions are made according to the examination mode, subject matter, the difficulty of the test questions.

6.5.8 购买 USMLE 资源网站

6.5.8 perchasing USMLE resources on websites

（1）淘宝网（http://s.taobao.com）

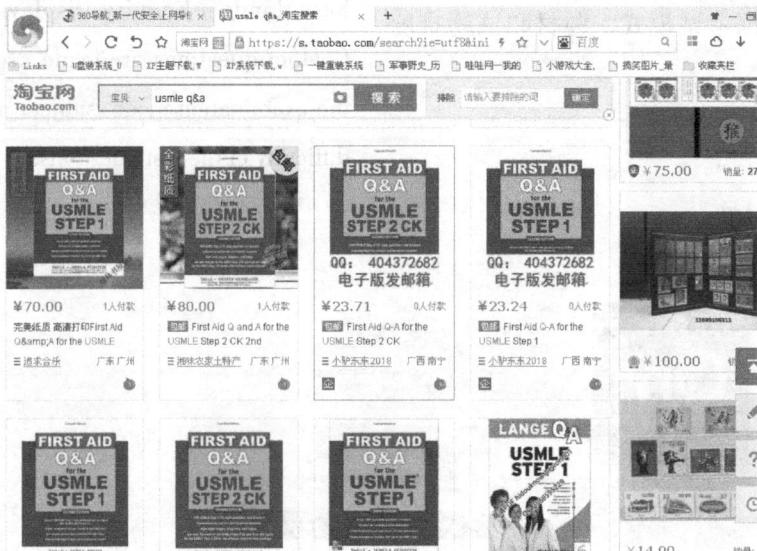

（2）京东商城（http://book.jd.com）

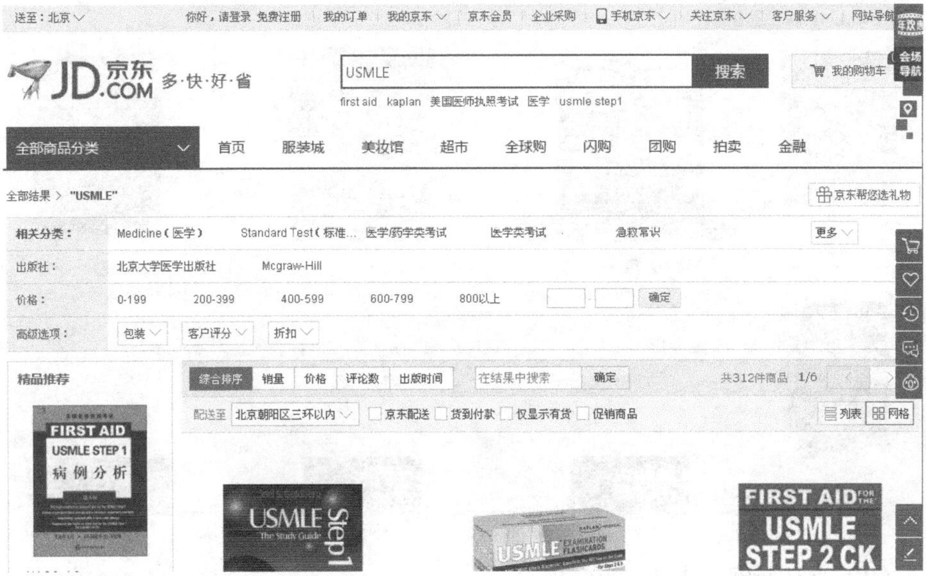

（3）澜瑞外文（http://www.lanree.com/）

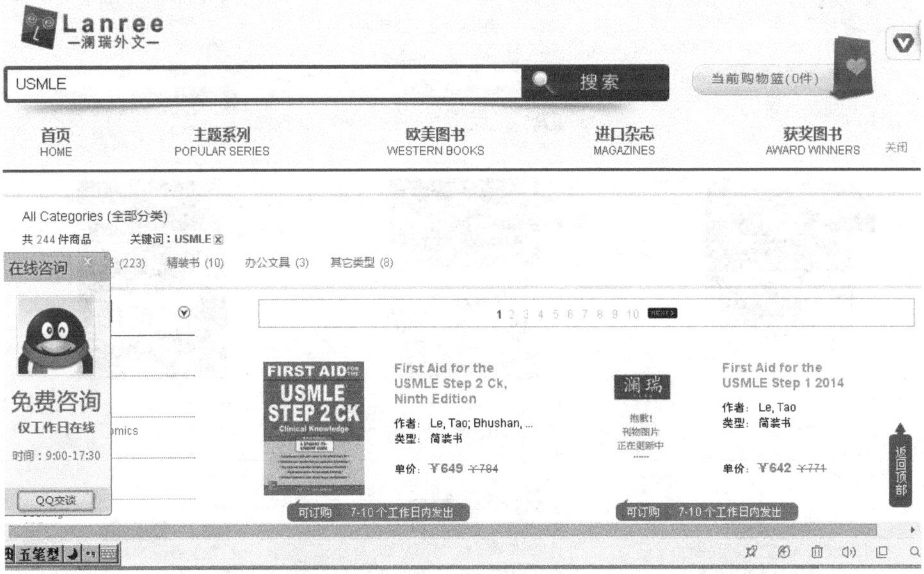

LANGE
¥186.10
Current Diagnosis &
Treatment Obstetrics &

FIRST AID
USMLE STEP 1
应试指南

¥152.30
美国医师执照考试丛书：
美国医师执照考试 USMLE

¥16.90
中华遗产（2015年12月）

澜瑞外文Lanree图书专营店
♡关注　加入购物车

FIRST AID
USMLE STEP 1
习题与解析

北京有货，下单后2-6天发货

¥165.30
美国医师执照考试 USMLE Step 1 习题与
已有 2 个评价
京东自营
♡关注　加入购物车

USMLE
STEP 2

京东自营
♡关注　加入购物车

Review for
USMLE
Step 3

¥337.90
NMS Review for USMLE Step 3
已有 0 个评价
京东自营
♡关注　加入购物车

USMLE

京东自营
♡关注　加入购物车

FIRST AID
USMLE STEP 2 CS
临床技能
Clinical Skills

¥125.60
美国医师执照考试：USMLE STEP
已有 2 个评价
京东自营
♡关注　加入购物车

KAPLAN MEDICAL
USMLE

（4）亚马逊网上书店（http://www.amazon.cn/）

Kaplan
平装
¥ 503.00 货到付款
部分地区今天或明天即可送达
此商品仅剩 2 件 - 欲购从速。
满99减10限光大卡 查看详细资料

加入购物车　加入心愿单

图书：查看所有 8 个商品

Kaplan
平装
¥ 1,139.30 货到付款
通常需要5-8周发货。
满99减10限光大卡 查看详细资料

加入购物车　加入心愿单

图书：查看所有 8 个商品
#1 最畅销商品 在Professional Test
Guides中

Microbiology 2015-12
Kaplan

平装
¥ 503.00 货到付款
部分地区今天或明天即可送达
此商品仅剩 1 件 - 欲购从速。
满99减10限光大卡 查看详细资料

加入购物车　加入心愿单

图书：查看所有 8 个商品

USMLE Step 1 Lecture Notes
2016: Biochemistry and Medical
Genetics 2015-12
Kaplan

平装
¥ 503.00 货到付款
部分地区今天或明天即可送达
此商品仅剩 2 件 - 欲购从速。
满99减10限光大卡 查看详细资料

加入购物车　加入心愿单

图书：查看所有 8 个商品

USMLE Step 1 Lecture Notes
2016: Pharmacology 2015-12
Kaplan

平装
¥ 503.00 货到付款
部分地区今天或明天即可送达
此商品仅剩 3 件 - 欲购从速。
满99减10限光大卡 查看详细资料

加入购物车　加入心愿单

图书：查看所有 8 个商品

USMLE Step 1 Lecture Note
2016: Behavioral Science ar
Social Sciences 2015-12
Kaplan

平装
¥ 503.00 货到付款
部分地区今天或明天即可送达
此商品仅剩 3 件 - 欲购从速。
满99减10限光大卡 查看详细资料

加入购物车　加入心愿单

图书：查看所有 8 个商品

（5）当当网（http://search.dangdang.com/）

（6）国外医学电子图书下载网站　　　（6）Foreign medical electronic book download website）

http://www.freebooks4doctors.com/

http://www.ncbi.nlm.nih.gov/sites/entrez?db=books

http://welovelmc.com/books.htm

http://library.nu/?utm_source=redirect&utm_medium=web&utm_campaign=gigapedia.org

6.6 USMLE 图书资源

6.6 USMLE Books Resources

6.6.1 First aid 系列图书

6.6.1 First aid series books

　　First aid 系列图书是 USMLE 考试复习中最重要、最实用的图书资料。它每年都根据 USMLE 考试大纲要求进

　　First aid series books are the most important and practical materials on the examination of the USMLE. It is required

行内容更新。该系列图书提供考生必须掌握和记住的组织器官系统的一般原则和高质量的临床图像。作为一本参考图书，它会提高考生学习效率，并且在图书后面向考生推荐 USMLE 考试用书。应该说，First aid 系列图书是重要的参考书。

to update the content annually according the USMLE outline. The book provides the general principles of organization organ system you must grasp and remember and clinical images of high quality. As a reference book, it will improve your learning efficiency, and recommend to you the materials using on USMLE examinations in the back of a book. It should be said, First aid series books are important reference books.

（1）First aid for the USMLE Step 1

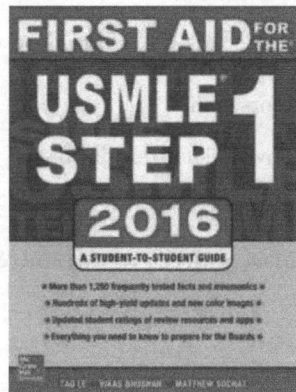

此书为考生提供了 USMLE 考试过程中涉及的必知和必背的医学一般原则和组织器官系统，用全彩的插图说明基本概念，在考前可以快速浏览，帮助考生提高学习效率。内容每年都

This book provides medical general principles and organ systems that should be grasped and remembered in the process of USMLE examination, using full-color illustrations to clarify the basic concepts,

会根据 USMLE 的考试大纲更新，确保考生通过 USMLE 考试。

and helping examinees browse quickly before exam. The book can improve your learning efficiency. Book contents will be updated annually according to the USMLE examination outline to ensure examinees passing the USMLE exam.

（2）First Aid for the USMLE Step 2 CS

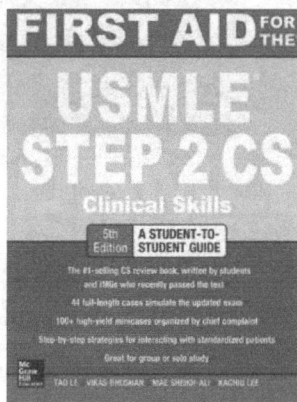

　　此书已根据 USMLE 考试大纲更新，反映了最新的考试形式，并且采纳了 USMLE 考生的建议，是一本很好的 USMLE 阶段 2 CS 考试指南。其内容包括成熟的学习和考试策略，40 例完整的实践病例完全模拟真实的考试时间管理，以提高处理临床突发事件的效率，与标准化病人的互动策略等。

　　This book has been updated according to the USMLE exam outline, reflecting the latest form of examination, and adopted the recommendations of USMLE examinees. It is a good guide to the USMLE Step 2 CS exam. The contents include mature learning and examination practice strategies, 40 full-length cases completely simulate real test Time management in order to improve the efficiency of clinical encourters, and standardized patient interaction strategies.

（3）First Aid Q&A for the USMLE Step 2 CK

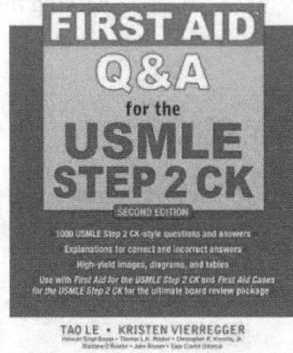

此书所包含的问题都是学生们在使用过程中认为比较好的问题，易于浏览，对正确答案和非正确答案有较好的解释。此书有许多有价值的图表。建议与 First Aid for the USMLE Step 2 CK 和 First Aid Cases for the USMLE Step 2 CK 配套使用。此书中的 1000 个问题和答案来自于 USMLERx Qmax Step 2 CK 试题库，试题完全模拟考试分 8 个考试模块。

This book contains the problems that students used well in the process of learning. It is easy to browse, and it gives full explanations of the correct and wrong answers. This book has a number of valuable pictures, charts and tables. It is suqqested that you match with two books First Aid the Step 2 CK and First Cases for the USMLE Step 2 CK during reading this book. There are 1000 questions and answers from the USMLERx Qmax Step 2 CK test bank, test questions fully simulated real exam test, which is divided into 8 test blocks.

（4）First Aid Cases for the USMLE Step 2 CK

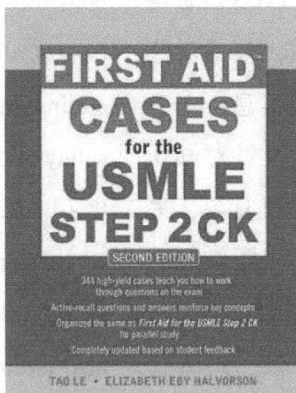

此书通过主动召回问题和答案的方式，根据考生的信息反馈做了更新，有344例考试类型的病例教考生如何通过。这344例案例当中有94例是新病例，是由已经通过考试的学生提供的。案例强调必须是与考试大纲要求一致的疾病和概念。此书还包括100个图表对病案进行补充。

This book updated the contents through active recall questions and answers and accepting the feedback of the students. There are 344 cases to teach you how to pass examination, in which 94 cases were new cases, provided by the students having passed the exam.Cases emphasize that concepts of diseases must be consistent with the outline of the examination. The book also includes 100 images, charts and tables to supplement the cases.

（5）First Aid for the USMLE Step 2 Ck

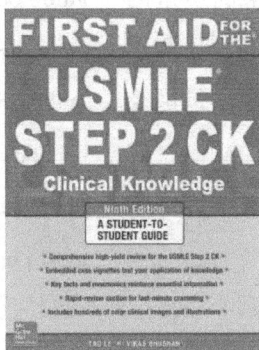

该书是 USMLE 阶段 2 CK 部分的高质量的复习书，它覆盖了 USMLE 考试大纲中的所有核心领域，包括对病人安全和质量改进的主题信息。书中有考试中必须记住的疾病及针对知识点进行的测试，能用来快速复习，另外，书中还包括数百个临床图像和彩色插图。

This book is the high quality review book for the USMLE Step 2 CK part, which covers all the core areas of the USMLE outline, including the information of patient safety and quality improvement topics. In this book,there are diseases which should be remembered and tests according to the key knowledge points. In addition, the book also includes hundreds of clinical images and color illustrations.

（6）First Aid for the USMLE Step 3

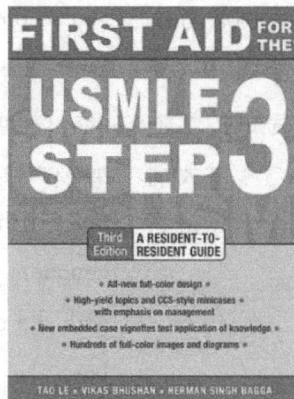

该书是一站式考试指南用书，它采用全新的彩色设计，收录高质量的话题及 CCS 风格的微型病例，强调了综合病理生理、诊断和管理，是最受欢迎的一本复习用书。

This book is one-stop examination guide book for examinees. It uses new full-color design, includes high quality topics and CCS style minicases, and it emphasizes on comprehensive pathology, physiology, diagnosis and management. It is one of the most popular review books.

（7）FIRST AID FOR THE USMLE STEP 1

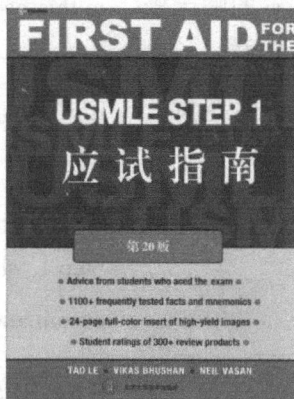

该书有 1100 多道考试前必须知道和记住的组织器官系统和一般原则，数百张高质量的临床图像，包括 24 页的全彩色图片。快速复习部分帮助考生在考试最后一分钟浏览，书中还有已经通过考试的学生给出的应试建议与应试策略。

This book has more than 1100 must-know and must-remember facts the organ system and general principles before the exam. There are hundreds of high quality clinical images, including 24 pages of full color pictures. Fast review section can help you browse last minute cramming, and the book also has tset-taking suggestions and strategies given by the students having passed the examination.

（8）First Aid Cases for the USMLE Step 1

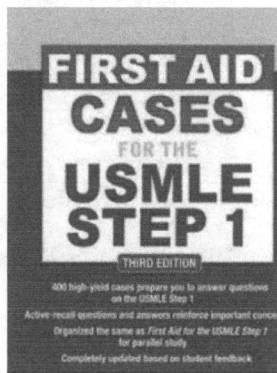

这本书里的 400 个高质量的病案能很好地帮助考生复习基本的临床概念。每个案例包括带有问答题的临床图像，可以加强对关键概念的理解。章节都是按照 Tao Le's First Aid for the USMLE Step 1 这本书编写的，其内容涵盖了整个考试范围。

The 400 high quality medical cases in this book will help you review the basic concepts of clinical practice. Each case includes clinical images with Q&As. Chapters are written in accordance with the book Tao Le's First Aid the USMLE Step 1, which covers the entire areas of the examination.

6.6.2 BRS 系列图书

BRS 系列图书被医学生广泛地用于 USMLE Step 1 考试学习中，BRE 提供了与临床相关的基础知识。下面按学科介绍几种常用的 USMLE 考试用书。

6.6.2 BRS series books

BRS books are Widely used by medical students studying for the USMLE Step 1, it provides basic knowledge as it relates to clinical situations. Now, several USMLE examinations books will be introduced according to the subject.

（1）BRS Pharmacology

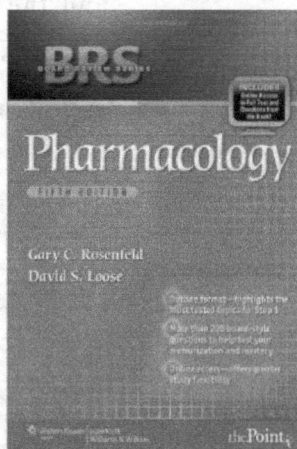

此书包括 13 个方面的内容：药物作用的一般原理；药物作用于自主神经系统；药物作用于肾系统；药物作用于心血管系统；作用于中枢神经系统的药物；内分泌素，麦角碱，抗炎药和免疫抑制剂；用于贫血和止血障碍的药物；作用于胃肠道的药物；作用于肺系统的药物；作用于内分泌系统的药物；用于治疗传染病的药物；癌症化疗；毒理学；综合考试。

This book includes 13 aspects: the general principle of drug action; drug effects on the autonomic nervous system; drug effects on the renal system; drug effects on the cardiovascular system; the central nervous system drugs; endocrine hormone, ergot, anti-inflammatory and immunosuppressive agents; drug for anemia and hemostatic disorders; drugs gastrointestinal tract; drug effects on the pulmonary system; drug effects on endocrine system; drug for the treatment of infectious diseases; cancer chemotherapy; toxicology; comprehensive examination.

（2）BRS Physiology

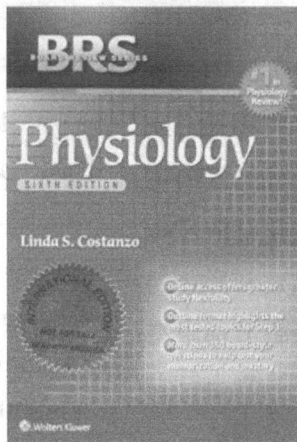

这本书提供了超过 350 个 USMLE 式问题的完整答案和解释，每章结束都有考试和在书的结尾有 USMLE 格式之间的联系。

This book provides a complete answer and explanation for more than 350

的综合考试，并有彩色插图和表格。考生可通过掌握关键的生理学内容，通过临床相关性看生理学与临床医学

（3）BRS Pathology

USMLE style questions, each chapter-ending with an exam and a USMLE format exam at the end of the book. Master the key physiological content through clinical relevance to learn the relationship between physiology and clinical medicine.

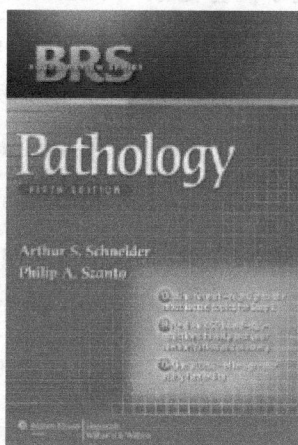

此书是为学生准备的 USMLE 阶段 1 和课程考试的病理检查用书。此书涵盖了基本的病理、疾病过程的主要概念，以及全身各器官系统的病理调查，主要通过简洁的描述和彩色插图来揭示图书内容。每一章节都附有 USMLE 格式的习题，便于发现自己在学习过程中的薄弱环节。图书后面还的一个综合性的考试题。

It is a book for students to prepare for pathological examination and USMLE Step 1 examinations. The book covers the basic concepts of Pathology, the course of the disease, and the investigation of the various organs of the body. By the simple descriptions and color illustrations, it reveals the contents of the book. Each chapter is accompanied by USMLE format exercises, in order to find their weaknesses in the learning process. At the end of the book, there is also a comprehensive examination questions.

（4）BRS Biochemistry, Molecular Biology and Genetics

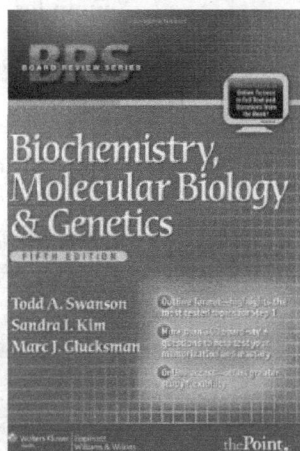

这本复习书有助于 USMLE 阶段 1
考试和生物化学、分子生物学、遗传
学课程的学习。每一章按大纲的形式
编写，包括教学的功能，如粗体关键
词、数字、表格、算法和突出的临床
相关性。每章有 USMLE 式问题和答
案，在书的最后有综合考试。

This review book is helpful for the
study of USMLE Step 1 and the coursework
of biochemistry, molecular biology and
genetics. According to the outline, each
chapter is written in the form of outline,
including the teaching function, such as
bold words, figures, tables, and highlights
the clinical relevance of algorithm. Each
chapter has USMLE type questions and
answers, and there is a comprehensive
examination in the end of the book.

（5）BRS Cell Biology and Histology

此书是 USMLE 和课程考试用书，
其形式是大纲格式的，具有丰富的电
子显微图。每章有高质量的复习题，
书的结尾有综合性考试题。第 6 版包
括 60 个新的全彩色照片和彩色线条图
新的彩色设计。内容和问题已经根据

This book is for USMLE and
coursework examinations, which is in the
form of an outline format. It is with richful
electron micrographs, and each chapter has
high quality review questions. And at the
end of the book, there is a comprehensive

大纲要求进行了更新。

examination. This sixth edition book includes a new color design for 60 new full-color photographs and color line drawings. Content and issues have been updated according to the outline.

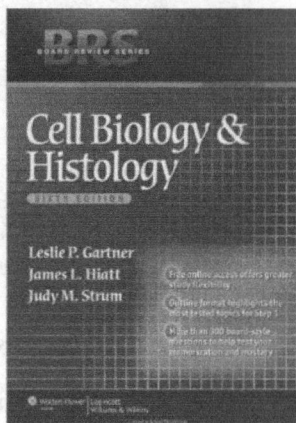

（6）BRS Embryology

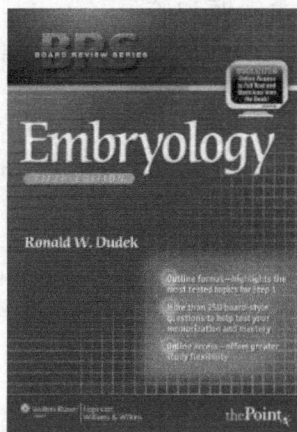

此书是 USMLE 和课程考试用书，其形式是大纲格式的，每章有高质量的复习题，书的结尾有综合性考试题。在人类胚胎的发展脉络下，阐述

This book is for USMLE and coursework examinations, which is in the form of an outline format. Each chapter has high quality review questions at the end of

了 USMLE 考试涉及的事实和概念，这本书还包括 X 射线检查、超声检查、CT 扫描及各种先天性畸形的照片。

the book, a comprehensive examination. It elaborated the facts and concepts tested on the USMLE examination within the context of the development of human embryos. This book also includes X−ray examination, ultrasonography, CT scan, and a variety of congenital malformations photos.

（7）BRS Genetics

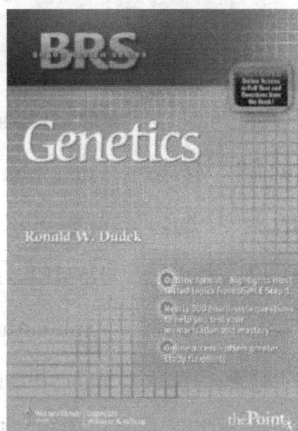

该书的形式是大纲格式的，包括教学的功能，如粗体关键词、表、算法和众多的插图，包括一个 16 页的彩色插图。这本书包含了近 300 道 USMLE 式问题来测试学生对概念的记忆与掌握程度。

It is in the form of an outline format, including the teaching function, such as bold words, tables, algorithms, and numerous illustrations, including a 16 page color illustrations. This book contains nearly 300 USMLE questions to test students' memory and mastery of concepts.

（8）BRS Neuroanatomy

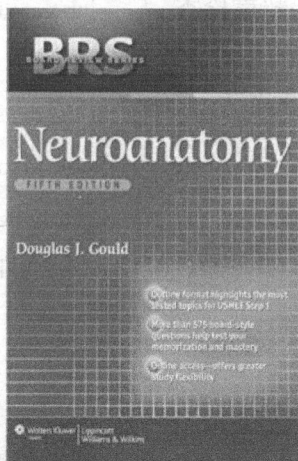

此书是课程和资格考试的医学人类神经解剖学的简要回顾，包括 USMLE 和 600 道带解释的复习题。这本书还包括新的全彩插图和设计元素，更新的临床相关性，超过 200 个关键术语的词汇和颅神经的附录。

This book is a brief review of curriculum and qualification examination of medical human neuroanatomy including USMLE, and 600 review questions with explanation.This book also includes full-color illustrations and new design elements, updated clinical correlations, more than 200 key terms, and appendix of cranial nerve.

（9）BRS Behavioral Science

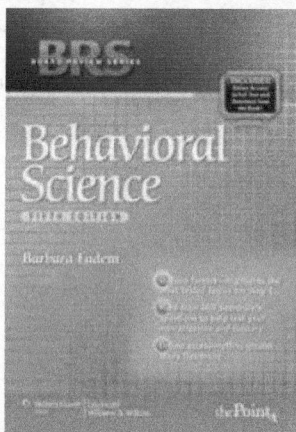

此书涵盖了 USMLEStep1 关于这个学科的所有资料，它以大纲的形式编写。此书包括至少 500 道 USMLE 式问题并伴随注解的答案。每章都有测试题，书的结尾有综合考试题。

This book covers all the information about the subject of USMLEStep1, which is written in outline. This book includes at least 500 USMLE questions and answers with annotations. Each chapter has test questions. At the end of the book, there is a comprehensive examination.

（10）BRS Gross Anatomy

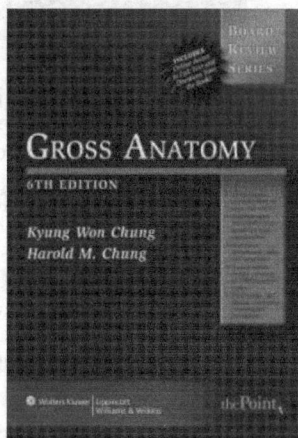

医学院一年级解剖学课程的初级课程复习与教材。在每一章的结尾提供 USMLE 式问题，在图书最后有综合考试答案和解释。它还有 150 个插图，50 个 X 射线临床图像，并在胚胎学章节强调"发展测试"。

This book is review and teaching materials of the primary course of anatomy in the first year of medical school. At the end of each chapter, it provides USMLE style questions. In the end of the book, there is a comprehensive test with answers and explanations. It also has 150 illustrations, 50 clinical X-ray images, and highlighted "development of testing" in the embryology section.

（11）BRS Microbiology and Immunolog

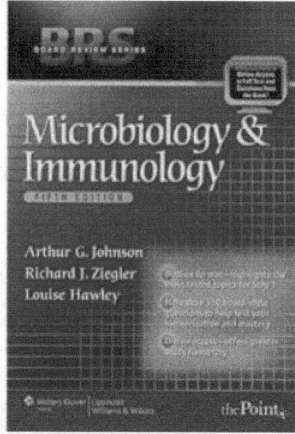

该书涵盖最常用的 USMLE 测试，包括 300~500 道 USMLE 格式复习题。全彩幻灯片设计和微生物学包括免疫学、寄生虫、真菌更多的信息。

The book covers the most commonly test used on USMLE, including 300 to 500 USMLE format review questions. It has full-color slide design and microbiology. It also includes more information about immunology, parasites and fungi.

6.6.3 High Yield 系列图书

（1）High-Yield 各学科图书

6.6.3 High Yield series books

（1）High-Yield subject books

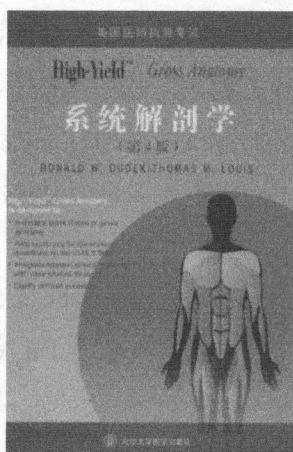

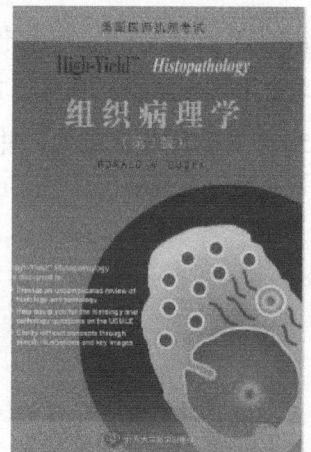

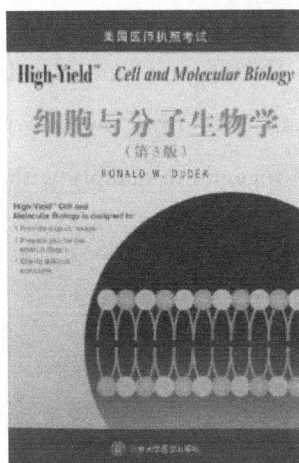

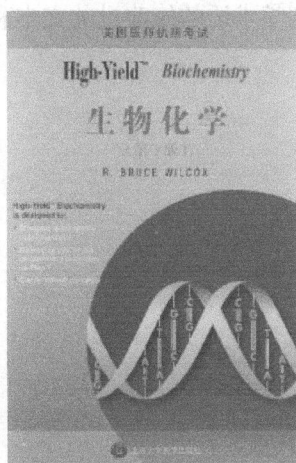

这套系列图书高度概括了考生需要快速掌握的核心知识，既有基础知识要点的介绍，又有以疾病为核心的综合归纳，并体现了相关学科的横向联系；语言规范、地道，既有利于读者快速掌握专业词汇，又有利于医学英语思维的培养，为中国学生参加美国执业医师资格考试发挥了辅助作用。

This series books summarize the core knowledge the examinees need to grasp quickly. In this book, there are not only basic knowledge introduction,but also the generalization of diseases as the core, which reflects related disciplines. Normative language is conducive to the readers to grasp the professional vocabulary, and also is conducive to the cultivation of medical English thinking. They play an auxiliary role on USMLE for Chinese students.

（2）High-Yield ™ Neuroanatomy

这本书用简洁的语言为学生课程考试和 USMLE 考试提供了神经解剖学的最重要的信息。这本书有一个关于神经解剖结构和疾病状态的词汇表，常见的神经病变表，确定临床相关解剖关系的扩展图，一个索引和符合解

This book provides the most important information for students of neuroanatomy course examination and USMLE examination in simple language. It has a vocabulary of neural anatomy and disease state, a table of common neurological

剖学术语的修改过的文本和图例。

lesions, expanded figure legends that identify clinically relevant anatomical relationships,an index and modified text and figure legends to comply with Terminologia Anatomica.

（3）High–Yield Embryolog

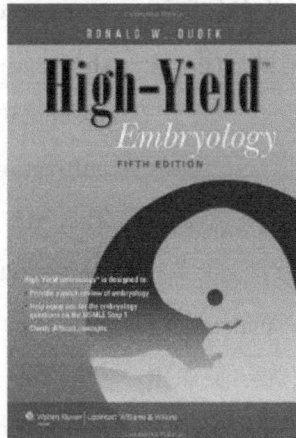

　　该书提供了 USMLE Step 1 考试中的胚胎学复习资料，知识集中，提高了考生的学习效率。概念采用大纲格式以表格、图、照片和 X 射线照片形

This book provides embryology review information on USMLE Step 1 examination. Knowledge concentration improves

式展现，便于突出重要材料。在每章的最后附加了 USMLE 式案例研究。

students learning efficiency. Concepts are presented in a streamlined outline format with tables, diagrams, photos, and radiographs to clarify important material.At the end of each chapter there is a USMLE case study.

（4）High–Yield: USMLE Step 1 综合复习

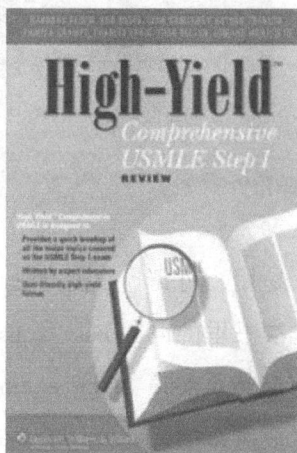

这是一本非常简洁的关于 USMLE 阶段 1 综合复习的书，是由有经验的作者团队编写的，其内容对于在 USMLE 考试中最有可能出现的知识进行综合检查。这本书用表格和插图的形式将难懂的概念进行总结，帮助考生快速浏览和复习。

This is a very concise book on the comprehensive review of USMLE Step 1, written by an experienced team of authors. Its content is most likely to appear in the USMLE examination. Using this book,you can have a comprehensive examination to the knowledge. This book summarizes the difficult concepts in the form of tables and illustrations, which can help students quickly browse and review.

6.6.4 Secrets Series

（1）SMLE Step 1 Secrets in Color

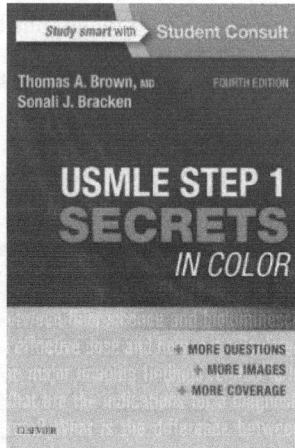

这本书简洁、高效、易用，可帮助考生顺利通过考试。这本书里的问题和答案简短，但强调的都是重点，包含相当多的信息。各章节按医学专业分开，包含一些黑白照片。即使只使用这个资源，科目考试也可以轻松通过。

This book is concise, efficient and easy to use, to help you successfully pass the exam. The questions and answers in this book are short, but the emphasis is on the focus, which contains a lot of information. Chapters separated by medical specialty, in which contain a number of black and white photos. If you only use this resource, you can easily pass the exam.

（2）USMLE Step 2 Secret

对于忙碌的学生来说这本书是一本完美的、易阅读的复习书。书中包含了在 USMLE Step 2 考试中必须掌握的重要知识概念。

It is an easy-to-read review perfect for busy students. In this book, it covers the important concepts you need to know on the USMLE Step 2 exam.

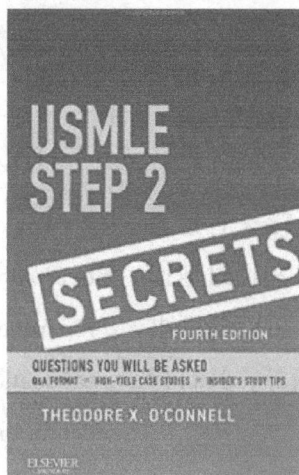

（3）USMLE Step 3 Preparation Secrets

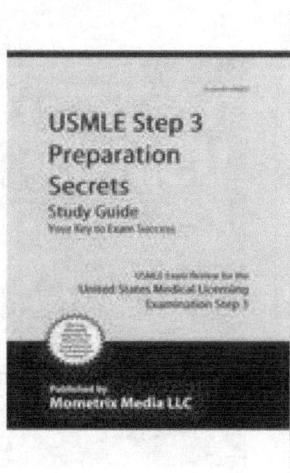

这本书是非常有帮助的，因为它包含了所有的在考试中考生需要知道的基本知识点，并且都有解释。它对于实时复习和巩固知识非常有帮助。它提到的最重要的知识点，语言易于理解。这本书还提到了关于考试过程中的物质、精神及情绪方面如何做准备。

This book is actually very helpful, because it contains all the basic topics I need to know in the exam, and all of them are explained. It is helpful to review and consolidate knowledge at any time. It refers to the most important topic, the language is easy to understand. The book also mentions how to prepare the material, mental and emotional aspects during the examination process.

6.6.5 Kaplan 出版的图书

40 多年来，Kaplan 医疗一直致力于帮助有抱负的医生准备和通过他们的医疗执照考试。Kaplan 出版的图书为医生和医学生提供了指导，其目标是帮助学生走向成功。

6.6.5 Kaplan published books

For more than 40 years, Kaplan has been working to help aspiring doctors prepare and pass their medical licensing examinations. Kaplan published books for doctors and medical students to provide guidance, its goal is to help students to success.

（1）USMLE Step 1 Qbook

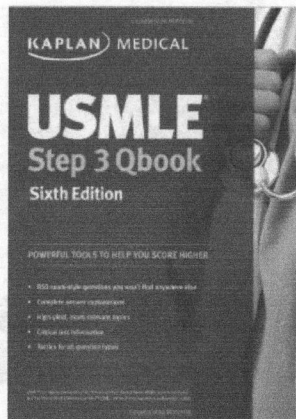

该书提供了 850 道类似考试的实践性问题，这些问题在别的地方找不到；对正确和不正确的答案都有解释；指导考生学习技巧和对每种类型的问题答题策略，涉及与考试相关度高的知识点，如解剖学、生理学、生物化学、微生物学、免疫学、病理学、病理生理学、药理学、行为科学 /

The book provides 850 exam-like practice questions, these problems can not be found in other places; to explain each correct and incorrect answers; to guide students how to learn and strategies for every question type, there are highly related topics in this book, such as anatomy, physiology, biology chemistry,

生物统计学。

microbiology, immunology, pathology, pathophysiology, pharmacology, behavioral science / biostatistics.

（2）USMLE Lecture Notes

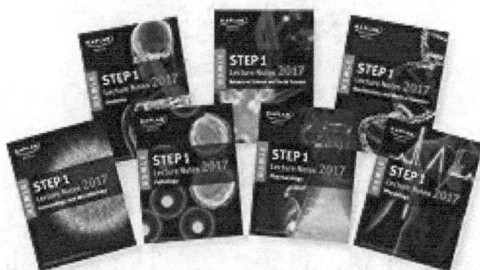

这是唯一的官方 Kaplan 讲稿，涵盖了考生想通过考试成为住院医师的综合信息。每年 Kaplan 全明星队伍对图书内容进行更新，整合临床相关性学科，在它们中间建立一座桥梁。书的内容以大纲的形式组织，提高了学习效率。更重要的是，每年数千名考生使用该书都成功通过了考试。该系列讲稿包含 7 卷——病理药理学、生理学，生物化学、医学遗传学、免疫学、微生物学、解剖学、行为科学和社会科学。

The only official Kaplan lecture covers the comprehensive information you want to pass the exam to become a resident. Each year, the Kaplan all star team updates the content of the book, integrates the relevant clinical disciplines, and builds a bridge between them. The content of the book is organized in outline form, which improves the learning efficiency. It is important that thousands of students use the book to pass the exam every year.The series Lecture Notes include 7 volumes——pathology, pharmacology, physiology, biochemistry and medical genetics, immunology and microbiology, anatomy and behavioral Science/Social sciences.

（3）USMLE Step 3 Qbook

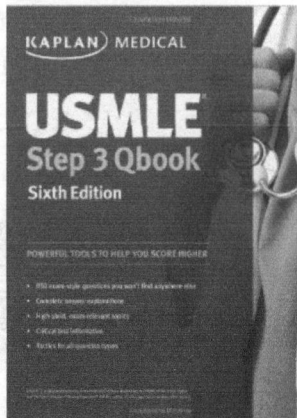

此书有850个考试样题，每道题都有详细的解释，让考生知道哪些问题回答的正确，哪些地方的知识还需要加强；可以使用在线题库；书中有专家给出的基于计算机考试的策略指导；此书覆盖的考试特定主题的范围：内科学、神经病学、妇产科、儿科学、精神病学、外科学。

The book has 850 exam-like questions, each question has a detailed explanation,which let you know whether your answer is correct, what knowledge you need to strengthen. You can use the online exam bank. There is a computer-based test strategy guidance provided by experts in the book. The book covers the range of topic specific test: internal medicine; neurology; department of obstetrics and gynecology; pediatrics; psychiatry; surgery.

（4）USMLE Step 2 CS Core Cases

该书全面修订，以反映最近的阶段2 CS考试的变化；新章节概述鉴别诊断和诊断推理过程；含有43例常见及具有挑战性的病案；内容主题包括健康体检、体检工作、电话、临终的问题、糖尿病检查、家庭暴力和HIV相关的问题；每个病例都会告诉考

This book comprehensively revised to reflect the recent changes in Step 2 CS test; new chapters overview of differential diagnosis and diagnosis reasoning; containing 43 frequently seen and challenging cases. The content topics include health checkups, work physicals,

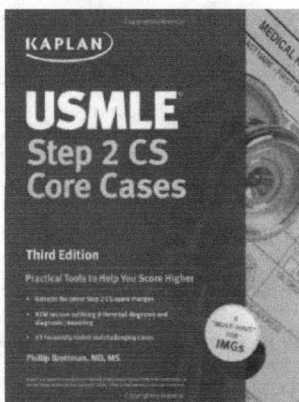

生：在进入病房之前要做什么；指导考生病史收集和体格检查；关于如何恰当地与病人联系的建议；考生可能面临的挑战性问题；病例讨论；样本病人笔记，包括新的鉴别诊断和诊断推理要素。

telephone calls, end-of-life issues, diabetes checkups, domestic violence, and HIV-related issues. Each cases will tell you :what to do before entering the room; guiding your medical history collection and physical examination; advice on how to close properly with a patient; you may face challenging problems; case discussion; samples with notes, including the differential diagnosis and diagnosis reasoning new elements.

（5）Kaplan Medical Internal Medicine Question Book

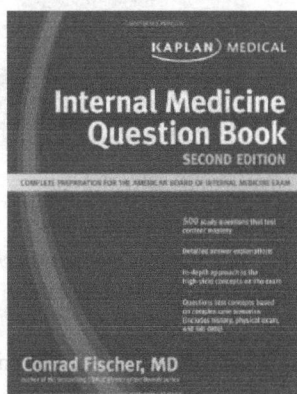

该书500例样题教会学生如何回答美国内科执业医认证考试中的最重要的话题。该书的特点是对病例的研究主要是这几个方面：从描述病人的病史、体检、实验室数据方面入手，熟练掌握问题答题内容，详细解答答案，确保清晰理解。该书的重点是回答和分析学生在实际考试中面临的问题，菲舍尔问题分析法是学生考试成功的关键。

The 500 cases in this book teach students how to answer the most important topics in American physicians practicing medicine certification exam. The characteristics of this book are to study cases mainly from the following aspects: history, physical examination, laboratory data. Study questions quiz content mastery, while detailed answer explanations ensure clear comprehension. The focus of this book is to answer and analyze the problems faced by the students in the actual test, Fischer's question analysis method is key for students' success on test.

（6）Master the Boards USMLE Step 2 CK

该书包含了考试小窍门和来自USMLE专家Conrad Fischer, MD的有针对性的评论。该书提供了考试中所需要了解的知识和匹配到考生想要的

This book contains the exam tips and targeted comments from the USMLE expert Conrad Fischer, MD's. It provides information about what you need to know

实习计划的信息。这本书的特点是：修订了 DSM Ⅴ 分类；新的对高血压 JNC 8 指南；丙型肝炎管理的最新指南；病人护理的循序渐进方法指导；识别不正确答案的小窍门；每一种疾病都有样题，样题的格式是：最可能的诊断是什么？什么是最好的初始测试？什么是最准确的诊断测试？治疗是什么？

in your exams and the information that matches your residency program you want. The characteristics of this book is: revised DSM Ⅴ classification; new JNC 8 guidelines on hypertension; the new guidelines for the management of hepatitis C patients; step by step approach to patient care; identifing the incorrect answer tips ; a sample of each disease. Its formate is: What is the most likely diagnosis? What is the best initial test? What is the most accurate diagnostic test? What is treatment?

（7）Master the Boards USMLE Step 3

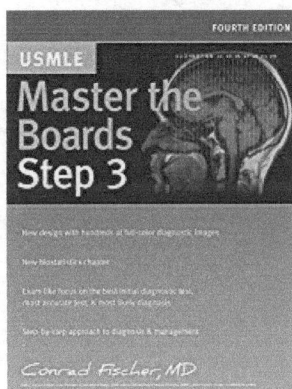

这本书包含了考试小窍门和来自 USMLE 专家 Conrad Fischer 的有针对性的评论。这本书帮考生确定考试高频率出现的概念，并且识别考试中最有可能的答案。书中的诊断图像都是全彩的，样题重点关注最佳初始诊断试验，最准确的测试，最可能的诊断，

This book contains the exam tips and targeted comments from the USMLE expert Conrad Fischer, MD' s. This book will help you determine the concept of the high frequency on the test and identify the most likely answer. The diagnostic images in the book are full-color, sample questions

循序渐进的方法来诊断和管理病案，以及简洁的病人安全注意事项和 CCS 考试技巧。

focus on the optimal initial diagnostic test, the most accurate test, the most likely diagnosis, step by step approach to the diagnosis and management of cases, and concise patient safety precautions and CCS exam tips.

第七章　加拿大医师资格考试
Chapter seven　MCCQE

7.1 加拿大医学会考试类型

加拿大医学会提供多项考试，以帮助加拿大和国际医学毕业生和医生成为合格的执业医师。国际医学毕业生（IMGs）要想到加拿大从事医生这个职业，必须先通过 MCCEE 的考试，除了 MCCEE 以外，需要考 MCCQE Part I、Part II, 详细的资料介绍可参阅加拿大医学委员会网站。（MCC http://mcc.ca/home/）。

7.1.1 加拿大考试评价医学委员会（MCCEE）

如果考生毕业于加拿大或美国以外的医学院校或者如果考生毕业于美国骨科医学院校，他（她）必须通过 MCCEE 考试才有资格在加拿大医学临

7.1 Types of MCC Exams

The Canadian Medical Association offers a number of tests to help Canadian and international medical graduates and doctors become qualified physicians. International medical graduates (IMGs) who want to be physicians in Canada, must pass the MCCEE exam. In addition to MCCEE, they also need to take MCCQE Part I & Part II, detailed information introduction can be browsed on Medical Council of Canada website. (MCC http://mcc.ca/home/).

7.1.1 Medical Council of Canada for Examination and Evaluation (MCCEE)

If examinees graduated from the Medical College of Canada or outside the United States, or if examinees graduated from the College of Medical Department of

床实践并申请住院医师。一旦考生已经通过了 MCCEE，可以申请加拿大医务委员会资格考试 MCCQE Part I.

加拿大考试评价医学委员会（MCCEE）是一个四个小时的计算机上的考试，它提供了英语和法语两种语言考试，在全球有 80 个国家 500 多个考试中心。

MCCEE 是对考生在医学主要学科上的基本医学知识的总体评估，也是为评估一个新的医学研究生在进入第一年实践培训时所需要的知识和技能而设计的。

MCCEE 由 180 道选择题组成，每道题有 5 个选项，其中只有一个是正确的答案。MCCEE 试题涉及以下领域：儿童保健、孕产妇保健、成人保健、心理健康和人口健康与伦理。考试中的一些问题也将侧重于一般实践。

一般情况下，考试时间设在星期一至星期五的时间，一些地方可能设在星期六或星期日。第一次申请考试

orthopedics, they must pass the MCCEE exam to be eligible medical clinical practice and apply for residency in Canada. Once examinees have passed the MCCEE, they can apply for MCCQE Part I.

The Medical Council of Canada Evaluating Examination (MCCEE) is a four-hour computer-based test. It offers two kinds of English and French language test. There are more than 500 test centres in 80 countries .

MCCEE is an overall evaluation of examinees on the basic medical knowledge of the subjects in the field of medicine, and also is designed to assess the knowledge and skills required by a new graduate student in the first year of practice training.

MCCEE is made up of 180 multiple-choice questions, each of which has five options, and only one is the correct answer. The following topics are covered in MCCEE: child care, maternal health, adult health, mental health,population health and ethics. Some of the questions in the exam will also focus on general practice.

In general, the examination time is scheduled from Monday to Friday, in some places it may be scheduled on Saturday or

的考生，需交纳考试费 1300 加元和申请费 250 加元。MCCEE 可随时申请，没有期限限制，但是如果一旦申请成功了，考试时间和日期就有期限了。考试地点设在全球能提供 MCCEE 考试的国家，这些国家可以在网站上看到。

7.1.2 国家评估合作委员会（NAC）

国际医学毕业生通过加拿大住院医师匹配服务（CaRMS）申请住院医师必须通过国家评估合作委员会（NAC）考试，只有通过了 MCCEE 考试的考生才能参加 NAC 考试。NAC 是一个为期一天的考试，是一个标准化的考试，NAC 测试在加拿大参加住院医师培训计划所需的知识、技能和态度。

这是一个客观的结构化临床考试（OSCE），其中包括一系列的站，每一站包括药、儿科、产科、妇科、精神病学、手术等方面的典型的临床问题。这个考试考生可在指定的中心用

Sunday. Examinees for the first exam need to pay the test fee 1300 Canadian dollars and the application fee 250 Canadian dollars. MCCEE can apply at any time, there is no time limit. But if the application is successful, the examination time and date have deadline. Examination places are located in the countries all over the world where can provide MCCEE exam. These countries can be seen on the website.

7.1.2 National Assessment Council（NAC）

IMGs apply for residency must be approved by the national assessment Cooperation Committee (NAC) exam through the Canadian resident matching service (CaRMS), only those exminees who passed the MCCEE exam can participate in the NAC exam. NAC is one-day standardized examination. NAC test examinns' knowledge, skills and attitudes that required in residency training programs in Canada.

This is an objective structured clinical examination (OSCE), which includes a series of stations. Each station includes pharmacy, pediatrics, obstetrics, gynecology, psychiatry, surgery and other aspects of the typical problems. You can

英语或法语进行考试。

NAC 考试不需要获得加拿大医务委员会执照，考试通过不能保证在加拿大获得住院医师培训的地位，它只是住院医师匹配项目的一部分。

考生可以通过自己的 physician-sapply.ca 帐户向 NAC 考试中心申请考试。无论考生在哪里参加考试，考试结果将被住院医师计划董事所接受。考生没必要在自己申请住院医师实习的省考试。

7.1.3 加拿大医学委员会资格考试（MCCQE）第一部分

MCC 管理两项资格考试：MCCQE Part I 和 MCCQE Part II。考生必须通过这两项考试后才能获得加拿大医学委员会执照 Licentiate of the Medical Council of Canada（LMCC）。考生只有通过了 MCCQE Part I，才有资格参加 MCCQE Part II 的考试。

take a test in English or in French at the designated center.

The NAC test does not require a license from the Medical Council of Canada. Passing the NAC exam can't guarantee residency status in Canada. It is only one part of the residency matching program.

Examinees can apply for an examination through their physicians apply. ca's account at the NAC test centre. No matter where you take the exam, the exam results will be accepted by the director of the residency program. Examinees do not need to apply for residency examination in your province.

7.1.3 Medical Council of Canada Qualifying Examination（MCCQE）Part I

Medical Council of Canada (MCC) manages two qualifying exams: MCCQE PartI and MCCQE PartII. You have to pass these two exams before you can get a license from Licentiate of the Medical Council of Canada (LMCC). Examinees only pass through MCCQE Part I, they are eligible to participate in the examination of MCCQE Part II.

加拿大医学委员会的资格考试第一部分是一个为期一天的、基于计算机的测试。这个测试主要是评估已经获得医学学位，将进入临床实践的考生的能力。MCCQE Part I 评估的知识、临床技能和态度，由加拿大目标医学委员会的考试大纲规定。

考生在上午利用3.5小时完成196多项选择题，下午有4个小时做临床决策部分，需要考生作出简短的答案。

7.1.4 加拿大医学委员会资格考试（MCCQE）第二部分

要想获得医生执业资格你必须通过 MCCQE Part II，还需要成功完成（或接近完成）12个月的研究生临床医学培训。

MCCQE Part II 是一个3小时的客观结构化临床考试，是为了评估考生的能力、专业知识、技能和态度而设计的。这些对于执业医师在加拿大进入独立的临床实践前至关重要。

MCCQE Part I is a part of one-day computer-based testing. The testing is mainly to assess students' capability, who got medical degree and will enter into clinical practice. The knowledge, clinical skills, and attitudes assessed in MCCQE Part I are desided by Canadian target medical board's outline.

The examinees complete 196 multiple-choice questions within three and half an hour in the morning, and complete clinical decision questions within 4 hours in the afternoon. In the exam, examinees should make brief answers.

7.1.4 Medical Council of Canada Qualifying Examination (MCCQE) Part II

To qualify as a doctor, you have to pass MCCQE Part II and need to successfully complete (or close to) 12 months of graduate clinical training.

MCCQE Part II is a 3-hour objective structured clinical examination (OSCE). It is designed to assess examinees' ability, the professional knowledge, skills and attitudes. These are crucial for practicing physicians in Canada before entering independent clinical practice.

这个考试包括一个 5 分钟临床工作站和一个 10 分钟临床工作站。在每一站都有一个简短的声明介绍问题和指导考生检查标准化病人并做一些其他工作，如采集主要的病史，引导体检，确定和解决病人的问题。考生可能要回答关于病人的具体问题，解释 X 射线或其他调查的结果，作出诊断和写出处方。

加拿大医学委员会资格考试第二部分包括问题在医药、儿科、妇产科、预防医学和社区卫生、精神病学、外科手术方面的问题，以及在同类学科中必不可少的一般医疗保健能力。

7.2 IMG 申请执业医师资格过程

"国际医学研究生"（IMG）可以指来自不同背景的医生。例如，一个国际医学研究生可能：在他 / 她的国家有几年的独立实践经验；最近刚刚完成医学院学业，毕业；已完成一个住院医师培训计划；来自于一个类似于加拿大的医学教育体系的国家。

The exam includes a 5-minute clinical station and a 10-minute clinical station. At each station, there is a brief statement of the problem and the guidance for the examinees to check the standardized patient as well as to do some other work, such as the acquisition of the main medical history, leading the physical examination, identifying and solving the patient's problem. Examinees may have to answer specific questions about the patient, explain the results of X-ray or other surveys, make a diagnosis and write recipe.

MCCQE Part II includes the problems in medicine, pediatrics, obstetrics and Gynecology, preventive medicine and community health, psychiatry, surgery and essential problems in similar subjects in the general health care ability.

7.2 IMG Application for Physician Qualification Process

"International medical graduate" (IMG) can refer to doctors from different backgrounds. For example, an IMG may have several years independent experience in his / her country; or graduated from medical school; or have completed a residency training program; or be from a

考生可以看 Registration to Practise Medicine in Canada 表了解执照获取的步骤，也可以看 the process of obtaining a licence 了解获取执照的步骤。一些步骤可一次性在加拿大完成。Working in Canada 网站也包括一些考生感兴趣的信息。

IMGs 来加拿大前可以开始做一些工作：确认考生的医学学位是否来自认可的医学院，网上自我评估考试，提交考生的凭据与加拿大医务委员会（MCC）医师证书库，参加加拿大医学委员会考试评价（MCCEE）考试。这些准备工作实际上就是申请医师资格的过程。

7.2.1 确认你的医学学位是否来自被认可的医学院

参考国际医学教育目录（IMED），考生的医学院的医学学位的名称和毕业的年份必须列入加拿大接受的 FAIMER 国际医学教育目录。

country whoes medical education system is similar to Canada.

Examinees can look at the table "Registration Practise Medicine in Canada" to understand the steps to get the license, or also can look at "the process obtaining a licence" to understand the steps to get a license. Some steps can be done once in Canada. The website "Working in Canada" also includes some information you are interested in.

IMGs can start doing some work before coming into Canada: making sure whether your medical degree is from a recognized medical school, self assessment online, submitting your credentials and the Medical Council of Canada (MCC) Physician Certificate Repository, taking the MCCEE examination . In fact, these preparations are the process of applying for physician qualification.

7.2.1 make sure whether your medical degree is from a recognized medical school

Reference to the International Medical Education Directory (IMED), The name of your medical school and the year of your graduation must be listed in the

International Medical Education Directory which acceped by Canadian FAIMER.

7.2.2 参加 SAE-EE 考试

IMGS 通过加拿大自我管理评价考试医学委员会（SAE-EE）测试考生是否准备好了参加加拿大医学委员会考试评价（MCCEE）。参加 SAE-EE 的考生将收到回答正确的问题数量和一个百分位数表，将其测试的结果与其他的考生测试结果进行比较。每个考试费用是 62 加元。

7.2.2 Take the SAE-EE exam

IMGs takes Self Administered Evaluating Examination (SAE-EE) to test whether they are eligible to participate in the MCCEE. IMGs who takes the SAE-EE will receive the number of questions correctly answered as well as a percentile table that compares their performance to the results achieved by other MCCEE examinees. Per examination's fee is C$62.

7.2.3 提交您的凭据

IMGs 可以用 MCC 的医师资格证书库建立保密的专业电子文档的凭证。IMGS 可以要求资格证书库与省 / 地区医疗监管部门、认证和合格机构分享他们的文档。MCC 要求首次向 MCCEE 申请考试的 IMGs 开放与医师资格证书库应用程序和发送最后的医学文凭的核证副本。文凭必须成功通过验证的考生有资格参加加拿大医学委员会资格考试（MCCQE）第二部分。

7.2.3 Submit your credentials

IMGS can use MCC's physician qualification Certificate Repository to establish a confidential professional electronic portfolio of their credentials. The IMGS can request the certificate repository to share their documents with the provincial / regional health care regulatory authorities, certification and compliance agencies. MCC requires the IMGs who are the first time to apply for a MCCEE examination to open an application with the Physician Credentials Repository and send a certified copy of their final medical

MCC 的医师资格证书库收取开库费，IMGs 一次性收取 250 加元，提交源核查的前 4 个医疗文件中的每一个都收取 100 加元。每个后续单据收取 60 加元，文件费除外。

7.2.4 参加加拿大医学委员会考试评价（MCCEE）

IMGs 必须通过 MCCEE 考试才能通过加拿大住院医师匹配服务申请住院医师的位置。MCCEE 考试可在 70 多个国家的 500 个网站上参加。MCCEE 考试的国家的名单，请参阅 Prometric centres—list of countries。如果 IMGS 获得了加拿大或美国专业委员会认证，可以向加拿大医学委员会申请 MCCEE 考试豁免。

第一次 MCCEE 考生收取 1550 加元；再次申请收取 1300 加元。MCC 要求所有首次参加 MCCEE 的考生打开

diploma. The diploma must be successfully validated for an examinee who is eligible to participate in the MCCQE Part II.

MCC's physician qualification certificate Repository charge to open a repository account. IMGs are charged a one-time account C$250, C$100 is charged for each of the first four medical documents submitted for source verification.Each subsequent document will be charged C$60, excluding the document fee.

7.2.4 Take MCCEE Exam

IMGs must pass the MCCEE exam in order to apply for a residency position through the Canadian resident matching service. The MCCEE exam is available on 500 sites in more than 70 countries. For a list of countries where the MCCEE is offered, please see Prometric centres—list of countries. If the IMGs have obtained a Canadian or US Specialized Committee certification, they may apply to the Medical Council of Canada for an exemption from the MCCEE.

First-time MCCEE examinees are charged C$1,550; C$1,300 is charged for IMGs who reapply for the MCCEE again.

MCC 的医师资格证书库应用程序和发送他们的医疗证书的核证副本。

各省有权要求额外的评估，以获得在其省的住院医师岗位资格。这些评估可能包括国家评估合作委员会客观结构化临床考试（NAC，OSCE）。考生必须参加 MCCEE 考试合格后，才有资格参加 NAC，OSCE 考试。某些司法管辖区可能会增加特定区域资格标准或可以要求加拿大医学会资格考试第一部分某些省级资助培训岗位。

7.3 加拿大医学委员会考试资源与技巧

考生在参加加拿大医学委员会多项考试过程中要查阅大量的相关资料，这里介绍一些相关的图书、视频和网站资源。

The MCC requires all first-time MCCEE examinees to open an application with the MCC's Physician Credentials Repository and send a certified copy of their medical diploma.

Provinces have the right to request additional assessments to obtain residency qualifications in their province. These assessments may include the National Assessment Cooperation Committee Objective Structured Clinical Examination (NAC, OSCE). Examinees must pass the MCCEE exam, then they qualified to participate in the NAC, OSCE exam. Some jurisdictions may increase the eligibility criteria for a particular area or may require the first part of the Canadian Medical Association qualifying examination.

7.3 Resources and Tips on MCC Exams

During the time of preparing to participate in a number of Canadian medical examination, examinees need to access to a large number of relevant information. Here are some of the books, videos and web resources to intruduce to examinees.

7.3.1 MCCQE Part I 资源介绍

（1）临床决策演示

MCCQE Part I 选择题和临床决策演示将告诉考生计算机测试如何进行的，让考生在考前了解软件的每个特性。选择题的演示包括 28 个问题，而临床决策的演示有 6 个病例。演示视频提供正确的答案，考生提交的任何答案都不会被评分。演示过程中剩余时间不能用在真正的考试中，整个考试过程中工作人员会通知考生的剩余时间。

（2）自我管理的资格考试第一部分

自我管理的资格考试第一部分（SAE‐QEI）是一个在线练习考试，用来测试考生参加 MCCQE Part I 的水平。SAE‐QEI 有三个不同版本，每个版本 96 题，难度水平相同（即 QEI 3 并不比 1 或 2 上的 QEI 更难）。而 SAE‐QEI 并不涵盖 MCCQE 第一部分的所有材料，它提供的问题类型和风格，可以在 MCCQE Part I 发现。

7.3.1 MCCQE Part I resources introduction

（1）clinical decision making demo

MCCQE Part I selection and clinical decision making demo will tell examinees how to do computer test and allow them to understand each characteristic of software in the exam. The presentation of the multiple-choice questions consisted of 28 questions, while the clinical decision was demonstrated in 6 cases. Demo video provides the correct answer, and any answer submitted will not be graded. During the presentation, the rest of the time can't be used in the real exam, and the staff will tell examinees the rest of the time.

（2）Self Administered Qualifying Examination Part I

Self Administered Qualifying Examination Part I（SAE – QEI）is an online practice test, which is designed to test examinees to participate in the level of MCCQE Part I. SAE – QEI has three different versions, each version has 96 questions. The level of difficulty are the same (ie, QEI 3 is not more difficult than QEI 1or 2). The SAE – QEI does not cover all the material in the MCCQE Part I, the

练习考试结束后，考生会接到一个即时反馈的电子邮件，内容是其回答问题的正确数量与其他测试者的结果相比较来判断考生的能力。考生应确保自己提供的电子邮箱准确性，以便接收自己的考试结果。

SAE - QEI 不包含临床决策部分的测试。目前，考生只能使用 SAE - QEI 准备测试 MCCQE Part I 选择题部分。

由加拿大医学委员会的资深开发人员 Tanya Rivard 开发的临床决策视频帮助考生了解和准备 MCCQE Part I 临床决策部分。视频中的图形元素不代表考试。MCCQE Part I 临床决策部分包括的问题，考生需要提供书面回答。

（3）经常被问到的问题

如果考生有关于 MCCQE Part I 的问题，例如什么时候应该到达考试地点，或者是否应该复习课程，考

type and style of the problem it provides can be found in the MCCQE Part I.

At the end of the practice exam, the examinee can receive an immediate feedback email that compares the correct number of questions you answer with the results of other testers. Examinees should ensure that the accuracy of their e-mail address in order to receive their examination results.

SAE – QEI does not contain tests for clinical decision making. Currently, examinees can only use SAE – QEI ready to test MCCQE Part I multiple–choice part.

The clinical decision making video is developed by senior developer Tanya Rivard of the Medical Council of Canada to help examinees understand and prepare for the MCCQE Part I clinical decision part.Graphic elements in the video do not represent the exam. Examinees need to provide written answers for the questions included in MCCQE Part I clinical decision section.

（3）Frequently asked questions

If you have questions about the MCCQE Part I, such as when you should arrive at the test place, or whether you

生可以去看网站上的 MCCQE Part I frequently asked questions.

（4）关于资格考试的 Objectives 文件

加拿大医学委员会将 Objectives 文件作为 MCCQE Part I and II 的资格考试基础，Objectives 文件适用于数据收集、诊断临床问题的解决和管理的原则，部分或全部是医生面临的临床情况。

Objectives 文件列出了考生必须知道的考试大纲。因此，Objectives 文件对 MCCQE Part I 的准备是有用的。在 MCCQE Part II 部分，考生回答考官问的问题，可以使用 DSM-5 或 DSM-IV-TR 找到适当的语言。DSM-5 是 2013 年 5 月，由美国精神病协会出版的心理疾病的诊断统计手册（第 5 版），DSM-IV-TR 是加拿大医学委员会与测试委员会工作回顾在 DSM-5 分类的变化，更新了考试内容中的语言。

should review the course, examinees can go to the site "the MCCQE Part frequently I asked questions".

（4）On Objectives

The Medical Council of Canada looks the Objectives file as qualification examination foundation of MCCQE Part I and MCCQE Part II. Objectives files are applicable to data collection, diagnostic clinical problem solving, and management principles, which are clinical situations faced by physicians.

Objectives files lists the outline of the examination the examinees must know. Therefore, the Objectives file is useful for the preparation of MCCQE Part I. In the MCCQE PartII section, examinees can use DSM-5 or DSM-IV-TR appropriate language to answer questions from a examiner. DSM-5 is *Psychological Disorders of the Diagnostic and Statistical Manual* of version fifth published by American Psychiatric Association in May 2013.DSM-IV-TR is the work of the Medical Council of Canada and the testing committee review changes in the DSM-5 classification and update the content of the examination in the language.

7.3.2 参考资料

MCC 列出了参考书和网上资料，对考生准备考试是有帮助的。

《美国精神病学协会 . 精神疾病诊断与统计手册（DSM–5）》，第 5 版，2013.

Andreasen, Nancy C., Black, Donald, W.《精神病学导论教科书》，第 6 版，美国精神病学出版公司，2014.

Behrman, K., 等主编 .Nelson《儿科学教材》，第 20 版，2016.

Benjamin, I., 等主编，《Andreoli and Carpenter's Cecil 基础医学》，第 9 版，W.B. Saunders，2015。

Decherney AH, Nathan L, Goodwin TM, Laufer N.《目前的诊断与治疗，妇产科》，第 11 版，麦格劳希尔，2012。

Hacker, N.F., Gambone, J.C., Moore, J.G. 妇产科学精要，第 6 版，2016。

Kasper, D., 等主编 , Harrison's 的内科原理，第 19 版，2015。

Lawrence, P.F.,《普通外科精要》，第 5 版，2012

Rudolph, A.M., 等主编，《Rudolph's 儿科学》，第 22 版，2011。

7.3.2 Reference materials

MCC lists the reference books and online information,which is helpful for examinees to prepare for the exam.

American Psychiatric Association, Diagnostic and Statistical Manual of Mental Disorders (DSM-5), 5th ed., 2013.

Andreasen, Nancy C., Black, Donald, W., *Introductory Textbook of Psychiatry*, 6th ed., American Psychiatric Publishing, Inc., 2014.

Behrman, K., et al (eds.), *Nelson Textbook of Pediatrics*, 20th ed., Elsevier, 2016.

Benjamin, I., et al. (eds.), *Andreoli and Carpenters' Cecil Essentials of Medicine*, 9th ed., W.B. Saunders, 2015.

Decherney AH, Nathan L, Goodwin TM, Laufer N, *Current Diagnosis & Treatment, Obstetrics & Gynecology*, 11th ed., McGraw Hill, 2012.

Hacker, N.F., Gambone, J.C., Moore, J.G.*Essentials of Obstetrics and Gynecology*, 6th ed., Elsevier, 2016.

Kasper, D., et al (eds.), *Harrison's Principles of Internal Medicine*, 19th ed., 2015.

Lawrence, P.F., *Essentials of General Surgery*, 5th ed., 2012.

Rudolph, A.M., et al. (eds.), *Rudolph's Pediatrics*, 22nd ed., 2011.

Schwartz, S.I., 等主编,《外科学原理》,
第 10 版, 2014

Schwartz, S.I., et al. (eds.), *Principles of Surgery*, 10th ed., 2014.

Eley, J., 等主编,《医学流行病学:人口健康和有效的卫生保健》, 第 5 版, 2015。

Eley, J., et al. (eds.), *Medical Epidemiology: Population Health and Effective Health Care*, 5th ed., 2015.

Heymann, D.L.,《控制传染病手册》, 第 20 版, 2014。

Heymann, D.L., *Control of Communicable Diseases Manual*, 20th ed., 2014.

加拿大公共卫生机构,《加拿大免疫指南, 2015》。http://www.phac-aspc.gc. ca/publicat/cig-gci/index-eng.php。

Public Health Agency of Canada, *Canadian Immunization Guide*, 2015. http://www.phac-aspc.gc.ca/publicat/cig-gci/index-eng.php.

加拿大健康研究所、自然科学与工程研究委员会、加拿大社会科学与人文研究委员会三个理事会政策声明:关于人类研究的伦理行为, 2014.12. http://www.pre.ethics.gc.ca/eng/policy-politique/initiatives/tcps2-eptc2/Default/

Canadian Institutes of Health Research, Natural Sciences and Engineering Research Council of Canada, and Social Sciences and Humanities Research Council of Canada, Tri-Council Policy Statement: Ethical Conduct for Research Involving Humans, December 2014. http://www.pre.ethics.gc.ca/eng/policy-politique/initiatives/tcps2-eptc2/Default/.

加拿大医学协会,《伦理 CMA 的代码 》, 2004, http://policybase.cma.ca/dbtw-wpd/policypdf/pd04-06.pdf

Canadian Medical Association; *CMA Code of Ethics*, 2004, http://policybase.cma.ca/dbtw-wpd/PolicyPDF/PD04-06.pdf

加拿大医疗保护协会《加拿大医生医疗法律手册》, 第 7 版, 2010。https://www.cmpa-acpm.ca/documents/10179/24891/com_16_mlh_for_physicians-e.pdf

Canadian Medical Protective Association, *Medico-Legal Handbook for Physicians in Canada*, 7th ed., 2010. Retrieved from: https://www.cmpa-acpm.ca/documents/10179/24891/com_16_MLH_for_physicians-e.pdf

加拿大医疗保护协会，《良好的做法指南：安全护理 – 减少医疗法律风险》。从 https://www.cmpa–acpm.ca/cmpapd04/docs/ela/goodpracticesguide/pages/index/index–e.html

Canadian Medical Protective Association, *Good Practices Guide: Safe care – Reducing Medical-Legal Risk*. Retrieved from https://www.cmpa–acpm.ca/cmpapd04/docs/ela/goodpracticesguide/pages/index/index–e.html

Evans, K.G.,《法医学手册的医生在加拿大》，第 6 版，2005。

Evans, K.G., A Medico–Legal Handbook for Physicians in Canada, 6th ed., 2005.

Evans, K.G., Consen,《加拿大医生指导》，第 4 版，2006。https://www.cmpa–acpm.ca/en/–/consent–a–guide–for–canadian–physicians

Evans, K.G., Consent, *A Guide for Canadian Physicians*, 4th ed., 2006. https://www.cmpa–acpm.ca/en/–/consent–a–guide–for–canadian–physicians.

Shah, C.P.,《公共卫生和预防医学在加拿大》，第 5 版，2003。

Shah, C.P., *Public Health and Preventive Medicine in Canada*, 5th ed., 2003.

第八章　中国香港执业医师考试
Chapter eight　LMCHK

8.1 LMCHK 考试内容

8.1.1 考试介绍

中国香港资格考试包括三个部分。第一部分：专业知识考试；第二部分：医学英语技能水平测试；第三部分：临床考试。

（1）专业知识考试

专业知识考试共分两个试卷，每卷各有120题多项选择题。这部分考试为测试考生的专业知识而设。考生需要考的科目有：基本科学Ⅰ、医学伦理社区医学、内科、外科、骨科、儿科及妇产科。考试内容所占比例见下表：

8.1 LMCHK Contents

8.1.1 LMCHK introduction

LMCHK consists of three parts: the first part: the professional knowledge test; the second part: the medical English skill level test; the third part: clinical examination.

（1）the professional knowledge test

Professional knowledge examination is divided into two papers, each volume has 120 multiple-choice questions. This part is designed to test the examinees' expertise. The subjects needed to test are: basic science I, medical ethics/community medicine, internal medicine, surgery, orthopedics, pediatrics and obstetrics and gynecology. The proportion of examination content is as follows:

考试内容比例（content proportion）	
试卷 I 120题（Paper I 120 SBA）	试卷 II（Paper II 120SBA）
内科学（Medicine）　60 SBA	外科学（Surgery）　45 SBA
儿科学（Pediatrics）　35 SBA	骨科（Oythopaedics）　15 SBA
精神病学（Psychiatry）　15SBA	妇产科（O&G）　35 SBA
基础科学 I（Basic Science）10 SBA	基础科学 II（Basic Science）10 SBA
	伦理 / 社区医学（Ethics/Community Medicine）15 SBA

（2）医学英语技能水平测试

主要确保考生的英语水平足够应付专业工作需要，是一项英语笔试。

（3）临床考试

这项考试为测试考生应用专业知识解决临床问题的能力而设。考生接受测试的范围包括内科、外科（包括骨科的病例）、妇产科及儿科。考生通过考试后，需在认可的医院或医疗机构担任住院实习医生，接受为期 12 个月的训练及评估。在这期间，考生会熟悉本地的医疗制度和常见疾病。成功完成住院实习训练的考生可向委员会申请注册。

（2）the medical English skill level test

To ensure that the examinees' English level is sufficient to meet the needs of professional work, it is a written test.

（3）clinical exam

This test is designed to test the ability of examinees to use professional knowledge to solve clinical problems. The examinees were tested in the Department of internal medicine, surgery (including orthopedics cases), obstetrics and Gynecology, and pediatrics. Examinees will be admitted to a hospital or medical institution as an intern for a period of 12 months training after the examination. During this period, examinees will receive clinical guidance in order to familiarize themselves with the local health care system and common

临床考试采用的是客观结构化考试（OSCE）。这种形式的考试是 1975 年 HAND 开发的，是通过模拟临床场景测试医学生临床实践技能的一种客观的、有序的、有组织的考核方法。OSCE 基本思想是"以操作为基础的测验"，它是一种在模拟临床场景下，使用模型、标准化病人甚至病人来测试医学生临床能力的考核方法。应试者考试过程中要经历多个站点，考试内容与形式多样。作为一种以技能为基础的考核工具，它已被证明是可行的、可靠和有效的考试模式。目前，它得到了广泛应用，尤其是被应用到医学本科考试中。

8.1.2 报考资格

除香港大学及香港中文大学的医科毕业生外，凡有意向香港医务委员会注册以获取执业医生资格的医科毕

diseases. Examinees who have successfully completed their internship training may apply to the Committee for registration.

The clinical examination is Objective Structured Clinical Examniation （OSCE）. This form of examination was developed in 1975 by HAND, which is a kind of objective, orderly and organized examination method to test the clinical practice skills of medical students by simulating clinical scenarios. The basic idea of OSCE is "an operation-based test", it is a kind of test method to test the clinical ability of medical students under the simulated clinical situation, using the model, standardized patients and even patients.In the course of examination, the examinees have to go through many stations, and the content and form of the examination are various. As a skill based assessment tool, it has been proved that OSCE is feasible, reliable and effective. At present, it has been widely used, especially in the medical examination.

8.1.2 The qualifications for application

In addition to the medical graduates of the University of Hong Kong and Chinese University Hong Kong, medical graduates

业生，必须通过委员会举办的执业资格考试，并且在认可的医院或医疗机构完成一段注册前住院实习评估。

任何医科毕业生在申请参加执业资格考试时应该符合以下条件：考生已向委员会提出申请，并为参加执业资格考试缴纳了费用；考生须完成不少于 5 年的由医务委员会批准的全日制医学训练；具有良好的品格。

全日制医学训练包括一段医务委员会批准的住院实习期，根据《医生注册条例》，如果考生参加执业资格考试的任何一部分连续五次而每次均不全格，委员会可禁止该人参加执业资格考试。

只要是符合条件的考生都可以参加考试，不只限于香港特别行政区居民或有香港特别行政区身份证的人，考生提交的申请资料包括：简历、

who have the intention to obtain the Medical Council of Hong Kong registered medical practitioner qualifications must pass the qualification examination committee held, and completed a residency in the pre registration assessment approved hospitals or medical institutions.

Any medical graduates who apply for the qualification examination should comply with the following conditions:examinees have been put forward to apply, and pay the fees to participate in the qualification examination; examinees are required to complete not less than 5 years of full-time medical training by the Medical Council approval;examinees should have a good character.

Full-time medical training includes a Medical Council approved residency, according to "Medical Registration Ordinance". If the examinees fail in any part of the qualification examination for five times, the Council may prohibit them to participate in qualification examination.

As long as the eligible examinees can take the exam, not limited to residents of Hong Kong or with Hong Kong identity cards, the application materials examinees

医学学位证书、成绩单、医院实习证书、对于执业资格考试申请表、良好的性格、身份证 / 护照。

submitted include:Resume, Medical degree certificate, Transcript, Hospital internship certificate, Application table for Liciensing exam, Good character, ID/passport.

8.1.3 中国香港地区医生培训流程

8.1.3 Hong Kong doctor training process

（1）Housemen（1 年）：实习生阶段。香港大学和香港中文大学的医学生 5 年毕业后，医管局统一安排一年的实习，内外妇儿都要实习。通过香港医生执照考试的任何考生同样也必须参加一年的实习。实习完后拿到医师执照，如果想当专科医生，就要到各公立医院的专科申请专科培训，当住院医生。

（1）Housemen (1 year): Intern phase. After graduating from the University of Hong Kong and CUHK for 5 years, the students will be arranged by the hospital authority for one year internship. Any candidate who has passed the Hong Kong medical licensing examination must also attend one year's internship. They will take practice in the department of medicine, surgery, gynecology, pediatrics. After the internship, the examinees will get a doctor's license, if they want to be a specialist. It is necessary to apply for specialist training in public hospitals as Medical Officer.

（2）Medical Officer（一般 6 年）：前 3 年在大内科或大外科轮转，3 年内考过 MRCP 或 MRCS，然后申请进专科培训，培训完后考过 FRCP 或 FRCS，成为专科医生。

（2）Medical Officer (usually 6 years): In the first three years, they are in the medical or surgical rotation, and pass the MRCP or MRCS, then apply into specialist training. After training, they pass the FRCP or FRCS, and then work as a specialist.

（3）Senior MO 或 Associate Consultant：（至少要 10 年）：专科医生主要负责专科的工作：查房、病房管理、医生培训。

（4）Consultant：主任顾问医生，最高级别的医生。

8.2 LMCHK 考试参考资料

8.2.1 参考书目

第一部分：专业知识考试

1. 内科

（1）《临床医学》，Parveen Kumar 和 Michael Clark 著

（2）《临床医学 1000 个问题和答案 》，Parveen Kumar 和 Michael Clark 著

（3）《亚洲临床医学教科书》，Joseph J.Y. Sung 著

（4）《牛津临床医学手册》，由 Murray Longmore、Ian Wilkinson、Tom Turmezei 和 Chee Kay Cheung 编写

2. 外科

（1）《Churchill 的外科学小册子》，A.T. Raftery、Michael S. Delbridge 编写

（3）Senior MO or Associate Consultant: (at least 10 years) : specialist is responsible for specialist work, making the rounds of the wards, wards management, doctors training

（4）Consultant: the chief consultant, the top doctor.

8.2 LMCHK Exam Reference Materials

8.2.1 Reference books

Part I: Examination in Professional Knowledge

1.Medicine

（1）*Clinical Medicine*, by Parveen Kumar and Michael Clark

（2）*1000 Questions and Answers from Clinical Medicine*, Parveen Kumar and Michael Clark

（3）*Textbook of Clinical Medicine for Asia*, by Joseph J.Y. Sung

（4）*Oxford Handbook of Clinical Medicine*, by Murray Longmore, Ian Wilkinson, Tom Turmezei, Chee Kay Cheung

2.Surgery

（1）*Churchill's Pocketbook of Surgery*, by A.T. Raftery, Michael S. Delbridge

（2）《基础外科训练应用基础科学》，Andraw T. Raftery 著

（3）《Apley 的骨科骨折简明系统》，Louis Solomon、David J. Warwick、Selvadurai Nayagam 著

（4）《1001 个手术选择题的答案：基于 Bailey and Love 的短期手术实践》，R.C.G. Russell、Norman S. Williams 和 Christopher J.K. Bulstrode 编写

（5）《牛津临床外科学手册》

（6）《Bailey & Love 的短期手术实践》

3. 妇产科

（1）《产科学》，Ten Teachers、Phil Baker 编写

（2）《妇科学》，Ten Teachers、Stanley G. Clayton 和 Ash Monga 编写

（3）《妇产科学中的 EMQS，MCQS，SAQS 和 OSCES》，Jerry Brocklesby 和 Christian Phillips 编写

4. 儿科

（1）《儿科学图解教材》，Tom Lisauer、Grayham Clayden 编写

（2）《图解儿科学自我评估》，Tom Lissauer、Graham Roberts、Caroline Foster 和 Michael Coren 编写

（2）*Applied Basic Science for Basic Surgical Training*, Andraw T. Raftery

（3）*Apley's Concise System of Orthopaedics and Fracture*, Louis Solomon, David J. Warwick, Selvadurai Nayagam

（4）*1001 Multiple Choice Questions and Answers in Surgery: Based on Bailey and Love's "Short Practice of Surgery"*, by R.C.G. Russell, Norman S. Williams, and Christopher J.K. Bulstrode

（5）*Oxford Handbook of Clinical Surgery*.

（6）*Bailey & Love's Short Practice of Surgery*

3.Obstetrics & Gynaecology

（1）*Obstetrics by Ten Teachers*, Phil Baker

（2）*Gynaecology* by Ten Teachers, Stanley G. Clayton and Ash Monga

（3）*EMQS, MCQS, SAQS and OSCES in Obstetrics and Gynaecology*, by Jerry Brocklesby and Christian Phillips

4.Paediatrics

（1）*Illustrated Textbook of Paediatrics*, byTom Lisauer, Grayham Clayden

（2）*Illustrated Self Assessment in Paediatrics*, by Tom Lissauer, Graham Roberts, Caroline Foster, Michael Coren

5. 精神科

《精神病学牛津核心文本》，Michael G. Gelder、Richard Mayou 和 John Geddes 编写

6. 药理学

《临床药理学》，D.R. Lawrence、P.N. Bennett 和 M.J. Brown 编写

第二部分：医学英语能力测试

《Macleod 临床考试》，Graham Douglas、Fiona Nicol 和 Colin Robertson 编写

第三部分：临床考试

1. 内科：

（1）《临床考试》，Nicholas J. Talley 和 Simon O' Connor 编写

（2）《内科考试》，Nicholas J. Talley 和 Simon O' Connor 编写

2. 外科：

（1）《通过临床手术的总决赛》，Gina Kuperberg 编写

（2）《Browse 外科疾病的症状和体征介绍》，Kevin Burnand、William Thomas、John Black 和 Norman Browse 编写

（3）《骨科临床检查》，Ronald MacRae 编写

（4）《产科：产科的秘密》，Helen L. Frederickson 和 Louise Wilkins-Hau 编写

5.Psychiatry

Psychiatry Oxford Core Texts, by Michael G. Gelder, Richard Mayou, John Geddes

6.Pharmacology

Clinical Pharmacology, by D.R. Lawrence, P.N. Bennett, M.J. Brown

Part II: Proficiency Test in Medical English

Macleod's Clinical Examination, by Graham Douglas, Fiona Nicol, Colin Robertson

Part III: Clinical Examination

1. Medicine:

（1）*Clinical Examination*,by Nicholas J. Talley, Simon O' Connor

（2）*Examination Medicine*, by Nicholas J. Talley, Simon O' Connor

2. Surgery:

（1）*Surgical Finals Passing the Clinical*, by Gina Kuperberg, John Lumley

（2）*Browse's Introduction to the Symptoms and Signs of Surgical Disease*, by Kevin Burnand, William Thomas, John Black, Norman Browse

（3）*Clinical Orthopaedics Examination*, by Ronald MacRae

（4）*Obstetrics & Gynaecology:OB/GYN Secrets*, by Helen L. Frederickson, Louise Wilkins-Hau

3. 儿科：

《研究生临床儿科学考试》，Terence Stephenson、Hamish Wallace 和 Angela Thomson 编写。

8.3 获得 LMCHK 资源的网站

在 LMCHK 考试过程中，获得权威性参考资源是必要的，以下列出的网站都是 LMCHK 考生利用率高的参考资源。

（1）丁香园（http://www.dx.cn/bbs/）

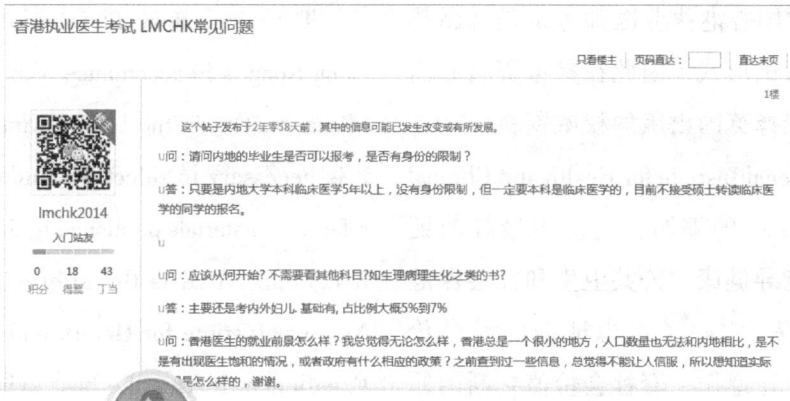

丁香园又名丁香园论坛，2002 年 5 月成立，是一个"独立、非营利、纯学术"的专业自由交流的医学学术平台网站。丁香园论坛设立了各医学专科讨论区，考试交流区，一些考试经验、考试策略、考试用书等都有分享，如关于 LMCHK 考试常见问题，LMCHK 考试复习攻略，LMCHK 考试经验分享等。

3.Paediatrics:

Clinical Paediatrics for Postgraduate Examination, Terence Stephenson, Hamish Wallace, Angela Thomson

8.3 The Website to Getting LMCHK Resources

In the LMCHK examination process, it is necessary to access the authoritative reference resources. The following list of sites are the high utilization of reference resources in LMCHK examinees.

Ding Xiangyuan, also known as the Ding Xiangyuan Forum was established on May 2002. It is an independent, non-profit, pure academic professional free exchange of medical academic platform website. The forum set up various medical specialties discussion, examination exchange area, some exam experience, test strategy, test books are shared, For example, on the LMCHK exam FAQ, LMCHK exam review Raiders, LMCHK exam experience sharing.

（2）NICE guidelines（https://www.nic.org.uk/）

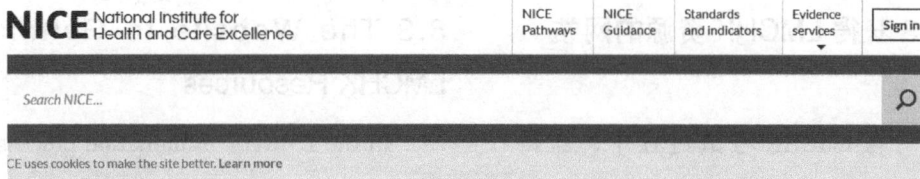

中国香港执业医师考试是遵循英国的考试形式，因此在参考资料方面应该选择英国出版的权威资料。NICE 是 National Instiute for Health and Clinical Excellence 的缩写。它使用最好的证据来指导健康、公共卫生和社会保健的决策。它除了考虑证据的科学价值外，还遵循一套社会价值判断的原则。NICE 指南以广泛的主题为依据，从预防和管理具体情况到规划更广泛的服务和干预，以改善社区的健康。该指南包括技术评估指南、介入操作指南、医疗技术指南、诊断指南、高度专门技术指南。

The examination of licensed doctors in Hong Kong is in accordance with the form of examination in the United Kingdom, so it is necessary to select the authoritative reference materials published in the United Kingdom. NICE is the abbreviation of National Instiute for Health and Clinical Excellence. It uses the best evidence to guide decisions on health, public health and social care. In addition to considering the scientific value of evidence, it also follows a set of principles of social value judgment. The NICE guidelines are based on a broad range of topics, from prevention and management of specific situations to planning for a wider range of services and interventions to improve community health. The guide includes Technology appraisals guidance, Interventional procedures guidance, Medical technologies guidance,Diagnostics guidance, Highly specialised technologies guidance.

（3）HKCOG guidelines（http://www.hkcog.org.hk/hkcog/pages__81.html）

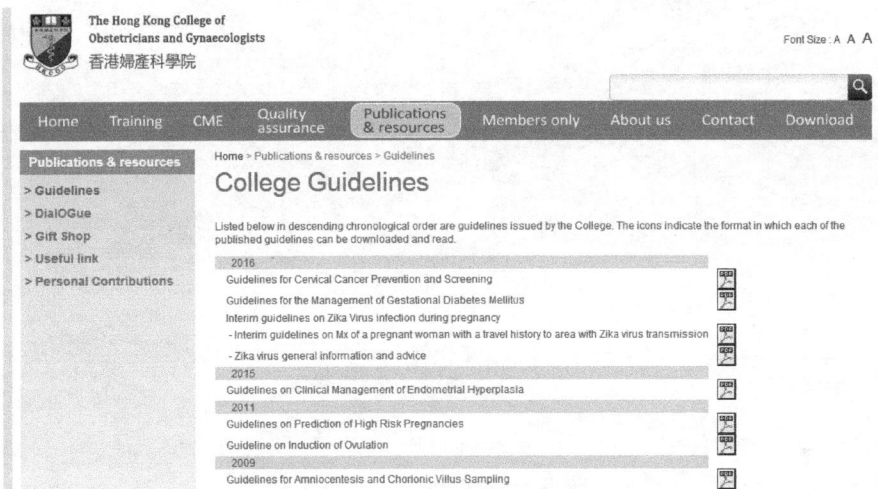

HKCOG guidelines 香港大学妇产科学院出版。每年出版新的指南，这些指南都是 PDF 格式的。例如，2016年出版的指南有宫颈癌预防和筛查指南，妊娠糖尿病管理指南，妊娠期病寨卡（Zika）毒感染的暂行指南，对传输到齐卡病毒区域具有旅游史的孕妇MX 的暂行指南，寨卡（Zika）病毒一般信息和建议。

HKCOG guidelines is published by The Hong Kong Colledge Obstetricians Gynaecologists A College Hong Kong Academy of Medicine College of Obstetrics and Gynecology. You can see the guidelines that are published every year. These guidelines' format are PDF format. For example, the guidelines published in 2016: guidelines for cervical cancer prevention and screening guidelines, guidelines for the management of diabetes in pregnancy, during pregnancy（Zika） disease Zika virus infection guidelines, pregnant women MX guide with travel history to transfer to the Provisional Regional Zika virus, Zika virus general information and advice.

第九章　澳大利亚执业医师考试
Chapter nine　MCQ OET

9.1 AMC MCQ 考试

想去澳大利亚从事医生职业的考生需要参加澳大利亚执业医师考试（MCQ OET）。由澳大利亚医学委员会（Australian Medical Council AMC）组织的 MCQ（multiple choice question）考试，由 AMC MCQ 和 AMC CLINICAL 组成。OET 是是澳大利亚成人教育局的职业英语考试，OET 考试包括听力、口语、阅读、写作四部分，要求考生在 OET 考试中的听力、口语、阅读、写作四个部分都拿到 B 以上的成绩。

9.1.1 AMC MCQ 考试内容

AMC 考试是一个两个阶段的连续性考试，包括一个高级形式的计算机自适应测试（CAT）——临床知识应用的 MCQ 考试，它是一个计算机管理

9.1 AMC MCQ Exam

If examinees want to go to Australia to engage in medical profession, they should participate in the Australian medical examination（MCQ OET）. MCQ（multiple choice question）examination organized by the Australian Medical Council（Australian Council AMC）, and composed of AMC MCQ and AMC CLINICAL. OET is the Occupational English Test of the Australian Bureau of adult education. The OET test includes four parts: listening, speaking, reading and writing. Examinees have to get more than B results in four parts.

9.1.1 AMC MCQ exam content

The AMC examination is a two-stage sequential test consisting of an advanced format Computer-Adaptive Test（CAT）——MCQ examination of applied

的完全集成的多选择问题考试；一个 OSCE 形式的有 16 个考站的临床技能评估考试。

AMC MCQ 考试包括多项选择题（MCQ）和基于计算机的考试两部分，主要测试医学知识，每一部分考试时间是 3.5 小时，150 道题。

MCQ 考试侧重于基础和应用医学知识的测试，涉及疾病过程，了解考生临床检查、诊断、治疗和管理的能力，以及在区分正确的诊断和合理的选择方面测试考生鉴别、判断和推理能力。

AMC 计算机自适应测验（CAT）考试是完全由计算机集成管理的多选择题，考试由 150 个 A 型选择题（从五个备选答案选择一个正确的答案）组成。120 个题是计分的 30 个题是不计分的。考生尽可能完成所有 150 个项目，但是必须完成 120 个得分项目。未能在考试中完成所有 120 个评分项目，检查结果记录为"不及格——未能获得足够的数据以获得结果"。

clinical knowledge, which is a computer-administered fully integrated multi-choice question examination and a 16 station OSCE format assessment of clinical skills.

AMC MCQ includes two parts: MCQ exam and computer-based exam, which mainly test examinees' medical knowledge, each part of the test time is 3.5 hours and has 150 questions.

MCQ examination focuses on the foundation and application of medical knowledge, disease process involved, to understand examinees' capacity of clinical examination, diagnosis, treatment and management, as well as the capacity of identify, judge and reasoning between the correct diagnosis and reasonable selection.

AMC Computer-Adaptive Test (CAT) is composed entirely of multiple-choice examination in computer integrated management. The test is made up of 150 A type choices (to choose a correct answer from five alternative answers), and of which the 120 items are the score, the 30 items are not scoring. Examinees complete all 150 items as possible, but must complete 120 scoring items. Failure to complete all 120 items in the examination, the results of the examination record as "failed——failed to obtain sufficient data to obtain results".

120 个得分项目的数量，见下表。

The number of 120 scoring items is as follows：

病人组（Patient Group）	项目数量（Items number）
成人健康（内科） Adult Health（Medicine）	35
成人健康（外科） Adult Health（Surgery）	25
妇女健康（妇产科） Women's Health（Obs&Gyn)	15
儿童健康 （Child Health）	15
精神健康 （Mental Health）	15
人口健康 （Population Health）	15
项目总数 （Total Number）	120

AMC MCQ 考试包括的 300 个问题涵盖了不同学科：一般实践、内科、妇产科、精神病学、儿科、外科。考生 MCQ 考试必须达到及格才能进入临床考试。

The AMC MCQ exam includes 300 items covering a wide range of disciplines: general practice, internal medicine, obstetrics and gynecology, psychiatry, pediatrics, surgery. Examninees must pass the MCQ exam successfully to enter the clinical examination.

9.1.2 AMC 的临床考试

临床考试测试考生的临床实践和沟通技巧，即评估考生采集病史、进行体检、诊断和制定管理计划，并与

9.1.2 AMC clinical exam

Clinical examinations test examinees for clinical practice and communication skills, which assess the examinees'

病人、病人家属、其他卫生工作者沟通的能力。考试连续进行 3~4 小时，一个下午或一个早上。如果需要的话，将进行 1~2 小时的临床重新测试。

在 AMC 的临床考试中，考生将在 20 个考站轮转（16 标记站和 4 个休息站）每一站考试时间是 10 分钟（8 分钟实际考试和 2 分钟的阅读信息）。站里的病人可以是真正的病人，也可以是标准化的病人，有时甚至考官也扮演病人。只要有可能，也可使用适当的老年病人。考生应该把标准化的病人或扮演成病人的考官看成病人，对待他们就像对待真正的病人一样。

16 个标记站的全部结果将被记录为及格或不及格。参加 AMC 临床考试的考生将被分成 Clear Pass、Marginal Performance、Clear Fail 三个级别。

ability of acquisition history, physical examination, diagnosis and management plan, and communication with patients, families and other health workers. Examinations are performed continuously for three to four hours, one afternoon or one morning. If necessary, one to two hours of clinical are testing.

In the AMC clinical examination, examinees will be in the 20 station rotary test (16 mark stations and 4 rest stations). Each station is 10 minutes (8 minutes for the actual exam and 2 minutes for reading information). The patient in the station can be real patients and also can be standardized patients. Sometimes even the examiner also plays the patient, if possible, elderly patients also can be used. Examinees should be treated standardized patients or examiner who play the patient as a true patient, and treat them like a real patient.

All the results of the 16 marking stations will be recorded as passing or failing. Examinees participating in the AMC clinical examination will be divided into three levels: Clear Pass, Marginal Performance and Clear Fail.

Clear Pass：通过了 16 个标记站里至少 12 个站的测试，其中至少通过 1 个妇产科站和 1 个儿科站。

Clear Pass: Passing at least 12 stations tests of 16 marking stations, during 12 stations, at least 1 obstetrics and gynecology station, and at least 1 pediatric station.

Marginal Performance：16 个标记站里通过 10 个或 11 个站的测试。

Marginal Performance: Passing at least 10 or 11 stations tests of 16 marking stations.

Clear Fail：16 个站里最多通过 9 个站的测试或者 3 个妇产科站都没通过，而其他站都通过，或者 3 个儿科站没能过，而其他站都能过了。这三种情况考试结果是不及格。

Clear Fail: Passing no more than 9 stations tests of 16 marking stations or passing all the stations but failing in 3 obstetrics and gynecology stations or 3 pediatric stations. The three cases means examinees failed in the exam.

更多关于临床考试的信息请看网站（http://amc-clinical.com/）上的详细信息。

For more information about the clinical examination, please refer to the website（http://amc-clinical.com/）.

9.1.3 AMC MCQ 考试技巧

9.1.3 AMC MCQ exam skills

在 MCQ 考试的 300 道题当中，只有 240 道题是计入总分的。考生应该尝试每一个问题并且仔细阅读每个问题和选项 / 答案。重要的是要调整自己的步伐，避免在一个问题上花太多时间。该网站提供了一个计算机考试软件教程，以帮助考生熟悉 MCQ 计算机考试。

Among the 300 questions in the MCQ exam, only 240 questions are included in the total score. Examinees should try every problem and read each question and options carefully. It's important to adjust your pace and avoid spending too much time on one question. The site provides a computer test software tutorials to help exminees familiar with the MCQ computer exam.

9.2 考试准备　　　　　　　　　　9.2 Preparation for the Exam

AMC MCQ 考试网（http://www.amc.org.au/assessment/mcq–exam）提供了考试过程中的必备资源。AMC 的一些出版物，不仅协助国际医学毕业生准备 AMC 的考试，也可作为临床实践的重要工具。考生可以从网上商店和其他有用的出版物的推荐阅读列表购买 AMC 的教科书，尝试 MCQ 在线试验考试。

AMC MCQ test network（http://www.amc.org.au/assessment/mcq–exam）provides the necessary resources in the examination process. Some AMC publications not only assist international medical graduates to prepare for the AMC exam, but also is an important tool in clinical practice. Examinees can purchase AMC textbooks from online stores and other useful publications on the recommended reading list. Try on MCQ online test.

9.2.1 AMC MCQ 参考书目　　　　9.2.1 AMC MCQ reference books

（1）*Good Medical Practice*

该书由澳大利亚医学委员会出版，该书由两位经验丰富的医生和一名经验丰富的律师撰写，这一新版本

The book is published by the Australian Medical Council, it is written by two experienced doctors and an

已被广泛修订和增加内容。该出版物推荐给准备考 AMC 的 IMGS 阅读。它也将作为一个医生在独立的临床实践的参考书，并作为指导医疗监管机构和律师，医生和社区成员的指南。

experienced lawyer, which has been extensively revised and expanded. The book is the core material of IMGS, medical students and doctors. The publication is recommended to the IMGS who prepare for the AMC exam. It will also serves as a reference book for physicians in independent clinical practice, and as a guide to medical regulators and lawyers, physicians and community members.

（2）*Handbook of Multiple Choice Questions*

这本书包含有将近 600 个多选题，从 AMC 国际医学毕业生（IMGS）考试题库选择，涵盖所有学科，并包含一个 150 个问题的测试卷。问题的范围涵盖以下学科：内科、外科、儿科、产科、妇科、精神科、人口卫生、社区与一般实践、流行病学、伦理学与法律。

This book contains nearly 600 multiple-choice questions, which are choosed from AMC international medical graduates（IMGS）exam question bank. The questions cover all disciplines, and contain a 150-question test. The scope of the problem covers the following disciplines: medicine, surgery, pediatrics, obstetrics, gynecology, psychiatry, population health, community and general practice, epidemiology, ethics and law.

（3）AMC Handbook of Clinical Assessment

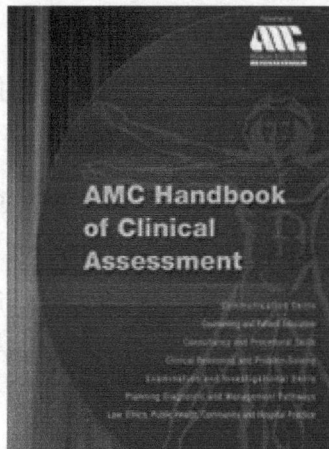

这本书内容包括：沟通技巧、临床咨询技能、道德与法律、更多的 150 自我评估任务和性能指引、8 个完整的自学考试。

This book includes: communication skills, clinical counseling skills, ethics and law, more than 150 self assessment tasks and performance guidelines, 8 complete self-study exams.

（4）Examination Reference Collection

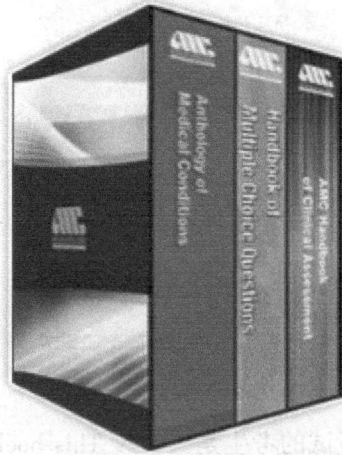

这套澳大利亚医学委员会参考材料文集包括 AMC 的医疗条件选集、AMC 多项选择题手册和 AMC 临床评估手册。AMC 医疗条件的选集含有即将毕业学生和临床医生需要的医学知识和技能，它代表了澳大利亚的各地医学院校课程。AMC 的多项选择题手册为医学本科生和研究生学员，IMG 提供了帮助，600 个自我测试的问题和评论几乎涉及所有学科和临床类型。AMC 的临床评估手册提供了独特的以问题为基础的练习，有助于临床评估。

The AMC reference collection includes anthology of medical conditions, AMC handbook of multiple-choice questions and AMC handbook of clinical assessment. Anthology of medical conditions contains knowledge and skills that graduating students and clinicians need, it represents the curriculum of medical schools in Australia. The AMC handbook of multiple-choice questions provides help for medical undergraduate students, graduate students and IMGs. 600 self test questions and comments involve almost all disciplines and clinical types. handbook of clinical assessment provides a unique problem-based exercise that contributes to clinical assessment.

（5）Clinical Examination Specification

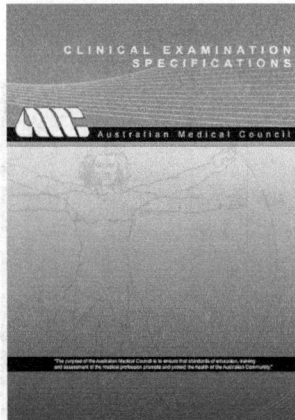

这本书对参加 AMC 考试的考生是重要的参考手册。下面是这本书包含的内容目录：

This book is an important reference manual for AMC examinees. Here are the contents of the book:

Contents

1. Guidelines and specifications
    1.1 Introduction
    1.2 Assessment aims and objectives
    1.3 Objective of the clinical examination
    1.4 Structure of the AMC Examination
    1.5 Standard of the AMC Examinations
    1.6 Appeals procedure

2. Clinical examination
    2.1 Requirements for the clinical examination
    2.2 Standard of performance required
    2.3 Format of the clinical examination
    2.4 Arrangements for the clinical examination
    2.5 Workplace based assessment
    2.6 Scheduling process for the clinical examination
    2.7 Venue
    2.8 Examination fees
    2.9 Structured clinical assessment
    2.10 Assessment criteria
    2.11 Assessment objective for the clinical examination
    2.12 Clinical examination content
    2.13 Retest
    2.14 Results

3. Marking in the structured clinical assessment examination
    3.1 Key steps
    3.2 Domains
    3.3 Determination of results

4. Administration arrangements at the NTC in Melbourne

5. Preparation for the structured clinical assessment examination
   5.1　Review of clinical skills
   5.2　Conduct of candidates presenting for examination
   5.3　The doctor patient relationship in Australia
   5.4　General preparation for the clinical examination
   5.5　Formal notification of clinical examination results and feedback
   5.6　AMC certificate
   5.7　Request for duplicate copies of AMC results

6. General information
   6.1　Change of address
   6.2　Further information

Appendix A:
Graduate outcome statements

Appendix B:
Summary of the format of the AMC Clinical Examination

Appendix C:
Structured clinical assessment station – sample

Appendix D:
Recommended reading

Appendix E:
General information for the structured clinical assessment

9.2.2 MCQ Examination 电子书目

1. 内科

（1）《普通医学临床问题》（第2版），ISBN 0443073236，shop. elsevier.com.au

（2）《医学原理与实践》（第18版），ISBN 0443059446。

（3）《内科医学原理》（第15版）ISBN 0070072744 网址：www.bookstore.mcgraw–hill.com/

（4）《临床技能：体检、体检、考核病人的问题》。ISBN 0522844677，www.mup.unimelb.edu.au

9.2.2 MCQ Examination electronic bibliography

1.Medicine

（1）*Clinical Problems in General Medicine*, 2nd ed., ISBN 0443073236. shop.elsevier.com.au

（2）*Principles and Practice of Medicine*, 18th ed, ISBN 0443059446.

（3）*Principles of Internal Medicine*, 15th ed. ISBN 0070072744

www.bookstore.mcgraw–hill.com/

（4）*Clinical Skills: The Medical Interview, Physical Examination and Assessment of the Patients' Problems*. ISBN 0522844677. www.mup.unimelb.edu.au

（5）《影像学指南》（第4版）ISBN 0959285415. www.ranzcr.edu.au

（6）《临床检查：物理诊断的系统指南》（第4版）ISBN 9780729539050, shop.elsevier.com.au

（7）《牛津医学教材》（第3版），ISBN 0192621408，www.oup.com/ us/ corporate/publishingprograms/ medical/?view=usa

2. 外科

（8）《外科学》（第3版），ISBN 9781405126274. www.wiley.com

（9）外科手术的MCQ选择题和简答题 ISBN 9780867930108. www.wiley.com

（10）《手术原则和实践—戴维森医学外科手术的原则和实践的补充》（第3版），ISBN 0443048606 www.us.elsevierhealth.com

（11）《辅助临床外科》（第6版），ISBN 044305603X. www.us.elsevier health.com

（12）《基础儿科学》（第4版），ISBN 0443059586. www.us.elsevierhealth.com

（13）《儿科学实践》（第5版），ISBN 044307139X. www.us.elsevierhealth.com

（5）*Imaging Guidelines*, 4th ed. ISBN 0959285415. www.ranzcr.edu.au

（6）*Clinical Examination: A Systematic Guide to Physical Diagnosis.* 4th ed. ISBN 9780729539050, shop. elsevier.com.au

（7）*Oxford Textbook of Medicine*, 3rd ed. ISBN 0192621408. www.oup. com/us/corporate/publishingprograms/ medical/?view=usa

2.Surgery

（8）*Textbook of Surgery*, 3rd ed. ISBN 9781405126274. www.wiley.com

（9）*MCQ's and Short Answer Questions for Surgery.* ISBN 978086793 0108. www.wiley.com

（10）*Principles and Practice of Surgery-A Surgical Supplement to Davidsons' Principles and Practice of Medicine*, 3rd ed. ISBN 0443048606 www. us.elsevierhealth.com

（11）*An Aid to Clinical Surgery*, 6th ed. ISBN 044305603X. www. us.elsevierhealth.com

（12）*Essential Paediatrics*, 4th ed. ISBN 0443059586. www.us.elsevierhealth.com

（13）*Practical Paediatrics*, 5th ed. ISBN 044307139X. www.us.elsevierhealth. com

（14）《澳大利亚免疫手册》（第7版）ISBN 0644475781

http://www.health.gov.au/internet/immunise/publishing.nsf/Content/Handbook-home

3. 妇产科

（15）《图解产科和新生儿的教科书》（第3版）ISBN 0702021237，www.us.elsevierhealth.com

（16）《图解妇科教科书》（第2版）ISBN 0729512118. www.us.elsevierhealth.com

（17）《儿科学手册》（第8版）ISBN 9781405174008 http://www.wiley.com

（18）《妇产科学基础》，ISBN 0723431507. www.mosby.com

4. 精神病科

（19）《牛津精神病学教材》（第3版）ISBN 0192625004（paperback）. www.oup.com/us/corporate/publishing programs/medical/?view=usa

（20）《DSM-IV-TR：精神疾病诊断与统计手册》（第4版修订），ISBN 0890420246. www.psych.org

（14）*The Australian Immunisation Handbook.* 7th ed. ISBN 0644475781

http://www.health.gov.au/internet/immunise/publishing.nsf/Content/Handbook-home

3.Obstetrics & Gynaecology

（15）*Obstetrics and the Newborn-An Illustrated Text*, 3rd ed. ISBN 0702021237. www.us.elsevierhealth.com

（16）*Illustrated Textbook of Gynaecology*, 2nd ed. ISBN 0729512118. www.us.elsevierhealth.com

（17）*Paediatric Handbook*, 8th ed. ISBN 9781405174008 http://www.wiley.com

（18）*Fundamentals of Obstetrics & Gynaecology.* ISBN 0723431507. www.mosby.com

4.Psychiatry

（19）*The Oxford Textbook of Psychiatry*, 3rd ed. ISBN 0192625004 (paperback). www.oup.com/us/corporate/publishingprograms/medical/?view=usa

（20）*DSM-IV-TR: Diagnostic and Statistical Manual of Mental Disorders*, 4th ed text revision. ISBN 0890420246. www.psych.org

9.2.3 临床考试电子书目

1. 内科

（1）《内科和外科的临床问题》（第 3 版）ISBN 0443073236. http://shop.el-sevier.com.au

（2）《临床检查：物理诊断的系统指南》，（第 7 版），ISBN 9780729539050. http://shop.elsevier.com.au

（3）《戴维森的医学原理与实践》，ISBN 9780702030857. www.us.el-sevierhealth.com

2. 外科

（4）《外科学》（第 3 版），ISBN 9781405126274. www.wiley.com

（5）《普通外科的临床问题》，ISBN 0409492132.

3. 儿童健康

（6）《实用儿科学》（第 7 版），ISBN 9780443102806. www.us.else-vierhealth.com

（7）《儿科学手册》（第 8 版），ISBN 9781405174008. www.wiley.com

（8）《澳大利亚免疫手册》（第 9 版），ISBN 1741864836.

www.health.gov.au/internet/immunise/publishing.nsf/Content/

9.2.3 Clinical examination electronic bibliography

1.Medicine

（1）*Clinical Problems in Medicine and Surgery*, 3rd ed. ISBN 0443073236. http://shop.elsevier.com.au

（2）*Clinical Examination: A Systematic Guide to Physical Diagnosis.* 7th ed. ISBN 9780729539050. http://shop.elsevier.com.au

（3）*Davidsons Principles and Practice of Medicine*, ISBN 9780702030857. www.us.elsevierhealth.com

2.Surgery

（4）*Textbook of Surgery*, 3rd ed. ISBN 9781405126274. www.wiley.com

（5）*Clinical Problems in General Surgery*. ISBN 0409492132.

3.Child Health

（6）*Practical Paediatrics*, 7th ed. ISBN 9780443102806. www.us.elsevierhealth.com

（7）*Paediatric Handbook*, 8th ed. ISBN 9781405174008. www.wiley.com

（8）*The Australian Immunisation Handbook*. 9th ed. ISBN 1741864836.

www.health.gov.au/internet/immunise/publishing.nsf/Content/

（9）《基础儿科学》（第4版），ISBN 0443059586. www.us.elsevierhealth.com

4. 妇女健康

（10）《妇产科基础》（第9版），ISBN 9780723435099. www.us.elsevier-health.com

（11）《图解产科和新生儿教材》（第3版），ISBN 0702021237. www.us.elsevierhealth.com

（12）《图解妇科教科书》（第2版），ISBN 0729512118. www.us.elsevierhealth.com

5. 精神健康

（13）《牛津精神病学教科书》（第6版），ISBN 0198566670.www.oup.com/us/corporate/publishingprograms/medical/?view=usa 29

（14）《精神障碍诊断与统计手册》（第5版），ISBN 0890420254 ISBN 089 0420246. www.psych.org

（15）《澳大利亚和新西兰精神科医师学会声明与指南》，www.ranzcp.org/Publications/Statements-Guidelines.aspx

（9）*Essential Paediatrics*, 4th ed. ISBN 0443059586. www.us.elsevierhealth.com

4.Women Health

（10）*Fundamentals of Obstetrics & Gynaecology*, 9th ed. ISBN 9780723435099. www.us.elsevierhealth.com

（11）*Obstetrics and the Newborn-An Illustrated Text*, 3rd ed. ISBN 0702021237. www.us.elsevierhealth.com

（12）*Illustrated Textbook of Gynaecology*, 2nd ed. ISBN 0729512118. www.us.elsevierhealth.com

5.Mental health

（13）*Shorter Oxford Textbook of Psychiatry*, 6th ed. ISBN 0198566670 (paperback). www.oup.com/us/corporate/publishingprograms/medical/?view=usa 29

（14）*DSM-V: Diagnostic and Statistical Manual of Mental Disorders*, 5th ed. ISBN 0890420254 ISBN 0890420246. www.psych.org

（15）*Statements and Guidelines Royal Australian and New Zealand College of Psychiatrists*（www.ranzcp.org/Publications/Statements-Guidelines.aspx）

6. 一般实践

（16）《一般实践》（第5版），ISBN 9780074717790. www.mhprofessional.com

（17）《实践技巧》（第5版），ISBN 9780070158986. www.mhprofessional.com

7. 人口健康：

（18）《一般预防活动指引》（红皮书）（第7版，2009），www.racgp.org.au/guidelines/redbook

（19）《把预防付诸实践—绿皮书》，（第2版），www.racgp.org.au/guidelines/greenbook

（20）《SNAP: 一般实践中行为危险因素的人口健康指南》，www.racgp.org.au/guidelines/snap

（21）《土著人和托雷斯海峡岛上居民的预防评估国家指南》，www.racgp.org.au/guidelines/nationalguide

（22）《澳大利亚一般戒烟做法指南》，www.racgp.org.au/guidelines/smokingcessation

（23）《澳大利亚免疫手册》，（第9版2008），www.racgp.org.au/guidelines/immunisation

6.General Practice

（16）*General Practice*, 5th ed. ISBN 9780074717790. www.mhprofessional.com

（17）*Practice tips*, 5th ed. ISBN 9780070158986. www.mhprofessional.com

7.Population Health:

（18）*Guidelines for preventive activities in general practice*（The Red Book）7th ed. 2009 www.racgp.org.au/guidelines/redbook

（19）*Putting Prevention Into Practice–The Green Book*, 2nd ed. www.racgp.org.au/guidelines/greenbook

（20）*SNAP: a Population Health Guide to Behavioural Risk Factors in General Practice*, www.racgp.org.au/guidelines/snap

（21）*National Guide to a Preventive Assessment in Aboriginal and Torres Strait Islander Peoples*, www.racgp.org.au/guidelines/nationalguide

（22）*Smoking Cessation Guidelines for Australian general practice*, www.racgp.org.au/guidelines/smokingcessation

（23）*The Australian Immunisation Handbook*, 9th ed. 2008, www.racgp.org.au/guidelines/immunisation

（24）《国家 HPV 疫苗接种计划 》，www.racgp.org.au/guidelines/immunisation/hpv

（25）《糖尿病管理的一般做法》（第 16 版）2010 / 11，www.racgp.org.au/guidelines/diabetes

（26）《完全的心血管疾病风险评估快速参考指南 30》，www.heartfoundation.org.au/SiteCollectionDocuments/A_AR_QRG_FINAL%20FOR%20WEB .pdf

（27）《痴呆病人的护理》，www.racgp.org.au/guidelines/dementia

（28）《难民卫生》，www.racgp.org.au/guidelines/refugeehealth

（29）《癌症委员会对特定癌症筛查和监视的建议：全科医师指南 》，www.cancer.org.au/File/HealthProfessionals/CCA-Screening-Card-for-GPs.pdf

（30）《良好的医疗实践：职业道德和法律》，ISBN 978-0-521-18341-3

（31）《高级的护理计划》，www.racgp.org.au/guidelines/advancecareplans

（24）*National HPV Vaccination Program*, www.racgp.org.au/guidelines/immunisation/hpv

（25）*Diabetes Management in General Practice* (16th edition) 2010/11 www.racgp.org.au/guidelines/diabetes

（26）*Absolute Cardiovascular Disease Risk Assessment—Quick Reference Guide 30*, www.heartfoundation.org.au/SiteCollectionDocuments/A_AR_QRG_FINAL%20FOR%20WEB .pdf

（27）*Care of Patients with Dementia*, www.racgp.org.au/guidelines/dementia

（28）*Refugee Health*, www.racgp.org.au/guidelines/refugeehealth

（29）*Cancer Councils' recommendations for screening and surveillance for specific cancers: Guidelines for general practitioners*, www.cancer.org.au/File/Health Professionals/CCA-Screening-Card-for-GPs.pdf

（30）*Good Medical Practice: Professionalism, Ethics and Law*, ISBN 978-0-521-18341-3

（31）*Advance Care Plans*, www.racgp.org.au/guidelines/advancecareplans

第十章　其他国家的医师资格考试
Chapter ten　Medical Licensing Examination in Other Countries

10.1 新西兰临床技能考试（NZREX Clinical）

10.1 New Zealand Residency Examination（NZREX）

新西兰临床技能考试（NZREX Clinical）是国际毕业生在新西兰获取住院医师职位的途径之一。NZREX Clinical 采用客观结构化临床考试形式，由 16 个考站的构成。这种考试每年两次，然而，由于申请的人数多，现在每年有 4~5 次考试，每一组测试 28 个考生。近 5 年的通过率为 60%。

国际医学毕业生要想在新西兰获取住院医师职位有很多途径，一种是申请者执有来自英国或爱尔兰共和国的初级资格，并且已完成主管部门的实习工作；一种是临时专用目的的途径；还有一种就是为国际医学毕业生

NZREX Clinical is one of the ways for international graduates to obtain residency positions in New Zealand. NZREX Clinical consists of 16 test stations which format is an objective structured clinical examination. The test is two times a year. However, due to the large number of applicants, there are now an annual examination of 4 to 5, it tests 28 examinees in each group, the pass rate is 60% in recent five years.

To obtain residency positions in New Zealand, the international medical graduates have many ways. One way is that the applicant holds primary qualification from the UK or Republic of Ireland, and has completed internship departments;

提供的 NZREX Clinical 考试途径。国际医学毕业生必须执有在 Avicenna 网站上列出的初级医疗证书才有资格参加 NZREX Clinical 考试。在 NZREX Clinical 考试之前，国际医学毕业生英语必须满足委员会制定的英语标准，并且通过了 USMLE Step 1 和 Step 2 CK 考试，或者通过澳大利亚医学委员会 MCQ 考试，或者通过了英国专业委员会和语言学委员会的 Part 1 评估。

申请 NZREX Clinical 考试成功者将进入一个在新西兰的临时注册期，在此期间，他们将被再次评估。为了在一般范围内有资格注册，通过 NZREX Clinical 的考生必须在新西兰公共医院成功完成 4 项流动实践，每一次流动为期三个月并且得到监督员的认可。所有流动实践都依照新西兰医学委员会的教学计划规定来实施。需要完成的四种流动实践包括 A 类内科流动，A 类外科流动，A、B 流动或 A、C 流动。

temporary special purpose way; another is to provide the NZREX Clinical test for international students. International students must have a primary medical certificate listed on the Avicenna website to be eligible for the NZREX Clinical exam. Before the NZREX Clinical exam, international students' English must meet the development of the English standard, and pass the USMLE Step 1 and Step 2 CK examination, or pass the Australian Medical Council MCQ examination, or pass the Part 1 assessment of British Specialized Committee and Linguistics Committee.

People who successfully applied for NZREX Clinical will enter a temporary registration period in New Zealand,and they will be assessed again. In order to be eligible for registration within the general scope, examinees having passed the NZREX Clinical exam must successfully complete four runs in the New Zealand public hospital. Each run is three months and It is signed off by its supervisor. All runs are categorised by the Medical Council of New Zealand according to their educational role. The four runs that need to be completed include category A medical run, A surgical run, A,B runs, A,C runs,

临床推理领域测试考生的能力，如整合不同方面的临床资料，正确解释病史、体检及考生与病人沟通的能力。

NZREX Clinical 考试是有 16 个考站的客观结构化考试，每一考站限时 12 分钟，其中 2 分钟阅读考站要求，能力测试包括病史（3 个病例），临床检查（4 个病例），调查研究（2 个病例），处理（3 个病例），临床推理 4 个病例），儿童健康（1 个病例），精神健康（1 个病例），妇女健康（1 个病例）。考站是动态的，以真实或模拟病人为基础，静态考站则是以试卷为基础。每次考试，平均有 3~4 个考站是静态考站，因为有些内容不适合采用真实或模拟病人，如解读 ECGs、X 射线和血液检查。所有的动态考站考察考生交流和专业技术能力。考生应表现出良好的职业素养包括：正直、尊重、文化能力、道德实践、非歧视与诚实。

The field of clinical reasoning tests examinees' capability, such as integrating different aspects of clinical data, the correct interpretation of the history, physical examination and communicating with the patient.

NZREX Clinical test is a kind of 16-station OSCE exam, it is within 12 minutes in each station. There are two minutes to read the examination station requirements. The contents of the test are history (three cases), clinical examination (four cases), research (two cases), management (three cases), clinical reasoning (four cases), child health (one case), mental health (a case), women's health (a case). The test station is dynamic, based on real or simulated patient, the static test station based on paper, there are 3 or 4 static stations in each exam, because some contents are not suitable for the use of real or simulated patients, such as the interpretation of ECGs, Xrays and blood examination. All the dynamic stations examine the examinees' communication and professional technical ability. Examinees should demonstrate good professional qualities: integrity, respect, cultural competence, ethical practice, non discrimination and honesty.

10.2 英国职业与语言评估委员会考试（PLAB）

在英国，要想成为一名医生，首先接受 5 年制的医学校学习，毕业后成绩要达到英国综合委员会（General Medical Council,GMC）制订的实习医生的标准，经过 1 年的实习，达到 GMC 制订的正式医生标准，然后便可注册执业医师。

参加英国执业医师资格考试的考生所取得的医学学历，必须是 WHO 名录中认可的医学院颁发的。医学院应届毕业生必须具备 12 个月的临床实习或者医院的工作经验。考生的英语要达标，雅思成绩最低分数线必须达到口语 7 分，听力 6 分，阅读 6 分，写作 6 分，总平均分 7 分。

对于 IMGS 来说，要想取得英国行医资格，首先要通过职业与语言评估委员会考试（Professional Linguistic Assessments Board, PLAB），PLAB 考试分为两部分。

10.2 Professional and Linguistic Assessments Board（PLAB）

In the UK, in order to become a doctor, firstly, you should graduate from a 5-year medical college. After graduation, your scores shoule reach the UK General Committee（General Medical Council, GMC）for the intern standard.After one year of practice, if you reach the official doctor standard developed by GMC, then you can register medical practitioners.

In the UK, the medical qualifications of the examinees who take Professional Linguistic Assessments Board（PLAB）must be issued by the school of medicine approved WHO list, medical school graduates must have twelve months' clinical practice experience or hospital work experience .Examinees' English should meet the standard, the lowest score of IELTS must reach 7 points in spoken English, 6 points in listening,reading and writing, the total average score is 7 points.

For IMGs, in order to obtain the qualifications of the British practice, first of all, they must pass PLAB exam, PLAB exam is divided into two parts.

第一部分是笔试，主要测试考生的临床医学知识和理论，共有200道单选题，是不同的病例以多选题的方式从每个病历里找出答案，考试时间为3小时。

第二部分考试形式为客观结构化临床考试，主要考察考生的临床应变能力。考生在考前至少要了解5000~10000种不同的病例考题。考生考试时会在17个不同的考站轮转，病人的基本信息和症状会贴在考站门前，考生要在规定时间内对病人作出诊断，并回答考官提出的问题。每一站5分钟。

根据考试大纲要求，考试范围包括心血管疾病，免疫性疾病，神经科疾病，呼吸系疾病，生殖系疾病，肾脏疾病，儿科疾病，胃肠道、肝胆系统及营养性疾病，眼科及耳鼻喉科疾病，皮肤病、过敏性疾病，血液病，外伤和急诊医学，代谢性疾病，心理疾病，矫形外科，老年疾病，围术期

The first part is the written test, which mainly test students' theory and clinical medicine knowledge. There are 200 questions, the case is different to many topics of the way from each medical record to find the answer, the examination time is 3 hours.

The second part of the examination is Objective Structured Clinical Examination (OSCE), it mainly tests the examinees' clinical ability. The examinees should understand no less than 5000–10000 different test cases before the exam. There are 17 different stations, basic information and symptom of the patient will be posted on the station's door.The examinee should make diagnosis of patients within the specified time, and answer the examiner's questions. There are 5 minutes per station.

According to the outline requirements, the scope of the examination includes: angiocardiopathy, immunopathy, neurological disease; respiratory disease; reproductive diseases, kidney diseases; pediatric diseases; gastrointestinal, hepatobiliary system and nutritional diseases; ophthalmology and department

处理。考试内容虽然很广泛，但是所考病例都是常见病例。

of ENT; dermatopathya; hypersensitivity disease; blood disease; trauma and emergency medicine; metabolic diseases; mental disease; mechanurgy; senile diseases; perioperative treatment. Examination content is very extensive, but all the test cases are common.

考试成绩只是合格或不合格，第一部分考试如果没通过，考试机构会通知考生四个月后重新考，第二部分考试如果连续四次不合格，考生第一部分的成绩及雅思成绩都会作废，从头开始考。

Examination results are qualified or unqualified，if you don't pass in the first part of the exam,the examination institution will notify you take it again after four months. If you don't pass in the second part of the exam four consecutive times, the first part score and the IELTS score will be zero, and examinees must take the exam again.

从 Medial Officer 到 Ricistar，申请者必须要通过英国皇家医师学会会员（Member of the Royal College of Physicians，MRCP）考试。

From Medical Officet to Rigistar applicants must pass the exam of Member the College of Physicians (MRCP).

英国 MRCP 考试共分为 Part 1（基础知识笔试）、Part 2A（临床知识笔试）、Part 2B（临床知识实践考核）三部分。Part 1 考生要完成两份考卷，每份考卷包括 100 道选择题。主要考察考生的基础知识，Part 2A 考生要完成三份考卷，每份考卷包括大约 100 道选择题。每道题目通常都给考生提供

MRCP examination is divided into PART 1 (basic knowledge written), PART 2A (clinical knowledge written), PART 2B (clinical knowledge practice assessment). Examinees must complete two exam papers in PART 1, each paper includes 100 multiple-choice questions, which test their basic knowledge. In PART 2A

了一个临床情景，还可能涉及临床检查的结果。Part 2B 为五站 OSCE 考试，考核的内容分别为呼吸系统和腹部检查，病史采集，心血管和神经系统检查，交流技巧和伦理知识，其他系统（皮肤、运动系统、内分泌系统和眼睛）检查。

exam, examinees must complete three exam papers, each paper includes about 100 multiple-choice questions. Each item usually provides a Clinical scenarios for the examinees, and may also involve the results of clinical examination. PART 2B is a five-station OSCE exam, the content of the examination are respiratory and abdominal examination, medical history, cardiovascular and neurological examination, communication skills and ethical knowledge, other systems examination（skin, motion system, endocrine system and eye）.

10.3 考试资源利用

10.3 Examination Resources Utilization

MRCP Part 1.co.uk

Home | Contact

News
Seven Steps To MRCP Part 1 Success
Preparing For The MRCP Part 1
Cultivating Healthy Study
General Journals
E-Journals
Recommended MRCP 1 Books
MRCP online course
MRCP e-video courses
MRCP exam format
MRCP exam fees
MRCP exam centres
MRCP results
Medical interview skills for physicians
Directory
Contact Us

E-learning News

MRCP Part 1 Book Review

Title Best of Five Clinical Scenarios for the MRCP: Volume 1, Part 1 (Paperback)
Author Punit S. Ramrakha, Iqbal Malik
ISBN: 1841101826
Pages: 296 pp

The material is divided by specialities which comprehensive revision questions. While space does not permit for an entire syllabus to be covered in one volume, this book contains eight chapters covering eight specialities and a total of 225 questions. This is the first in a series of books to complement each other and provide students with a comprehensive revision guide for the MRCP Part 1 examination. You will also receive access to the online e-course version of the book.

Title Best of Five Clinical Scenarios for the MRCP Part 1 Vol. 2
Author: Julian Nash
ISBN: 1-904583-02-4
Pages: 332pp

This MRCP Part 1 book covers the most important specialties seen on the MRCP exam. Each of the specialties most-tested topics are

这是 MRCP Part 1 的考试资源网，该网站提供了 MRCP Part 1 的考试策略，考试资料，考试用期刊、图书、在线课堂等。

This is the MRCP PART 1 examina-tion Resources Network, the site provides MRCP PART 1 examination strategy, examination information, journals, books, online classes for the examination.

10.3.1 参考图书

10.3.1 Reference books

（1）Best of Five Clinical Scenarios for the MRCP: Volume 1, 2Part 1（Paperback）

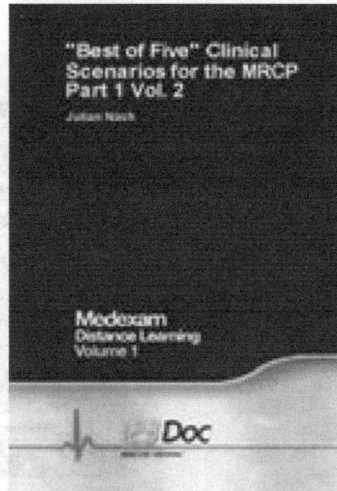

这套系列书为参加 MRCP 的考生提供了复习指南。两本书在内容上相互补充。第一卷按专业划分，共 8 章，涵盖八个专业 225 个问题。第二卷涵盖了 MRCP 考试中最重要的专业内容。每个专业最常见的话题以问题的形式说明，并有详细的教学笔记，用列表的形式将热点话题和要点列出方便记忆和联想，帮助考生顺利通过 MRCP 考试。8 个专业的内容包括：临床药理

This series of books provides a review guide for the examinees to participate in the MRCP. Two books complement each other in content. The first volume is divided by specialities, there are eight chapters, covering eight professional 225 questions. The second volume covers the most important professional content in the MRCP exam. The most common topic of each subject are illustrated by questions,

学、糖尿病和内分泌学、遗传学、免疫学、医学生物化学、分子生物学、风湿病、统计与流行病学。

with detailed teaching notes and a list of hot topics and key points listed in the convenient memory and association, which can help examinees successfully passed the MRCP exam. Eight major contents include: clinical pharmacology, diabetes and endocrinology, genetics, immunology, biochemistry, molecular biology, rheumatism, statistics and epidemiology.

（2）MRCP Part 1 UK Qbook

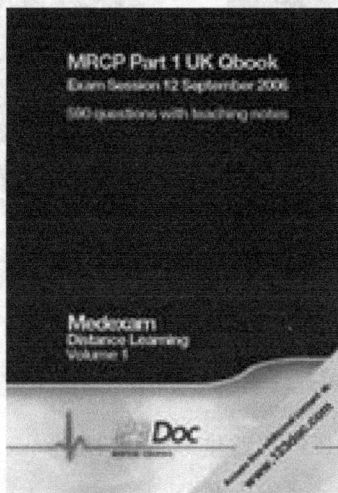

这是一本题库，汇编了590个过去考试的问题和教学笔记，由123Doc教育（www.123doc.com）领导小组的医学讲师开发。所有的材料已经过测试，而且不断修订确保考生通过MRCP Part 1考试。专业包括：心脏病学、肿瘤学、精神病学、临床药理学、皮肤病、肠胃病学、内分泌与代谢、呼

This is a Qbank on PRCP PART 1, compilation of 590 past examinations based questions and teaching notes. It is developed by a leading medical team of 123Doc Education (www.123doc.com). All materials have been tested and revised to ensure examinees passing the MRCP Part 1 exam. The specialties include:

吸、血液学、遗传学、传染病、免疫学、遗传学、分子医学、生物化学、肾病学、神经解剖学、眼科、风湿病和统计。

cardiology, oncology, psychiatry,clinical pharmacology, dermatology, gastroenterology, endocrinology and metabolism, rrespiratory, hematology, genetics, infectious diseases, immunology, genetics, molecular medicine, biochemistry, nephrology, neuroanatomy, ophthalmology, rheumatology and statistics.

（3）MRCP Part 2 UK Qbook

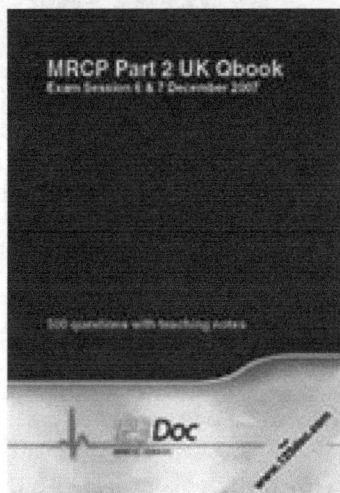

这本书是 MRCP Part 1 的延续，包含 500 个考试复习题，由一个医学专家团队编写，所有内容都在课堂上进行了测试，并根据最新的皇家学院大纲重写。17 个重点专业包括：临床药理学、呼吸内科。青少年医学、精神病学、心脏病学、内分泌与代谢、消化、免疫学、血液学、传染病、皮

This book is a continuation of the MRCP PART 1, including 500 exam review questions, written by a team of medical experts. All the contents were tested in the classroom, rewritten according to the latest Royal Academy outline. The 17 specialties highlighted include: clinical pharmacology, respiratory medicine. Adolescent medicine,

肤病学、肾脏病学、神经病学、肿瘤学、眼科、放射科。

psychiatry, cardiology, endocrinology and metabolism, digestion, immunology, hematology, infectious diseases, skin diseases, nephrology, neurology, oncology, ophthalmology, radiology.

（5）Qbase Medicine: 1 MCQs for the MRCP Part 1, Ramrakh

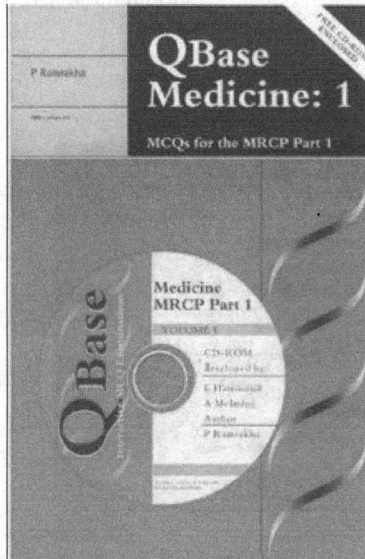

这本书是专为考生复习 MRCP Part 1 准备的。这本书包含了 300 个问题，按照 MRCP Part 1 考试大纲概述分成 5 个单独的试卷，每个试卷包含 60 个问题。每个试卷有答案和解释。这本书有一个随书光盘，包含考试形式的 300 个多选题。

This book is designed for examinees to review MRCP PART 1. It contains 300 questions which are divided into 5 separate papers according to the outline of the MRCP PART 1 exam, each paper contains 60 questions with answer and explanation. There is a CD-ROM with the book, including 300 MCQ questions in the form of examination.

10.3.2 期刊

10.3.2 Journals

（1）内分泌学

（1）Endocrinology

《BMC 内分泌失调》	*BMC Endocrine Disorders*
《心血管疾病的糖尿病》	*Cardiovascular Diabetology*
《临床糖尿病》	*Clinical Diabetes*
《内分泌期刊》	*Endocrine Journal*
《内分泌调节》	*Endocrine Regulations*
《内分泌》	*Endocrinology Rounds*
《欧洲内分泌学杂志》	*European Journal of Endocrinology*
《国际糖尿病与代谢杂志》	*International Journal of Diabetes & Metabolism*
《神经内分泌学》	*Neuroendocrinology Letters*
《比较内分泌日本协会通讯》	*Newsletter of Japan Society for Comparative Endocrinology*
《生殖生物学与内分泌》	*Reproductive Biology and Endocrinology*
《糖尿病患者的声音》	*Voice of the Diabetic*
《基础年杂志》	*Foundation Years Journal*

（2）心脏病学

（2）Cardiology

《电子超声心动图杂志》	*E-chocardiography Journal*
《希腊心脏病学杂志》	*Hellenic Journal of Cardiology*
《高血压的研究》	*Hypertension Research*
《儿科心脏病学图像》	*Images in Paediatric Cardiology*
《印度心脏杂志》	*Indian Heart Journal*
《印度起搏与电生理期刊》	*Indian Pacing and Electrophysiology Journal*
《意大利心脏杂志》	*Italian Heart Journal*
《日本心脏杂志》	*Japanese Heart Journal*
《临床与基础心脏病学杂志》	*Journal of Clinical and Basic Cardiology*

《波兰心脏杂志》	*Polish Heart Journal*
《心血管医学评论》	*Reviews in Cardiovascular Medicine*
《得克萨斯心脏研究所杂志》	*Texas Heart Institute journal*
《基础年杂志》	*Foundation Years Journal*
（3）血液学	（3）Haematology
《BMC 的血液病》	*BMC Blood Disorders*
《血液》	*Haema*
《血液病 2002》	*Haematology 2002*
《白血病洞察通讯》	*Leukemia Insights Newsletter*
《血栓杂志》	*Thrombosis Journal*
《土耳其血液杂志》	*Turkish Journal of Haematology*
《土耳其血液学和肿瘤学杂志》	*Turkish Journal of Haematology and Oncology*
《基础年杂志》	*Foundation Years Journal*
（4）肾脏学	（4）Nephrology
《腹膜透析进展》	*Advances in Peritoneal Dialysis*
《BMC 肾脏》	*BMC Nephrology*
《香港肾脏病杂志》	*Hong Kong Journal of Nephrology*
《印度肾脏病杂志》	*Indian Journal of Nephrology*
《肾脏病杂志》	*Journal of Nephrology*
《肾脏病》	*Nephrology Rounds*
《基础年杂志》	*Foundation Years Journal*
（5）肿瘤学	（5）Oncology
《BMC 癌症》	*BMC Cancer*
《乳腺癌研究》	*Breast Cancer Research*
《临床医生的癌症杂志》	*CA: A Cancer Journal for Clinicians*
《国际癌细胞》	*Cancer Cell International*
《癌症控制：Moffitt 癌症中心杂志》	*Cancer Control: Journal of the Moffitt Cancer Center*

《癌症论坛—澳大利亚癌症委员会
杂志》

Cancer Forum - Journal of The Cancer
Council Australia

《肿瘤免疫》

Cancer Immunity

《癌症科学（原日本癌症期刊研究）》

Cancer Science (formely Japanese
Journal of Cancer Research)

《临床肿瘤学》

Clinical Oncology

《电子版肿瘤学杂志》

Electronic Journal of Oncology

《癌症治疗学范围》

Horizons in Cancer Therapeutics

《国际肿瘤学杂志》

International Journal of Oncology

《日本分子肿瘤标记研究杂志》

Japan Journal of Molecular Tumor
Marker Research

《癌症研究与治疗杂志》

Journal of Cancer Research and
Therapeutics

《癌变杂志》

Journal of Carcinogenesis

《支持肿瘤学杂志》

Journal of Supportive Oncology

《分子肿瘤》

Molecular Cancer

《肿瘤学家》

Oncologist

《肿瘤报告》

Oncology Reports

《放射肿瘤学杂志》

Radiology and Oncology Journal

《土耳其癌症杂志》

Turkish Journal of Cancer

《世界外科肿瘤学杂志》

World Journal of Surgical Oncology

（6）肠胃病学

（6）Gastroenterology

《肝脏病学年报》

Annals of Hepatology

《胃肠肝病学档案》

Archives of Gastroenterohepatology

《BMC 胃肠病学》

BMC Gastroenterology

《比较肝脏病学》

Comparative Hepatology

《腹泻对话》

Dialogue on Diarrhoea

《国际肝胆胰疾病》

HBPD INT Hepatobiliary & Pancreatic
Diseases International

《印度胃肠病学杂志》

Indian Journal of Gastroenterology

《胰腺杂志》   *JOP. Journal of the Pancreas*

《腹泻病研究》   *Journal of Diarrhoeal Diseases Research*

《韩国肠胃病杂志》   *Korean Journal of Gastroenterology*

《韩国肝病学杂志》   *Korean Journal of Hepatology*

《胃肠疾病评论》   *Reviews in Gastrointestinal Disorders*

《土耳其胃肠病学杂志》   *Turkish Journal of Gastroenterology*

《世界华人消化杂志》   *World Chinese Journal of Digestology*

《世界胃肠病学杂志》   *World Journal of Gastroenterology*

（7）风湿病学   （7）Rheumatology

《关节炎研究与治疗》   *Arthritis Research & Therapy*

《关节炎研究》   *Arthritis Research*

《风湿病通报》   *Bulletin on the Rheumatic Diseases*

《加拿大风湿病协会杂志》   *Journal of the Canadian Rheumatology Association*

（8）传染病学   （8）Infectious Diseases

《BMC 传染病》   *BMC Infectious Diseases*

《巴西传染病杂志》   *Brazilian Journal of Infectious Diseases*

《真菌感染的临床进展》   *Clinical updates in Fungal Infections*

《感染性疾病的临床进展》   *Clinical updates in Infectious Diseases*

《儿科感染性疾病的临床进展》   *Clinical updates in Pediatric Infectious Diseases*

《双螺旋》   *Double Helix*

《新出现的传染病》   *Emerging Infectious Diseases*

《欧洲肺结核》   *Euro TB*

《疱疹》   *Herpes*

《传染病简讯》   *Infectious Diseases News Brief*

《日本传染病杂志》   *Japanese Journal of Infectious Diseases*

《麻风病评论》   *Leprosy Review*

《热带疾病研究出版物》   *Tropical Disease Research publications*

《世界卫生组织传染病报告》 *WHO Report on Infectious Diseases*

《微生物细胞工厂》 *Microbial Cell Factories*

《微生物学》 *Microbiology*

《今日微生物》 *Microbiology Today*

《微生物学和免疫学》 *Microbiology and Immunology*

《微生物学与分子生物学评论》 *Microbiology and Molecular Biology Reviews*

《分子微生物学》 *Molecular Microbiology*

《拉丁美洲寄生虫学》 *Parasitologia latinoamericana*

《波兰微生物学杂志》 *Polish Journal of Microbiology*

（9）分子医学 （9）Molecular Medicine

《国际分子医学杂志》 *International Journal of Molecular Medicine*

《分子医学》 *Molecular Medicine*

（10）药理学 （10）Pharmacology

《美国科学促进会杂志》 *AAPS Journal*

《美国科学促进会药剂学技术》 *AAPS PharmSci Tech*

《澳大利亚药品不良反应通报》 *Australian Adverse Drug Reactions Bulletin*

《BMC 临床药理学》 *BMC Clinical Pharmacology*

《加拿大医院药学杂志》 *Canadian Journal of Hospital Pharmacy*

《印度药理学杂志》 *Indian Journal of Pharmacology*

《药物治疗通报杂志》 *Journal of Informed Pharmacotherapy*

《药理学杂志》 *Journal of Pharmacological Sciences*

《生理学与药理学杂志》 *Journal of Physiology and Pharmacology*

《现代药物发现》 *Modern Drug Discovery*

《波兰药理学杂志》 *Polish Journal of Pharmacology*

《精神药理学通报》　　　　　　　　Psychopharmacology Bulletin

《美国药剂师》　　　　　　　　　　U.S. Pharmacist

《药物信息世界》　　　　　　　　　World of Drug Information

（11）皮肤病学　　　　　　　　　　（11）Dermatology

《皮肤病学年鉴》　　　　　　　　　Annales de Dermatologie

《BMC 皮肤病》　　　　　　　　　　BMC Dermatology

《皮肤病学》　　　　　　　　　　　Dermatology Times

《皮肤病学杂志在线》　　　　　　　Dermatology on line journal

《印度皮肤病、性病、麻风病杂志》　Indian Journal of Dermatology Venereology and Leprology

（12）免疫学　　　　　　　　　　　（12）Immunology

《BMC 免疫学》　　　　　　　　　　BMC Immunology

《免疫疗法与疫苗杂志》　　　　　　Journal of Immune Based Therapies and Vaccines

《医学免疫学》　　　　　　　　　　Medical Immunology

（13）神经病学　　　　　　　　　　（13）Neurology

《BMC 神经病学》　　　　　　　　　BMC Neurology

《BMC 神经科学》　　　　　　　　　BMC Neuroscience

《巴罗神经学研究所季刊》　　　　　Barrow Neurological Institute Quarterly

《行为与脑科学》　　　　　　　　　Behavioral and Brain Sciences

《中枢神经系统图谱》　　　　　　　CNS Spectrums

《加拿大阿尔茨海默病评论》　　　　Canadian Alzheimer Disease Review

《皮质》　　　　　　　　　　　　　Cortex

《癫痫电流》　　　　　　　　　　　Epilepsy Currents

《国际 MS 护理杂志》　　　　　　　International Journal of MS Care

《肌肉骨骼与神经相互作用杂志》　　Journal of Musculoskeletal and Neuronal Interactions

《神经科学杂志》　　　　　　　　　Journal of Neurological Sciences

《小儿神经病学杂志》　　　　　　　Journal of Pediatric Neurology

《尼泊尔神经科学杂志》	*Nepal Journal of Neuroscience*
《神经解剖学》	*Neuroanatomy*
《印度神经病学》	*Neurology India*
《神经病学与临床神经生理学》	*Neurology and Clinical Neuro-physiology*
《神经心理药理学》	*Neuropsychopharmacology*
《神经网络》	*Neuroscience-Net*
（14）遗传学	（14）Genetics
《BMC 遗传学》	*BMC Genetics*
《BMC 医学遗传学》	*BMC Medical Genetics*
《巴西遗传学杂志》	*Brazilian Journal of Genetics*
《基因与遗传系统》	*Genes and Genetic Systems*
《基因漂移》	*Genetic Drift*
《基因疫苗与治疗》	*Genetic Vaccines and Therapy*
《遗传学与分子生物学》	*Genetics and Molecular Biology*
《遗传学与分子研究》	*Genetics and Molecular Research*
《印度人类遗传学杂志》	*Indian Journal of Human Genetics*
《应用遗传学杂志》	*Journal of Applied Genetics*

10.3.3 e-cours 在线

10.3.3 Online e-cours

281

123doc MRCP PART 1 是高度灵活的，可以让考生随时随地学习在线课程。课程包括：4169 MRCP PART 1 MCQ，34 MRCP PART 1 电子讲议，100 多个新的过去考试的主题，记忆列表，按主题或难度等级学习，无限定时模拟考试与评级，和在线导师通过电子邮件讨论问题。

123Doc MRCP PART 1 online e-course is highly flexible, allowing you to study anytime, from any computer connected to the internet. The course includes: 4,169 MRCP PART 1 MCQ, BOF questions, 34 MRCP PART 1 electures (sold separately), 100+ new past exam theme BOF questions, MCQ questions, lists to memorize, study by topic or by difficulty level, unlimited timed mock exams with rating, option to email comments about a question to our online tutor.

SCI 收录的期刊名全称和缩写对照
SCI Journal Titles and Abbreviations

以 A 字母开头的期刊	Journals beginning with A letters
Adv. Carbohydr. Chem. Biochem.	Advances in Carbohydrate Chemistry and Biochemistry
Adv. Chem. Phys.	Advances in Chemical Physics
Adv. Chem. Ser.	Advances in Chemistry Series
Adv. Chromatogr.	Advances in Chromatography
Adv. Colloid Interface Sci.	Advances in Colloid and Interface Science
Adv. Compos.Mater	Advanced Composite Materials
Adv. Cryog. Eng.	Advances in Cryogenic Engineering
Adv. Eng. Mater.	Advanced Engineering Materials
Adv. Enzyme Regul.	Advances in Enzyme Regulation
Adv. Enzymol. Relat. Areas Mol. Biol.	Advances in Enzymology and Related Areas of Molecular Biology
Adv. Filtr. Sep. Technol.	Advances in Filtration and Separation Technology
Adv. Funct. Mater.	Advanced Functional Materials
Adv. Heterocycl. Chem.	Advances in Heterocyclic Chemistry
Adv. Inorg. Chem.	Advances in Inorganic Chemistry
Adv. Mass Spectrom.	Advances in Mass Spectrometry Adv. Synth. Catal.
Adv. Synth. Catal.	Advanced Synthesis and Catalysis
Adv. Mater.	Advanced Materials
Adv. Mater. Opt. Electron.	Advanced Materials for Optics and Electronics
Adv. Mater. Processes	Advanced Materials and Processes
Adv. Mater. Res.	Advances in Materials Research

Adv. Organomet. Chem.	Advances in Organometallic Chemistry
Adv. Phys. Org. Chem.	Advances in Physical Organic Chemistry
Adv. Polym. Sci.	Advances in Polymer Science
Adv. Polym. Tech.	Advances in Polymer Technology
Adv. Powder Technol.	Advanced Powder Technology
Adv. Powder. Metall. Part. Mater.	Advances in Powder Metallurgy and Particulate Materials
Adv. Space Res.	Advances in Space Research
Adv. X–Ray Anal.	Advances in X–Ray Analysis
Adverse Drug React. Toxicol. Rev.	Adverse Drug Reactions and Toxicological Reviews
Aerosol Sci. Technol.	Aerosol Science and Technology
Al Ch E J.	AICh E Journal
Al Ch E Symp. Ser.	AICh E Symposium Series
Am. Ceram. Soc. Bull.	American Ceramic Society Bulletin
Am. Ind. Hyg. Assoc. J.	American Industrial Hygiene Association Journal
Am. J. Respir. Cell Mol. Biol.	American Journal of Respiratory Cell and Molecular Biology
Am. Lab.	American Laboratory
Am. Mineral.	American Mineralogist
Ammonia Plant Saf. Relat. Facil	Ammonia Plant Safety and Related Facilities
An. Asoc. Quim. Argent.	Anales de la Asociacion Quimica Argentina
An. Quim.	Anales de Quimica
Anal. Biochem.	Analytical Biochemistry
Anal. Chem.	Analytical Chemistry
Anal. Chim.	Annali di Chimica
Anal. Chim. Acta	Analytica Chimica Acta
Anal. Commun.	Analytical Communications
Anal. Lett.	Analytical Letters

Anal. Sci.	Analytical Sciences
Angew. Chem. Int. Ed.	Angewandte Chemie International Edition
Angew. Makromol. Chem.	Angewandte Makromolekulare Chemie
Ann. Chim. (Rome)	Annali di Chimica
Ann. Chim. – Sci. Mat.	Annales de Chimie – Science des Materiaux
Ann. Clin. Biochem.	Annals of Clinical Biochemistry
Ann. N.Y. Acad. Sci.	Annals of the New York Academy of Sciences
Annu. Rep. Med. Chem.	Annual Reports in Medicinal Chemistry
Annu. Rep. Prog. Chem. Sect. A: Inorg. Chem.	Annual Reports on the Progress of Chemistry, Section A: Inorganic Chemistry
Annu. Rep. Prog. Chem. Sect. B: Org. Chem.	Annual Reports on the Progress of Chemistry, Section B: Organic Chemistry
Annu. Rep. Prog. Chem. Sect. C: Phys. Chem.	Annual Reports on the Progress of Chemistry, Section C: Physical Chemistry
Annu. Rev. Biochem	Annual Review of Biochemistry
Annu. Rev. Biophys. Biomol. Struct.	Annual Review of Biophysics and Biomolecular Structure
Annu. Rev. Cell Dev. Biol.	Annual Review of Cell and Developmental Biology
Annu. Rev. Energy Env.	Annual Review of Energy and the Environment
Annu. Rev. Mater. Sci.	Annual Review of Materials Science
Annu. Rev. Pharmacool. Toxicol.	Annual Review of Pharmacology and Toxicology
Annu. Rev. Phys. Chem.	Annual Review of Physical Chemistry
Anti–Cancer Drug Des.	Anti–Cancer Drug Design
Anticancer Res.	Anticancer Research
Antimicrob. Agents Chemother.	Antimicrobial Agents and Chemotherapy
Antisense Nucleic Acid Drug Dev.	Antisense and Nucleic Acid Drug Development
Antiviral Chem. Chemother.	Antiviral Chemistry and Chemotherapy
Appita J.	Appita Journal

Appl. Biochem. Biotechnol.	Applied Biochemistry and Biotechnology
Appl. Catal., A	Applied Catalysis A
Appl. Catal., B	Applied Catalysis B
Appl. Clay Sci.	Applied Clay Science
Appl. Compos. Mater.	Applied Composite Materials
Appl. Environ. Microbiol.	Applied and Environment Microbiology
Appl. Geochem	Applied Geochemistry
Appl. Magn. Reson.	Applied Magnetic Resonance
Appl. Microbiol. Biotechnol.	Applied Microbiology and Biotechnology
Appl. Opt.	Applied Optics
Appl. Organomet. Chem.	Applied Organometallic Chemistry
Appl. Phys. A	Applied Physics A
Appl. Phys. B	Applied Physics B
Appl. Phys. Lett.	Applied Physics Letters
Appl. Radiat. Isot.	Applied Radiation and Isotopes
Appl. Sci. Res.	Applied Scientific Research
Appl. Spectrosc.	Applied Spectroscopy
Appl. Supercond.	Applied Superconductivity
Appl. Surf. Sci.	Applied Surface Science
Appl. Therm. Eng.	Applied Thermal Engineering
Aquat. Toxicol.	Aquatic Toxicology
Arch. Biochem. Biophys.	Archives of Biochemistry and Biophysics
Arch. Environ. Contam. Toxicol.	Archives of Environment Contamination and Toxicology
Acc. Chem. Res.	Accounts of Chemical Research
ACH – Models Chem.	ACH – Models in Chemistry
ACI Mater. J.	ACI Materials Journal
ACS Symp. Ser.	ACS Symposium Series

Acta Biochim. Pol.	Acta Biochimica Polonica
Acta Biotechnol.	Acta Biotechnologica
Acta Chem. Scand.	Acta Chemica Scandinavica
Acta Chim. Sinica	Acta Chimica Sinica
Acta Cienc. Indica, Chem.	Acta Cienceia Indica Chemistry
Acta Cienc. Indica, Phys.	Acta Ciencia Indica Phyics
Acta Crystallogr., Sect. A: Found. Crystallogr.	Acta Crystallographica Section A: Foundations
Acta Crystallogr., Sect. B:Struct. Sci	Acta Crystallographica Section B: Structural Science
Acta Crystallogr., Sect. C: Cryst. Struct. Commun.	Acta Crystallographica Section C: Crystal Structure Communications
Acta Crystallogr., Sect D: Biol.Crystallogr.	Acta Crystallographica Section D: Biological Crystallography
Acta Crystallogr. Sect. E: Struct. Rep. Online	Acta Crystallographica Section E Structure Reports Online
Acta Hydroch. Hydrob.	Acta Hydrochimica et Hydrobiologica
Acta Mater.	Acta Materialia
Acta Metall.	Acta Metallurgica
Acta Phys. Pol., A	Acta Physica Polonica A
Acta Phys. Pol., B	Acta Physica Polonica B
Acta Polym.	Acta Polymerica
Acta Polytech. Scand., Chem.Technol. Ser	Acta Polytechnica Scandinavica – Chemical Technology Series
Adhes. Age	Adhesives Age
Adsorpt. Sci. Technol.	Adsorption Science and Technology
Adv. Appl. Microbiol.	Advances in Applied Microbiology
Adv. At. Mol. Opt. Phy.	Advances in Atomic Molecular and Optical Physics

Adv. Biochem. Eng./Biotechnol.	Advances in Biochemical Engineering / Biotechnology
Arch. Environ. Health	Archives of Environment Health
Arch. Insect Biochem. Physiol.	Archives of Insect Biochemistry and Physiology
Arch. Microbiol.	Archives of Microbiology
Arch. Pharm.	Archiv der Pharmazie
Arch. Pharmacal Res.	Archives of Pharmacal Research
Arch. Physiol. Biochem.	Archives of Physiology and Biochemistry
Arch. Toxicol.	Archives of Toxicology
Arch. Virol	Archives of Virology
Artif. Cells, Blood Substitues, Immobilization Biotechnol.	Artificial Cells Blood Substitutes and Immobilization Biotechnology
Arzneim.–Forsch.	Arzneimittel–Forschung/Drug Research
Asian J. Chem.	Asian Journal of Chemistry
Asian J. Spectro.	Asian Journal of Spectroscopy
ASTM Spec. Tech. Publ.	ASTM Specical Technical Publication
Astron. Astrophys.	Astronomy and Astrophysics
Astron. J.	Astronomy Journal
Astrophys J.	Astrophysics Journal
At. Data Nucl. Data Tables	Atomic Data and Nuclear Data Tables
At. Energ.	Atomic Energy
At. Spectrosc.	Atomic Spectroscopy
Atmos. Environ.	Atmospheric Environment
Atomization Sprays	Atomization and Sprays
Aust. J. Chem.	Australian Journal of Chemistry
以 B 字母开头的期刊	Journals beginning with B letters
Back to Top Behav. Pharmacol.	Back to Top Behavioural Pharmacology

Ber.Chemische Berichte	Ber. Bunsen–Ges. Phys. Chem Berichte der Bunsen–Gesellschaft Physical Chemistry Chemical Physics
Biocatal. Biotransform.	Biocatalysis and Biotransformation
Biochem. Arch.	Biochemical Archives
Biochem. Biophys. Res. Commun.	Biochemical and Biophysical Research Communications
Biochem. Cell Biol.	Biochemistry and Cell Biology–Biochimie et Biologie Cellulaire
Biochem. Eng. J.	Biochemical Engineering Journal
Biochem. Genet.	Biochemical Genetics
Biochem. J	Biochemical Journal
Biochem. Med. Metab. Biol.	Biochemical Medicine and Metabolic Biology
Biochem. Mol. Biol. Int.	Biochemistry and Molecular Biology International
Biochem. Mol. Med.	Biochemical and Molecular Medicine
Biochem. Pharmacol.	Biochemical Pharmacology
Biochem. Soc. Symp.	Biochemical Society Symposium
Biochem. Soc. Trans.	Biochemical Society Transactions
Biochem. Syst. Ecol.	Biochemical Systematics and Ecology
Biochim. Biophys. Acta	Biochimica et Biophysica Acta
Bioconjugate Chem.	Bioconjugate Chemistry
Bioelectrochem. Bioenerg.	Bioelectrochemistry and Bioenergetics
Biog. Amines	Biogenic Amines
Biol. Chem.	Biological Chemistry
Biol. Chem. Hoppe–Seyler	Biological Chemistry Hoppe–Seyler
Biol. Membr.	Biological Membranes
Biol. Pharm. Bull.	Biological and Pharmaceutical Bulletin
Biol. Trace Elem. Res.	Biological Trace Element Research

Biomass Bioenergy	Biomass and Bioenergy
Biomed. Chromatogr.	Biomedical Chromatography
Bio–Med. Mater. Eng.	Bio–Medical Materials and Engineering
Biomed. Microdevices	Biomedical Microdevices
Biomol. Eng	Biomolecular Engineering
Bioorg. Chem.	Bioorganic Chemistry
Bioorg. Khim	Bioorganicheskaya Khimiya（Russian Journal of Bioorganic Chemistry）
Bioorg. Med. Chem.	Bioorganic and Medicinal Chemistry
Bioorg. Med. Chem. Lett.	Bioorganic and Medicinal Chemistry Letters
Biopharm. Drug Dispos.	Biopharmaceutics and Drug Disposition
Biophys. Chem.	Biophysical Chemistry
Biophys. J .	Biophysical Journal
Bioprocess. Eng.	Bioprocess Engineering
Biorem. J.	Bioremediation Journal
Bioresour. Technol.	Bioresource Technology
Biosci. Rep.	Bioscience Reports
Biosci., Biotechnol., Biochem.	Bioscience Biotechnology and Biochemistry
Biosens. Bioelectron.	Biosensors and Bioelectronics
Biotech. Histochem.	Biotechnic and Histochemistry
Biotechnol. Adv.	Biotechnology Advances
Biotechnol. Appl. Biochem.	Biotechnology and Applied Biochemistry
Biotechnol. Bioeng.	Biotechnology and Bioengineering
Biotechnol. Biotechnol. Equip.	Biotechnology and Biotechnological Equipment
Biotechnol. Lett	Biotechnology Letters
Biotechnol. Progr.	Biotechnology Progress
Biotechnol. Tech.	Biotechnology Techniques
Bol. Soc. Chil. Quim.	Boletin de la Sociedad Chilena de Quimica

Br. Ceram. Trans.	British Ceramic Transactions
Br. Corros. J.	British Corrosion Journal
Br. J. Pharmacol.	British Jornal of Pharmacology
Brennst.–Warme–Kraft	Brennstoff–Warme–Kraft
Bull. Chem. Soc. Jpn.	Bulletin of the Chemical Society of Japan
Bull. Electrochem.	Bulletin of Electrochemistry
Bull. Environ. Contam. Toxicol.	Bulletin of Environment Contamination and Toxicology
Bull. Hist. Chem.	Bulletin for the History of Chemistry
Bull. Korean Chem. Soc.	Bulletin of the Korean Chemical Society
Bull. Mater. Sci.	Bulletin of Materials Science
Bull. Pol. Acad. Sci., Chem.	Bulletin of the Polish Academy of Sciences Chemistry
Bull. Soc. Chim. Belg.	Bulletin des Societes Chimiques Belges
Bull. Soc. Chim. Fr.	Bulletin de la Societe Chimique de France

以 C 字母开头的期刊   Journals beginning with C letters

Chem. Rev.	Chemical Reviews
Chem. Senses	Chemical Senses
Chem. Soc. Rev.	Chemical Society Reviews
Chem. Speciation Bioavailability	Chemical Speciation and Bioavailability
Chem. Tech.	Chem Tech
Chem. Tech.（Leipzig）	Chemische Technik
Chem. Technol. Fuels Oils	Chemistry and Technology of Fuels and Oils
Chem. Vap. Deposition	Chemical Vapor Deposition
Chem. Week	Chemical Week
Chem. unserer Zeit	Chemie in unserer Zeit
Chemom. Intell. Lab. Syst.	Chemometrics and Intelligent Laborary Systems
Chin. Chem. Lett.	Chinese Chemical Letters

Chin. J. Chem .	Chinese Journal of Chemistry
Chin. J. Chem. Eng.	Chinese Journal of Chemical Engineering
Chin. J. Nucl. Phys.	Chinese Journal of Nuclear Physics
Chin. J. Polym. Sci.	Chinese Journal of Polymer Science
Chin. Sci. Bull.	Chinese Science Bulletin
Chromatogr. Sci. Ser.	Chromatographic Science Series
CIM Bull.	CIM Bulletin
Clays Clay Miner.	Clays and Clay Minerals
Clin. Biochem.	Clinical Biochemistry
Clin. Chem.	Clinical Chemistry
Clin. Chim. Acta	Clinica Chimica Acta
Collect. Czech. Chem. Commun.	Collection of Czechoslovak Chemical Communications
Colloid J.	Colloid Journal
Colloid. Polym. Sci.	Colloid and Polymer Science
Colloids Surf., A	Colloids and Surfaces A
Colloids Surf., B	Colloids and Surfaces B
Comb. Chem. High Throughput Screening	Combinatorial Chemistry and High Throughput Screening
Combust. Flame	Combustion and Flame
Combust. Sci. Technol.	Combustion Science and Technology
Comments Inorg. Chem.	Comments on Inorganic Chemistry
Comp. Biochem. Physiol. A: Physiol.	Comparative Biochemistry and Physiology A: Physiology
C.R. Acad. Sci., Ser. III	Comptes Rendus de l' Academie des Sciences Serie III: Sciences de la Vie
C.R. Acad. Sci., Ser. IIa: SciTerre Planets	Comptes Rendus de l' Academie des Sciences Serie IIa:Sciences de la Terre et des Planets
C.R. Acad. Sci., Ser. IIb: Mec., Phys., Chim., Astron.	Comptes Rendus de l' Academie des Sciences Serie IIb:Mecanique Physique Chimie Astronomie

C.R. Acad. Sci., Ser. IIc: Chim.	Comptes Rendus de l'Academie des Sciences Serie IIc:Chemie
Cah. Inf. Tech./Rev Metall	Cahiers d'Informations Techniques / Revue de Metallurgie
Calphad	Calphad – Computer Coupling of Phase Diagrams and Thermochemistry
Can. Ceram. Q.	Canadian Ceramics Quarterly
Can. J. Anal. Sci. Spectros.	Canadian Journal of Analytical Sciences and Spectroscopy
Can. J. Biochem.	Canadian Journal of Biochemistry
Can. J. Chem.	Canadian Journal of Chemistry
Can. J. Chem. Eng.	Canadian Journal of Chemical Engineering
Can. J. Microbiol.	Canadian Journal of Microbiology
Can. J. Phys.	Canadian Journal of Physics
Can. J. Physiol. Pharmacol.	Canadian Journal of Physiology and Pharmacology
Can. Metall. Q.	Canadian Metallurgical Quarterly
Can. Min. J.	Canadian Mining Journal
Can. Mineral.	Canadian Mineralogist
Carbohydr. Chem.	Carbohydrate Chemistry
Carbohydr. Lett.	Carbohydrate Letters
Carbohydr. Polym.	Carbohydrate Polymers
Carbohydr. Res.	Carbohydrate Research
Cat. Rev. – Sci. Eng.	Catalysis Reviews – Science and Engineering
Catal. Commun.	Catalysis Communications
Catal. Lett.	Catalysis Letters
Catal. Today	Catalysis Today
Cell Biochem. Funct.	Cell Biochemistry and Function
Cell. Physiol. Biochem.	Cellular Physiology and Biochemistry
Cell. Polym.	Cellular Polymers

Cellul. Chem. Technol.   Cellulose Chemistry and Technology

Cem. Concr. Compos.   Cement and Concrete Composites

Cem. Concr. Res.   Cement and Concrete Research

Ceram. Int.   Ceramics International

Ceram. Silik.   Ceramics – Silikaty

Ceram. Trans.   Ceramic Transactions

Cereal Chem.   Cereal Chemistry

Chem. –Anlagen Verfahren   Chemie Anlagen und Verfahren

Chem. Anal. (Warsaw)   Chemia Analityczna

Chem. Aust.   Chemistry in Australia

Chem. Ber.   Chemische Berichte

Chem. Ber. Recl   Chemische Berichte–Recueil

Chem. Biochem. Eng. Q.   Chemical and Biochemical Engineering Quarterly

Chem. Biol. Interact.   Chemico–Biological Interactions

Chem. Br.   Chemistry in Britain

Chem. Commun.   Chemical Communications

Chem. Eng. (London)   Chemical Engineer (London)

Chem. Eng. (New York)   Chemical Engineering (New York)

Chem. Eng. Commun.   Chemical Engineering Communications

Chem. Eng. J.   Chemical Engineering Journal

Chem. Eng. News   Chemical and Engineering News

Chem. Eng. Process.   Chemical Engineering and Processing

Chem. Eng. Prog.   Chemical Engineering Progress

Chem. Eng. Res. Des.   Chemical Engineering Research and Design

Chem. Eng. Sci.   Chemical Engineering Science

Chem. Eng. Technol.   Chemical Engineering and Technology

Chem. Eur. J.   Chemistry– A European Journal

Chem. Express	Chemistry Express
Chem. Fibers Int.	Chemical Fibers International
Chem. Eur. J.	Chemistry A European Journal
Chem. Geol.	Chemical Geology
Chem. Heterocycl. Compd.	Chemistry of Heterocyclic Compounds
Chem. Ind. (london)	Chemistry and Industry
Chem. Ing. Tech.	Chemie Ingenieur Technik
Chem. Lett.	Chemistry Letters
Chem. Listy	Chemicke Listy
Chem. Mater.	Chemistry of Materials
Chem. Nat. Compd.	Chemistry of Natural Compounds
Chem. Pap. – Chem. Zvesti	Chemical Papers – Chemicke Zvesti
Chem. Pharm. Bull.	Chemical and Pharmaceutical Bulletin
Chem. Phys.	Chemical Physics
Chem. Phys. Carbon	Chemistry and Physics of Carbon
Chem. Phys. Lett.	Chemical Physics Letters
Chem. Phys. Lipids	Chemistry and Physics of Lipids
Chem. Process.	Chemical Processing
Chem. Res. Toxicol.	Chemical Research in Toxicology
Comp. Biochem. Physiol. B: Biochem. Mol. Biol.	Comparative Biochemistry and Physiology B: Biochemistry and Molecular Biology
Comp. Biochem. Physiol. C: Pharmacol. Toxicol.	Comparative Biochemistry and Physiology C: Pharmacology Toxicology and Endocrinology
Compos. Eng.	Composites Engineering
Compos. Interfaces	Composite Interfaces
Compos. Sci. Technol.	Composites Science and Technology
Compos. Struct.	Composite Structures

Composites Part A — Composites Part A: Applied Science and Manufacturing

Composites Part B — Composites Part B: Engineering

Comput. Chem.（Oxford） — Computers and Chemistry

Comput. Chem. Eng. — Computers and Chemical Engineering

Comput. Mater. Sci. — Computation Materials Science

Comput. Phys. Commun. — Computer Physics Communications

Comput. Theor. Polym. Sci. — Computational and Theoretical Polymer Science

Concepts Magn. Reson. — Concepts in Magenetic Resonance

Concr. Eng. Int. — Concrete Engineering International

Concr. Int. — Concrete International

Concr. Sci. Eng. — Concrete Science and Engineering

Condens. Matter Phys. — Condensed Matter Physics

Condens. Matter Theor. — Condensed Matter Theories

Continuum Mech. Thermodyn. — Continuum Mechanics and Thermodynamics

Contrib. Mineral. Petrol. — Contributions to Mineralogy and Petrology

Coord. Chem. Rev. — Coordination Chemistry Reviews

Corros. Rev. — Corrosion Reviews

Corros. Sci. — Corrosion Science

CPP Chem. Plants and Process. — CPP Chemical Plants and Processing

Crit. Rev. Anal. Chem. — Critical Reviews in Analytical Chemistry

Crit. Rev. Biochem. Mol. Biol. — Critical Reviews in Biochemistry and Molecular Biology

Crit. Rev. Biotechnol. — Critical Reviews in Biotechnology

Crit. Rev. Env. Sci. Technol. — Critical Reviews in Environment Science and Technology

Crit. Rev. Solid State Mater. Sci. — Critical Reviews in Solid State and Materials Sciences

Crit. Rev. Toxicol.	Critical Reviews in Toxicology
Croat. Chem. Acta	Croatica Chemica Acta
Cryst. Eng.	Crystal Engineering
Cryst. Growth Des.	Crystal Growth and Design
Cryst. Res. Technol.	Crystal Research and Technology
Curr. Opin. Biotechnol.	Current Opinion in Biotechnology
Curr. Opin. Chem. Biol.	Current Opinion in Chemical Biology
Curr. Opin. Colloid Interface Sci.	Current Opinion in Colloid and Interface Science
Curr. Opin. Pharmacol.	Current Opinion in Pharmacology
Curr. Opin. Solid State Mater. Sci.	Current Opinion in Solid State and Materials Science
Curr. Org. Chem.	Current Organic Chemistry
Curr. Plant Sci. Biotechnol. Agric.	Current Plant Science in Biotechnology and Agriculture
Curr. Top. Membr.	Current Topics in Membranes
Curr. Top. Med. Chem.	Current Topics in Medicinal Chemistry

以 D 字母开头的期刊　　　　　　　　　　Journals beginning with D letters

Dent. Mater.	Dental Materials
Diamond Films Technol.	Diamond Films and Technology
Diamond Relat. Mater.	Diamond and Related Materials
Dokl. Akad. Nauk	Doklady Akademii Nauk
Drug Chem. Toxicol.	Drug and Chemical Toxicology
Drug Dev. Ind. Pharm.	Drug Development and Industrial Pharmacy
Drug Dev. Res.	Drug Development Research
Drug Discovery Today	Drug Discovery Today
Drying Technol.	Drying Technology

以 E 字母开头的期刊　　　　　　　　　　Journals beginning with E letters

Electrochem. Soc. Interface	Electrochemical Society Interface

Electrochem. Solid–State Lett.	Electrochemical and Solid–State Letters
Electrochim. Acta	Electrochimica Acta
Electron. Lett	Electronics Letters
Electron Technol.	Electronic Technology
EMBO J.	EMBO Journal
Energy Convers. Manage.	Energy Conversion and Management
Energy Fuels	Energy and Fuels
Eng. Min. J.	Engineering and Mining Journal
Environ. Carcinog. Ecotoxicol. Rev.	Environment Carcinogenesis and Ecotoxicology Reviews
Environ. Geochem. Health	Environmental Geochemistry and Health
Environ. Geol.	Environmental Geology
Environ. Health Perspect.	Environmental Health Perspectives
Environ. Microbiol.	Environmental Microbiology
Environ. Monit. Assess.	Environmental Monitoring and Assessment
Environ. Pollut.	Environmental Pollution
Environ. Prog.	Environmental Progress
Environ. Res.	Environmental Research
Environ. Sci. Technol.	Environmental Science and Technology
Environ. Technol.	Environmental Technology
Environ. Toxicol. Chem.	Environmental Toxicology and Chemistry
Environ. Toxicol. Pharmacol.	Environmental Toxicology and Pharmacology
Environ. Toxicol. Water Qual.	Environmental Toxicology and Water Quality
Enzyme Microb. Technol.	Enzyme and Microbial Technology
Enzyme Protein	Enzyme and Protein
Erdol and Kohle Erdgas, Petrochem.	Erdol and Kohle Erdgas, Petrochemie
Eur. J. Biochem.	European Journal of Biochemistry

Eur. J. Clin. Chem. Clin. Biochem.	European Journal of Clinical Chemistry and Clinical Biochemistry
Eur. J. Inorg. Chem.	European Journal of Inorganic Chemistry
Eur. J. Lipid Sci. Technol.	European Journal of Lipid Science and Technology
Eur. J. Mass Spectrom.	European Journal of Mass Spectrometry
Eur. J. Med. Chem.	European Journal of Medical Chemistry
Eur. J. Mineral.	European Journal of Mineralogy
Eur. J. Org. Chem.	European Journal of Organic Chemistry
Earth. Planet. Sci. Lett.	Earth and Planetary Science Letters
Ecol. Eng.	Ecological Engineering
Econ. Geol.	Economic Geology and the Bulletin of the Society of Economic Geologists
Ecotoxicol. Environ. Saf.	Ecotoxicology and Environment Safety
Educ. Chem.	Education in Chemistry
Electro– Magnetobiol.	Electro– and Magnetobiology
Electrochem. Commun.	Electrochemistry Communications
Eur. J. Pharmacol.	European Journal of Pharmacology
Eur. J. Solid State Inorg. Chem.	European Journal of Solid State and Inorganic Chemistry
Eur. Mass Spectrom.	European Mass Spectrometry
Eur. Polym. J.	European Polymer Journal
Europhys. Lett.	Europhysics Letters
Exp. Fluids	Experiments in Fluids
Exp. Therm Fluid Sci.	Experimental Thermal and Fluid Science
Explor. Min. Geol.	Exploration and Mining Geology
以 F 字母开头的期刊	Journals beginning with F letters
Faraday Discuss.	Faraday Discussions
FASEB J.	FASEB Journal

Fatigue Fract. Eng. Mater. Struct.	Fatigue and Fracture of Engineering Materials and Structures
FEBS Lett.	FEBS Letters
FEMS Immunol. Med. Microbiol.	FEMS Immunology And Medical Microbiology
FEMS Microbiol. Ecol.	FEMS Microbiology Ecology
FEMS Microbiol. Lett.	FEMS Microbiology Letters
FEMS Microbiol. Rev.	FEMS Microbiology Review
Ferroelectr. Rev.	Ferroelectrics Review
Ferroelectr. Lett.	Ferroelectrics Letters
Fett – Lipid	Fett – Lipid
Fiber Integr. Opt.	Fiber and Integrated Optics
Field Anal. Chem. Technol.	Field Analytical Chemistry and Technology.
Filtr. Sep.	Filtration and Separation
Fiz. Met. Metalloved.	Fizika Metallov i Metallovedenie
Fluid/Part. Sep. J.	Fluid/Particle Separation Journal
Fluid Phase Equilib.	Fluid Phase Equilibria
Fold Des.	Folding and Design
Food Addit. Contam.	Food Additives and Contaminants
Food Biotechnol.	Food Biotechnology
Food Chem.	Food Chemistry
Food Chem. Toxicol.	Food and Chemical Toxicology
Food Sci. Technol. Int.	Food Science and Technology International
Free Radical Biol. Med.	Free Radical Biology and Medicine
Free Radical Res.	Free Radical Research
Fresenius Environ. Bull.	Fresenius Environment bulletin
Fresenius J. Anal. Chem.	Fresenius Journal of Analytical Chemistry
Front Sci. Ser.	Frontier Science Series
Fuel Process. Technol.	Fuel Processing Technology

Fuel Sci. Technol. Int.　　　　　　　Fuel Science and Technology International

Fullerene Sci. Technol.　　　　　　　Fullerene Science and Technology

Funct. Integr. Genomics　　　　　　Functional and Integrative Genomics

Fundam. Appl. Toxicol.　　　　　　　Fundamental and Applied Toxicology

Fusion Eng. Des.　　　　　　　　　Fusion Engineering and Design

Fusion Technol.　　　　　　　　　Fusion Technology

以 G 字母开头的期刊　　　　　　Journals beginning with G letters

Galvanotechnik　　　　　　　　　Galvanotechnik

Gas Sep. Purif.　　　　　　　　　Gas Separation and Purification

Gazz. Chim. Ital.　　　　　　　　Gazzetta Chimica Italiana

Gefahrstoffe – Reinhalt. Luft　　　　Gefahrstoffe Reinhaltung der Luft

Genet. Anal. – Biomol. Eng.　　　　Genetic Analysis – Biomolecular Engineering

Geochem. Geophys. Geosyst.　　　　Geochemistry, Geophysics, Geosystems

Geochem. J.　　　　　　　　　　Geochemical Journal

Geochem. Trans.　　　　　　　　Geochemical Transactions

Geochem.: Explor. Environ., Anal.　　Geochemistry: Exploration, Environment, Analysis

Geochim. Cosmochim. Acta　　　　Geochimica et Cosmochimica Acta

Geol Geofiz　　　　　　　　　　Geologiya i Geofizika

Geomicrobiol. J.　　　　　　　　Geomicrobiology Journal

Glass Ceram.　　　　　　　　　Glass and Ceramics

Glass Phys. Chem　　　　　　　Glass Physics and Chemistry

Glass Res.　　　　　　　　　　Glass Research

Glass Sci. Technol.　　　　　　　Glass Science and Technology

Glass Technol.　　　　　　　　　Glass Technology

Global Biogeochem. Cycles　　　　Global Biogeochemical Cycles

Global J. Pure Appl. Sci.　　　　　Global Journal of Pure and Applied Sciences

Glycoconjugate J.　　　　　　　　Glycoconjugate Journal

Green Chem.	Greem Chemistry
Ground Water Monit. Rem.	Ground Water Monitoring and Remediation

以 H 字母开头的期刊 Journals beginning with H letters

Handb. Exp. Pharmacol.	Handbook of Experimental Pharmacology
Hazard. Waste Hazard. Mater.	Hazardous Waste and Hazardous Materials
He Iv. Chim. Acta	He Ivetica Chimica Acta
Health Phys.	Health Physics
Heat Mass Transfer.	Heat and Mass Transfer
Heat Treat. Met.	Heat Treatment of Metals
Heteroat. Chem	Heteroatom Chemistry
Heterocycl. Commun.	Heterocyclic Communications
Heterogen. Chem. Rev.	Heterogeneous Chemistry Reviews
High Energ. Chem.	High Energy Chemistry
High Perform. Polym.	High Performance Polymers
High Temp. Mater. Processes（London）	High Temperature Materials and Processes
High Temp. Mater. Processes（New York）	High Temperature Material Processes
Holz Roh Werkst.	Holz als Roh und Werkstoff
Hoppe−Seyler's Z. Physiol. Chem.	Hoppe−Seyler's Zeitschrift fur Physiologische Chemie
HRC J. High Resolut. Chromatogr.	HRC Journal of High Resolution Chromatography
Hung. J. Ind. Chem.	Hungarian Journal of Industrial Chemistry
Hydrocarbon Process., Int. Ed.	Hydrocarbon Processing, International Edition
Hyperfine Interact.	Hyperfine Interactions

以 I 字母开头的期刊 Journals beginning with I letters

IEEE Sens. J.	IEEE Sensors Journal
Ind. Diamond Rev.	Industrial Diamond Review
Ind. Eng. Chem.	Industrial and Engineering Chemistry

Ind. Eng. Chem., Anal. Ed.	Industrial and Engineering Chemistry, Analytical Edition
Ind. Eng. Chem. Fundam.	Industrial and Engineering Chemistry Fundamentals
Ind. Eng. Chem. Res.	Industrial and Engineering Chemistry Research
Indian J. Biochem. Biophys.	Indian Journal of Biochemistry and Biophysics
Indian J. Chem. Technol.	Indian Journal of Chemical Technology
Indian J. Chem., Sect A	Indian Journal of Chemistry Section A: Inorganic, Bio-inorganic, Physical, Theoretical and Analytical Chemistry
Indian J. Chem., Sect B	Indian Journal of Chemistry Section B: Organic Chemistry including Medicinal Chemistry
Indian J. Eng. Mater. Sci.	Indian Journal of Engineering and Materials Science
Indian J. Heterocycl. Chem.	Indian Journal of Heterocyclic Chemistry
Indian J. Pure Appl. Phys.	Indian Journal of Pure and Applied Physics
Indian J. Technol.	Indian Journal of Technology
Ing. Quim.	Ingeniera Quimica (Madrid)
Infrared Phys. Technol.	Infrared Physics and Technology
Inorg. Chem.	Inorganic Chemistry
Inorg. Chem. Commun.	Inorganic Chemistry Communications
Inorg. Chim. Acta	Inorganica Chimica Acta
Inorg. Mater.	Inorganic Materials
Inorg. React. Mech.	Inorganic Reaction Mechanisms
Inorg. Synth.	Inorganic Syntheses
Insect Biochem. Mol. Biol.	Insect Biochemisry and Molecular Biology
Instrum Sci. Technol.	Instrumentation Science and Technology
Int. Biodeterior. Biodegrad.	International Biodeterioration and Biodegradation

Int. DATA Ser., Sel. Data Mixtures, Ser. A	International DATA Series, Selected Data on Mixtures, Series A
Int. J. Adhes. Adhes.	International Journal of Adhesion and Adhesives
Int. J. Biochem.	International Journal of Biochemistry
Int. J. Biochem. Cell Biol.	International Journal of Biochemistry and Cell Biology
Int. J. Bio–Chromatogr.	International Journal of Biochromatography
Int. J. Biol. Macromol.	International Journal of Biological Macromolecules
Int. J. Cast Met. Res.	International Journal of Cast Metals Research
Int. J. Chem. Kinet.	International Journal of Chemical Kinetics
Int. J. Electrochem. Sci.	International Journal of Electrochemical Science
Int. J. Environ. Anal. Chem.	International Journal of Environment Analytical Chemistry
Int. J. Fatigue	International Journal of Fatigue
Int. J. Heat Fluid Flow	International Journal of Heat and fluid flow
Int. J. Heat Mass Transfer	International Journal of Heat and Mass Transfer
Int. J. Hydrogen Energy	International Journal of Hydrogen Energy
Int. J. Immunopharmacol	International Journal of Immunopharmacology
Int. J. Impact Eng.	International Journal of Impact Engineering
Int. J. Inorg. Mater.	International Journal of Inorganic Materials
Int. J. Mass spectrom.	International Journal of Mass Spectrometry
Int. J. Mass Spectrom. Ion Processes	International Journal of Mass Spectrometry and Ion Processes
Int. J. Miner. Process.	International Journal of Mineral Processing
Int. J. Mod Phys B	International Journal of Modern Physics B
Int. J. Multiphase Flow	International Journal of Multiphase Flow
Int. J. Numer. Methods Fluids	International Journal for Numerical Methods in Fluids
Int. J. Oncol.	International Journal of Oncology

Int. J. Pept. Protein Res.	International Journal of Peptide and Protein Research
Int. J. Pharm.	International Journal of Pharmaceutics
Int. J. Phytorem.	International Journal of Phytoremediation
Int. J. Plast.	International Journal of Plasticity
Int. J. Polym. Anal. Charact.	International Journal of Polymer Analysis and Characterization
Int. J. Polymer. Mater.	International Journal of Polymeric Materials
Int. J. Powder Metall.	International Journal of Powder Metallurgy
Int. J. Quantum Chem	International Journal of Quantum Chemistry
Int. J. Radiat Biol.	International Journal of Radiation Biology
Int. J. Refract. Met. Hard Mater.	International Journal of Refractory Metals and Hard Materials
Int. J. Self–Propag. High–Temp Synth.	International Journal of Self–Propagating High–Temperature Synthesis
Int. J. Thermophys.	International Journal of Thermophysics
Int. Mater. Rev.	International Materials Reviews
Int. Polym. Proc.	International Polymer Processing
Int. Rev. Phys. Chem.	International Reviews in Physical Chemistry
Interface Sci.	Interface Science
Internet J. Vib. Spectro.	Internet Journal of Vibrational Spectroscopy
Internet J. Chem.	Internet Journal of Chemistry
Inz. Chem. Procesowa	Inzynieria Chemiczna Procesowa
Ironmaking Steelmaking	Ironmaking and Steelmaking
ISIJ Int.	ISIJ International
Isr. J. Chem.	Israel Journal of Chemistry
以 J 字母开头的期刊	Journals beginning with J letters
J. Adhes.	Journal of Adhesion
J. Adhes. Sci. Technol.	Journal of Adhesion Science and Technology

J. Adv. Mater.	Journal of Advanced Materials
J. Aerosol Sci	Journal of Aerosol Science
J. Agric. Food. Chem.	Journal of Agricultural and Food Chemistry
J. Air Waste Manage. Assoc.	Journal of the Air and Waste Management
J. Alloys Compd.	Journal of Alloys and Compounds
J. Am. Ceram. Soc.	Journal of the American Ceramic Society
J. Am. Chem. Soc.	Journal of the American Chemical Society
J. Am. Oil Chem. Soc.	Journal of the American Oil Chemists Society
J. Am. Soc. Brew. Chem.	Journal of the American Society of Brewing Chemists
J. Am. Soc. Mass. Spectrom.	Journal of the American Society for Mass Spectrometry
J. Amer. Chem. Soc.	Journal of the American Chemical Society
J. Anal. Appl. Pyrolysis	Journal of Analytical and Applied Pyrolysis
J. Anal. At. Spectrom.	Journal of Analytical Atomic Spectrometry
J. Anal. Chem	Journal of Analytical Chemistry
J. Anal. Toxicol.	Journal of Analytical Toxicology
J. Antibiot.	Journal of Antibiotics
J. Antimicrob. Chemother.	Journal of Antimicrobial Chemotherapy
J. AOAC Int.	Journal of AOAC International
J. Appl. Bacteriol.	Journal of Applied Bacteriology
J. Appl. Biomater.	Journal of Applied Biomaterials
J. Appl. Crystallogr.	Journal of Applied Crystallography
J. Appl. Electrochem.	Journal of Applied Electrochemistry
J. Appl. Phycol.	Journal of Applied Phycology
J. Appl. Phys.	Journal of Applied Physics
J. Appl. Polym. Sci.	Journal of Applied Polymer Science
J. Appl. Spectrosc.	Journal of Applied Spectroscopy

J. Appl. Toxicol.	Journal of Applied Toxicology
J. Asian Nat. Prod. Res.	Journal of Asian Natural Products Research
J. Autom. Chem.	Journal of Automatic Chemistry
J. Autom. Methods Manage. Chem.	Journal of Automated Methods & Management in Chemistry
J. Bacteriol.	Journal of Bacteriology
J. Bioact. Compat. Polym.	Journal of Bioactive and Bompatible Polymers
J. Biochem.	Journal of Biochemistry
J. Biochem. Bioph. Methods	Journal of Biochemical and Biophysical Methods
J. Biol. Chem.	Journal of Biological Chemistry
J. Biol. Inorg. Chem.	Journal of Biological Inorganic Chemistry
J. Biolumin. Chemilumin.	Journal of Bioluminescence and Chemiluminescence
J. Biomater. Appl.	Journal of Biomaterials Applications
J. Biomater. Sci., Polym. Ed.	Journal of Biomaterials Science Polymer Edition
J. Biomed. Mater. Res.	Journal of Biomedial Materials Research
J. Biomol. NMR	Journal of Biomolecular NMR
J. Biomol. Struct. Dyn.	Journal of Biomolecular Structure and Dynamics
J. Biotechnol.	Journal of Biotechnology
J. Can. Pet. Technol.	Journal of Canadian Petroleum Technology
J. Carbohydr. Chem.	Journal of Carbohydrate Chemistry
J. Cardiovasc. Pharmacol.	Journal of Cardiovascular Pharmacology
J. Catal.	Journal of Catalysis
J. Cell. Biochem.	Journal of Cellular Biochemistry
J. Cell Biol.	Journal of Cell Biology
J. Cell. Physiol.	Journal of Cellular Physiology
J. Cell Sci.	Journal of Cell Science
J. Ceram. Soc. Jpn.	Journal of the Ceramic Society of Japan

J. Chem. Crystallogr.	Journal of Chemical Crystallography
J. Chem. Ecol.	Journal of Chemical Ecology
J. Chem. Educ.	Journal of Chemical Education
J. Chem. Eng. Data	Journal of Chemical and Engineering Data
J. Chem. Eng. Jpn.	Journal of Chemical Engineering of Japan
J. Chem. Inf. Comput. Sci.	Journal of Chemical Information and Computer Science
J. Chem. Neuroanat.	Journal of Chemical Neuroanatomy
J. Chem. Phys.	Journal of Chemical Physics
J . Chem. Res., Synop .	Journal of Chemical Research Synopsis
J. Chem. Soc.	Journal of the Chemical Society
J. Chem. Soc. Pak.	Journal of the Chemical Society of Pakistan
J. Chem. Soc., Chem. Commun.	Journal of the Chemical Society, Chemical Communications
J. Chem. Soc., Dalton Trans.	Journal of the Chemical Society, Dalton Transactions
J. Chem. Soc., Faraday Trans.	Journal of the Chemical Society, Faraday Transactions
J. Chem. Soc., Perkin Trans. 1	Journal of the Chemical Society, Perkin Transactions 1
J. Chem. Soc., Perkin Trans. 2	Journal of the Chemical Society, Perkin Transactions 2
J. Chem. Technol. Biotechnol.	Journal of Chemical Technology and Biotechnology
J. Chem. Thermodyn.	Journal of Chemical Thermodynamics
J. Chemom.	Journal of Chemometrics
J. Chim. Phys. Phys.– Chim. Biol.	Journal de Chimie Physique et de Physico–Chimie Biologique
J. Chin. Chem. Soc.	Journal of the Chinese Chemical Society

J. Chin. Inst. Chem. Eng,	Journal of the Chinese Institute of Chemical Engineers
J. Chromatogr.	Journal of Chromatography
J. Chromatogr. A	Journal of Chromatography A
J. Chromatogr. B	Journal of Chromatography B
J. Chromatogr. Sci.	Journal of Chromatographic Science
J. Clin. Endocrinol. Metab.	Journal of Clinical Endocrinology and Metabolism
J. Clin. Microbiol.	Journal of Clinical Microbiology
J. Cluster Sci.	Journal of Cluster Science
J. Coat. Technol.	Journal of Coatings Technology
J. Colloid Interface Sci.	Journal of Colloid and Interface Science
J. Comb. Chem.	Journal of Combinatorial Chemistry
J. Compos. Mater.	Journal of Composite Materials
J. Compos. Tech. Res.	Journal of Composites Technology and Research
J. Comput. Aided Mater. Des.	Journal of Computer–Aided Materials Design
J. Comput. Aided Mol. Des.	Journal of Computer–Aided Molecular Design
J. Comput. Chem.	Journal of Computational Chemistry
J . Contam. Hydrol.	Journal of Contaminant Hydrology
J. Controlled Release	Journal of Controlled Release
J. Coord. Chem.	Journal of Coordination Chemistry
J. Cryst. Growth	Journal of Crystal Growth
J. Dairy Sci.	Journal of Dairy Science
J. Dispersion Sci. Technol.	Journal of Dispersion Science and Technology
J. Elastomers Plast.	Journal of Elastomers and Plastics
J. Electroanal. Chem.	Journal of Electroanalytical Chemistry
J. Electroceram.	Journal of Electroceramics
J. Electrochem. Soc.	Journal of the Electrochemical Society
J. Electron. Mater.	Journal of Electronic Materials

J. Electron Microsc.	Journal of Electron Microscopy
J. Electron. Spectrosc. Relat. Phenom.	Journal of Electron Spectroscopy and Related Phenomena
J. Electrostat.	Journal of Electrostatics
J. Endocrinol.	Journal of Endocrinology
J. Endotoxin Res.	Journal of Endotoxin Research
J. Eng. Mater. Technol.	Journal of Engineering Materials and Technology
J. Environ. Biol.	Journal of Environment biology
J. Environ. Eng.	Journal of Environment Engineering
J. Environ. Health	Journal of Environment Health
J. Environ. Manage.	Journal of Environment Management
J. Environ. Monit.	Journal of Environmental Monitoring
J. Environ. Qual.	Journal of Environment Quality
J. Environ. Radioact.	Journal of Environment Radioactivity
J. Environ. Sci. Health., Part A	Journal of Environment Science and Health, Part A Environmental Science
J. Environ. Sci. Health., Part B	Journal of Environment Science and Health, Part B Pesticides
J. Enzym Inhib.	Journal of Enzyme Inhibition
J. Essent. Oil Res.	Journal of Essential Oil Research
J. Ethnopharmacol.	Journal of Ethnopharmacology
J. Eur. Ceram. Soc.	Journal of the European Ceramic Society
J. Exp. Biol.	Journal of Experimental Biology
J. Exp. Bot.	Journal of Experimental Botany
J. Exposure Anal. Environ. Epidemiol.	Journal of Exposure Analysis and Environment Epidemiology
J. Ferment. Bioeng.	Journal of Fermentation and Bioengineering
J. Fire Sci.	Journal of Fire Sciences
J. Fluid Mech.	Journal of Fluid Mechanics

J. Fluids Eng.	Journal of Fluids Engineering
J. Fluorine Chem.	Journal of Fluorine Chemistry
J. Food Biochem.	Journal of Food Biochemistry
J. Food Eng.	Journal of Food Engineering
J. Food Lipids	Journal of Food Lipids
J. Food Prot.	Journal of Food Protection
J. Food Sci.	Journal of Food Science
J. Gen. Appl. Microbiol.	Journal of General and Applied Microbiology
J. Gen. Microbiol.	Journal of General Microbiology
J. Hazard. Mater.	Journal of Hazardous materials
J. Heat Transfer	Journal of Heat Transfer
J. Heterocycl. Chem.	Journal of Heterocyclic Chemistry
J. High. Resolut. Chromatogr.	Journal of High Resolution Chromatography
J. Histochem. Cytochem.	Journal of Histochemistry and Cytochemistry
J. Hypertens.	Journal of Hypertension
J. Imaging Sci. Technol.	Journal of Imaging Science and Technology
J. Inclusion Phenom. Mol. Recognit. Chem.	Journal of Inclusion Phenomena and Molecular Recognition in Chemistry
J. Ind. Microbiol.	Journal of Industrial Microbiology
J. Indian Chem. Soc.	Journal of the Indian Chemical Society
J. Ind. Microbiol. Biotechnol.	Journal of Industrial Microbiology and Biotechnology
J. Inorg. Biochem.	Journal of Inorganic Biochemistry
J. Inorg. Nucl. Chem.	Journal of Inorganic and Nuclear Chemistry
J. Inorg. Organomet. Polym.	Journal of Inorganic and Organometallic Polymers
J. Inst. Chem.	Journal of Institute of Chemists (India)
J. Inst. Environ. Sci.	Journal of the Institute of Environment Sciences

J. Inst. Water Environ. Manage.	Journal of the Institution of Water and Environment Management
J. Intell. Mater. Syst. Struct.	Journal of Intelligent Material Systems and Structures
J. Interferon Cytokine Res.	Journal of Interferon and Cytokine Research Medicine
J. Mater. Sci. Technol.	Journal of Materials Science and Technology
J. Mater. Synth. Process.	Journal of Materials Synthesis and Processing
J. Math. Chem.	Journal of Mathematical Chemistry
J. Med. Chem.	Journal of Medicinal Chemistry
J. Membr. Biol.	Journal of Membrane Biology
J. Membr. Sci.	Journal of Membrane Science
J. Microbiol. Biotechnol.	Journal of Microbiology and Biotechnology
J. Microbiol. Methods	Journal of Microbiological Methods
J. Microcolumn Sep.	Journal of Microcolumn Separations
J. Microelectromech. Syst.	Journal of Microelectronic Systems
J. Microencapsulation	Journal of Microencapsulation
J. Mol. Biol.	Journal of Molecular Biology
J. Mol. Catal.	Journal of Molecular Catalysis
J. Mol. Catal. A: Chem.	Journal of Molecular Catalysis A: Chemical
J. Mol. Catal. B: Enzym.	Journal of Molecular Catalysis B: Enzymatic
J. Mol. Graphics Modell.	Journal of Molecular Graphics and Modelling
J. Mol. Liq.	Journal of Molecular Liquids
J. Mol. Microbiol. Biotechnol.	Journal of Molecular Microbiology and Biotechnology
J. Mol. Model.	Journal of Molecular Modeling
J. Mol. Spectrosc.	Journal of Molecular Spectroscopy
J. Mol. Struct.	Journal of Molecular Structure
J. Nanopart. Res.	Journal of Nanoparticle Research

J. Nat. Prod.	Journal of Natural Products
J. Near Infrared Spectrosc.	Journal of Near Infrared Spectroscopy
J. Neurochem.	Journal of Neurochemistry
J. Neurosci.	Journal of Neuroscience
J. Neurosci. Res.	Journal of Neuroscience Research
J. New Mater. Electrochem. Syst.	Journal of New Materials for Electrochemical Systems
J. Non-Cryst. Solids	Journal of Non-Crystalline Solids
J. Non-Equilib. Thermodyn.	Journal of Non-Equilibrium Thermodynamics
J. Nucl. Mater.	Journal of Nuclear Materials
J. Nucl. Sci. Technol.	Journal of Nuclear Science and Technology
J. Opt. Soc. Am. B: Opt. Phys.	Journal of the Optical Society of America B: Optical Physics
J. Org. Chem.	Journal of Organic Chemistry
J . Organomet. Chem.	Journal of Organometallic Chemistry
J. Pet. Sci. Technol.	Journal of Petroleum Science and Technology
J. Pharm. Biomed. Anal.	Journal of Pharmaceutical and Biomedical Analysis
J. Pharm. Pharmacol.	Journal of Pharmacy and Pharmacology
J. Pharm. Sci.	Journal of Pharmaceutical Sciences
J. Pharmacol. Exp. Ther.	Journal of Pharmacology and Experimental Therapeutics
J. Pharmacol. Toxicol. Methods	Journal of Pharmacological and Toxicological Methods
J. Phase Equilib.	Journal of Phase Equilibrium
J. Photochem. Photobiol., A	Journal of Photochemistry and Photobiology A
J. Photochem. Photobiol., B	Journal of Photochemistry and Photobiology B
J. Photopolym. Sci. Technol.	Journal of Photopolymer Science and Technology
J. Phys. A: Math. Gen.	Journal of Physics A: Mathematical and General

J. Phys. B: At., Mol. Opt. Phys.	Journal of Physics B: Atomic Molecular and Optical Physics
J. Phys. Chem.	Journal of Physical Chemistry
J. Phys. Chem. A	Journal of Physical Chemistry A
J. Phys. Chem. B	Journal of Physical Chemistry B
J. Phys. Chem. Ref. Data	Journal of Physical and Chemical Reference Data
J. Phys. Chem. Solids	Journal of Physics and Chemistry of Solids
J. Phys. D: Appl. Phys.	Journal of Physics D: Applied Physics
J. Phys. G: Nucl. Part. Phys.	Journal of Physics G: Nuclear and Particle Physics
J. Phys. I	Journal de Physique I
J. Phys. II	Journal de Physique II
J. Phys. III	Journal de Physique III
J. Phys. IV	Journal de Physique IV
J. Phys. Org. Chem.	Journal of Physical Organic Chemistry
J. Phys. Soc. Jpn.	Journal of the Physical Society of Japan
J. Phys.: Condens. Matter	Journal of Physics: Condensed Matter
J. Planar. Chromatogr. – Mod. TLC	Journal of Planar Chromatography – Modern TLC
J. Plant Biochem. Biotechnol.	Journal of Plant Biochemistry and Biotechnology
J . Polym. Eng.	Journal of Polymer Engineering
J. Polym. Environ.	Journal of Polymers and the Environment
J. Polym. Mater.	Journal of Polymer Materials
J. Polym. Sci., Part A: Polym. Chem.	Journal of Polymer Science Part A: Polymer Chemistry
J. Polym. Sci., Part B: Polym. Phys.	Journal of Polymer Science Part B: Polymer Physics
J. Porous Mater.	Journal of Porous Materials
J. Porphyrins Phthalocyanines	Journal of Porphyrins and Phthalocyanines
J. Power Sources	Journal of Power Sources

J. Prakt. Chem. /Chem–Ztg	Journal fur Praktische Chemie – Chemiker Zeitung
J. Propul. Power	Journal of Propulsion and Power
J. Protein Chem.	Journal of Protein Chemistry
J. Pulp Pap. Sci.	Journal of Pulp and Paper Science
J. Quant. Spectrosc. Radiat. Transfer	Journal of Quantitative Spectroscopy and Radiative Transfer
J. Radioanal. Nucl. Chem.	Journal of Radioanalytical and Nuclear Chemistry
J. Radioanal. Nucl. Chem. Art.	Journal of Radioanalytical and Nuclear Chemistry Articles
J. Radioanal. Nucl. Chem. Lett.	Journal of Radioanalytical and Nuclear Chemistry Letters
J. Raman Spectrosc.	Journal of Raman Specroscopy
J. Rapid Methods Autom. Microbiol.	Journal of Rapid Methods and Automation in Microbiology
J. Reinf. Plast. Compos.	Journal of Reinforced Plastics and Composites
J. Rheol.	Journal of Rheology
J. S. Afr. Inst. Min. Metall.	Journal of the South African Institute of Mining and Metallurgy
J. Sci. Food Agric.	Journal of the Science of Food and Agriculture
J. Sci. Ind. Res.	Journal of Scientific and Industrial Research
J. Serb. Chem. Soc.	Journal of the Serbian Chemical Society
J. Sep. Sci.	Journal of Separation Science
J. Sol–Gel Sci. Technol.	Journal of Sol–Gel Science and Technology
J. Solid State Chem.	Journal of Solid State Chemistry
J. Solid State Electrochem.	Journal of Solid State Electrochemistry
J. Solution Chem.	Journal of Solution Chemistry
J . Interferon Res.	Journal of Interferon Research
J. Jpn. Inst. Met.	Journal of the Japan Institute of Metals

J. Korean Chem. Soc.	Journal of the Korean Chemical Society
J. Labelled Compd. Radiopharm.	Journal of Labelled Compounds and Radiopharmaceuticals
J. Lipid Mediators	Journal of Lipid Mediators
J. Lipid Mediators Cell Signalling	Journal of Lipid Mediators and Cell Signalling
J. Lipid Res.	Journal of Lipid Research
J. Liq. Chromatogr.	Journal of Liquid Chromatography
J. Liq. Chromatogr. Related Technol.	Journal of Liquid Chromatography and Related Technologies
J. Low Temp. Phys.	Journal of Low Temperature Physics
J. Lumin.	Journal of Luminescence
J. Macromol. Sci., Phys.	Journal of Macromolecular Science – Physics
J. Macromol. Sci., Polym. Rev.	Journal of Macromolecular Science Polymer Reviews
J. Macromol. Sci., Pure Appl. Chem.	Journal of Macromolecular Science Pure and Applied Chemistry
J. Macromol. Sci., Rev. Macromol. Chem. Phys.	Journal of Macromolecular Science – Reviews in Macromolecular Chemistry and Physics
J. Magn. Magn. Mater.	Journal of Magnetism and Magnetic Materials
J. Magn. Reson., Ser A	Journal of Magnetic Resonance Series A
J. Magn. Reson., Ser B	Journal of Magnetic Resonance Series B
J. Mass Spectrom.	Journal of Mass Spectrometry
J. Mater. Chem.	Journal of Materials Chemistry
J. Mater. Civ. Eng.	Journal of Materials in Civil Engineering
J. Mater. Cycles Waste Manage.	Journal of Material Cycles and Waste Management
J. Mater. Eng. Perform.	Journal of Materials Engineering and Performance
J. Mater. Process. Manuf. Sci.	Journal of Materials Processing and Manufacturing Science
J. Mater. Process. Technol.	Journal of Materials Processing Technology

J. Mater. Res.	Journal of Materials Research
J. Mater. Sci. Lett.	Journal of Materials Science Letters
J. Mater. Sci. – Mater. Electron.	Journal of Materials Science – Materials in Electronics
J. Mater. Sci. – Mater. Med.	Journal of Materials Science Materials in Medicine
J. Mater. Sci. Technol.	Journal of Materials Science and Technology
J. Mater. Synth. Process.	Journal of Materials Synthesis and Processing
J. Math. Chem.	Journal of Mathematical Chemistry
J. Med. Chem.	Journal of Medicinal Chemistry
J. Membr. Biol.	Journal of Membrane Biology
J. Membr. Sci.	Journal of Membrane Science
J. Microbiol. Biotechnol.	Journal of Microbiology and Biotechnology
J. Microbiol. Methods	Journal of Microbiological Methods
J. Microcolumn Sep.	Journal of Microcolumn Separations
J. Microelectromech. Syst.	Journal of Microelectronic Systems
J. Microencapsulation	Journal of Microencapsulation
J. Mol. Biol.	Journal of Molecular Biology
J. Mol. Catal.	Journal of Molecular Catalysis
J. Mol. Catal. A: Chem.	Journal of Molecular Catalysis A: Chemical
J. Mol. Catal. B: Enzym.	Journal of Molecular Catalysis B: Enzymatic
J. Mol. Graphics Modell.	Journal of Molecular Graphics and Modelling
J. Mol. Liq.	Journal of Molecular Liquids
J. Mol. Microbiol. Biotechnol.	Journal of Molecular Microbiology and Biotechnology
J. Mol. Model.	Journal of Molecular Modeling
J. Mol. Spectrosc.	Journal of Molecular Spectroscopy
J. Mol. Struct.	Journal of Molecular Structure

J. Steroid Biochem. Mol. Biol.	Journal of Steroid Biochemistry and Molecular Biology
J. Strain Anal. Eng. Des.	Journal of Strain Analysis for Engineering Design
J. Struct. Chem.	Journal of Structural Chemistry
J. Supercrit. Fluids	Journal of Supercritical Fluids
J. Synth. Org. Chem Jpn.	Journal of Synthetic Organic Chemistry, Japan
J. Test. Eval.	Journal of Testing and Evaluation
J. Therm. Anal.	Journal of Thermal Analysis
J. Therm. Anal. Calorim.	Journal of Thermal Analysis and Calorimetry
J. Therm. Spray Technol.	Journal of Thermal Spray Technology
J. Thermophys Heat Transfer	Journal of Thermophysics and Heat Transfer
J. Thermoplast. Compos. Mater.	Journal of Thermoplastic Composite Materials
J. Toxicol. Environ. Health	Journal of Toxicology and Environment Health
J. Toxicol., Clin. Toxicol.	Journal of Toxicology – Clinical Toxicology
J. Toxicol., Cutaneous Ocul. Toxicol.	Journal of Toxicology – Cutaneous and Ocular Toxicology
J. Toxicol., Toxin Rev.	Journal of Toxicology – Toxin Reviews
J. Trace Elem. Exp. Med.	Journal of Trace Elements in Experimental Medicine
J. Trace Elem. Med Biol.	Journal of Trace Elements in Medicine and Biology
J. Trace Microprobe Tech.	Journal of Trace and Microprobe Techniques
J. Vac. Sci. Technol., A	Journal of Vacuum Science and Technology A
J. Vac. Sci. Technol., B	Journal of Vacuum Science and Technology B
J. Wood Chem. Technol.	Journal of Wood Chemistry and Technology
JACS	Journal of the American Chemical Society
JOM	JOM Journal of the Minerals Metals and Materials Society

JPC J. Planar Chromatogr. – Mod. TLC	JPC Journal of Planar Chromatography Modern TLC
Jpn. J. Appl. Phys., Part 1	Japanese Journal of Applied Physics Part 1
Jpn. J. Appl. Phys., Part 2	Japanese Journal of Applied Physics Part 2
Jpn. J. Cancer Res.	Japanese Journal of Cancer Research
Jpn. J. Pharmacol.	Japanese Journal of Pharmacology
Jpn. J. Toxicol. Environ. Health	Japanese Journal of toxicology and Environment health
J. Polym. Eng.	Journal of Polymer Engineering
J. Polym. Environ.	Journal of Polymers and the Environment
J. Polym. Mater.	Journal of Polymer Materials
J. Polym. Sci., Part A: Polym. Chem.	Journal of Polymer Science Part A: Polymer Chemistry
J. Polym. Sci., Part B: Polym. Phys.	Journal of Polymer Science Part B: Polymer Physics
J. Porous Mater.	Journal of Porous Materials
J. Porphyrins Phthalocyanines	Journal of Porphyrins and Phthalocyanines
J. Power Sources	Journal of Power Sources
J. Prakt. Chem. /Chem–Ztg	Journal fur Praktische Chemie – Chemiker Zeitung
J. Propul. Power	Journal of Propulsion and Power
J. Protein Chem.	Journal of Protein Chemistry
J. Pulp Pap. Sci.	Journal of Pulp and Paper Science
J. Quant. Spectrosc. Radiat. Transfer	Journal of Quantitative Spectroscopy and Radiative Transfer
J. Radioanal. Nucl. Chem.	Journal of Radioanalytical and Nuclear Chemistry
J. Radioanal. Nucl. Chem. Art.	Journal of Radioanalytical and Nuclear Chemistry Articles
J. Radioanal. Nucl. Chem. Lett.	Journal of Radioanalytical and Nuclear Chemistry Letters

J. Raman Spectrosc.	Journal of Raman Specroscopy
J. Rapid Methods Autom. Microbiol.	Journal of Rapid Methods and Automation in Microbiology
J. Reinf. Plast. Compos.	Journal of Reinforced Plastics and Composites
J. Rheol.	Journal of Rheology
J. S. Afr. Inst. Min. Metall.	Journal of the South African Institute of Mining and Metallurgy
J. Sci. Food Agric.	Journal of the Science of Food and Agriculture
J. Sci. Ind. Res.	Journal of Scientific and Industrial Research
J. Serb. Chem. Soc.	Journal of the Serbian Chemical Society
J. Sep. Sci.	Journal of Separation Science
J. Sol−Gel Sci. Technol.	Journal of Sol−Gel Science and Technology
J. Solid State Chem.	Journal of Solid State Chemistry
J. Solid State Electrochem.	Journal of Solid State Electrochemistry
J. Solution Chem.	Journal of Solution Chemistry
J. Organomet. Chem.	Journal of Organometallic Chemistry
J. Pet. Sci. Technol.	Journal of Petroleum Science and Technology
J. Pharm. Biomed. Anal.	Journal of Pharmaceutical and Biomedical Analysis
J. Pharm. Pharmacol.	Journal of Pharmacy and Pharmacology
J. Pharm. Sci.	Journal of Pharmaceutical Sciences
J. Pharmacol. Exp. Ther.	Journal of Pharmacology and Experimental Therapeutics
J. Pharmacol. Toxicol. Methods	Journal of Pharmacological and Toxicological Methods
J. Phase Equilib.	Journal of Phase Equilibrium
J. Photochem. Photobiol., A	Journal of Photochemistry and Photobiology A
J. Photochem. Photobiol., B	Journal of Photochemistry and Photobiology B
J. Photopolym. Sci. Technol.	Journal of Photopolymer Science and Technology

J. Phys. A: Math. Gen.	Journal of Physics A: Mathematical and General
J. Phys. B: At., Mol. Opt. Phys.	Journal of Physics B: Atomic Molecular and Optical Physics
J. Phys. Chem.	Journal of Physical Chemistry
J. Phys. Chem. A	Journal of Physical Chemistry A
J. Phys. Chem. B	Journal of Physical Chemistry B
J. Phys. Chem. Ref. Data	Journal of Physical and Chemical Reference Data
J. Phys. Chem. Solids	Journal of Physics and Chemistry of Solids
J. Phys. D: Appl. Phys.	Journal of Physics D: Applied Physics
J. Phys. G: Nucl. Part. Phys.	Journal of Physics G: Nuclear and Particle Physics
J. Phys. I	Journal de Physique I
J. Phys. II	Journal de Physique II
J. Phys. III	Journal de Physique III
J. Phys. IV	Journal de Physique IV
J. Phys. Org. Chem.	Journal of Physical Organic Chemistry
J. Phys. Soc. Jpn.	Journal of the Physical Society of Japan
J. Phys.: Condens. Matter	Journal of Physics: Condensed Matter
J. Planar. Chromatogr. – Mod. TLC	Journal of Planar Chromatography – Modern TLC
J. Plant Biochem. Biotechnol.	Journal of Plant Biochemistry and Biotechnology
J. Nanopart. Res.	Journal of Nanoparticle Research
J. Nat. Prod.	Journal of Natural Products
J. Near Infrared Spectrosc.	Journal of Near Infrared Spectroscopy
J. Neurochem.	Journal of Neurochemistry
J. Neurosci.	Journal of Neuroscience
J. Neurosci. Res.	Journal of Neuroscience Research
J. New Mater. Electrochem. Syst.	Journal of New Materials for Electrochemical Systems
J. Non–Cryst. Solids	Journal of Non–Crystalline Solids

J. Non-Equilib. Thermodyn.	Journal of Non-Equilibrium Thermodynamics
J. Nucl. Mater.	Journal of Nuclear Materials
J. Nucl. Sci. Technol.	Journal of Nuclear Science and Technology
J. Opt. Soc. Am. B: Opt. Phys.	Journal of the Optical Society of America B: Optical Physics
J. Org. Chem.	Journal of Organic Chemistry
JSME Int J., Ser. A	JSME International Journal Series A:
JSME Int J., Ser. B	JSME International Journal Series B: Fluids and Thermal Engineering
JSME Int J., Ser. C	JSME International Journal Series C: Mechanical Systems Machine Elements and Manufacturing

以 K 字母开头的期刊 — Journals beginning with K letters

Kautsch. Gummi Kunstst.	Kautschuk Gummi Kunststoffe
Key Eng. Mater.	Key Engineering Materials
Khim. Fiz.	Khimicheskaya Fizika
Kinet. Catal.	Kinetics and Catalysis
Kinet. Katal.	Kinetika i Kataliz
Kolloidn Zh	Kolloidn Zhurnal
Koord. Khim.	Koordinatsionnaya Khimiya (Russian Journal of Coordination Chemistry)
Korean J. Chem. Eng.	Korean Journal of Chemical Engineering
Kovove Mater.	Kovove Materialy Metallic Materials

以 L 字母开头的期刊 — Journals beginning with L letters

Lab. Autom. Inf. Manage.	Laboratory Automation and Information Management
Lab. Invest.	Laboratory Investigation
Lab. Rob. Autom.	Laboratory Robotics and Automation
Laser Chem.	Laser Chemistry
LC-GC	LC-GC The Magazine of Separation Science

Lett. Appl. Microbiol.	Letters in Applied Microbiology
Lett. Pept. Sci.	Letters in Peptide Science
Liebigs Ann. Chem.	Liebigs Annalen der Chemie
Liebigs Ann. Recl.	Liebigs Annalen – Recueil
Life Sci.	Life Sciences
Liq. Cryst.	Liquid Crystals
Lubr. Eng.	Lubrication Engineering
Lubr. Sci.	Lubrication Science

以 M 字母开头的期刊 — Journals beginning with M letters

Macromol. Chem. Phys.	Macromolecular Chemistry and Physics
Macromol. Rapid Commun.	Macromolecular Rapid Communications
Macromol. Symp.	Macromolecular Symposium
Macromol. Theory Simul.	Macromolecular Theory and Simulations
Magn. Reson. Chem.	Magnetic Resonance in Chemistry
Magn. Reson. Mater. Phys., Biol. Med.	Magnetic Resonance Materials in Physics, Biology and Medicine
Magy. Kem. Foly.	Magyar Kemiai Folyoirat
Main Group Chem.	Main Group Chemistry
Main Group Met. Chem.	Main Group Metal Chemistry
Manuf. Chem.	Manufacturing Chemist
Mar. Biol.	Marine Biology
Mar. Biotechnol.	Marine Biotechnology
Mar. Chem.	Marine Chemistry
Mar. Environ. Res.	Marine Environment Research
Mar. Pollut. Bull.	Marine Pollutution Bulletin
Mass Spectrom. Rev.	Mass Spectrometry Reviews
Mater. Charact.	Materials Characterization
Mater. Chem. Phys.	Materials Chemistry and Physics

Mater. Corros.	Materials and Corrosion
Mater. Des.	Materials and Design
Mater. Eval.	Materials Evaluation
Mater. Forum	Materials Forum
Mater. High Temp.	Materials at High Temperatures
Mater. Lett.	Materials Letters
Mater. Manuf. Processes	Materials and Manufacturing Processes
Mater. Org.	Materials and Organisms
Mater. Performance	Materials Performance
Mater. Res. Bull.	Materials Research Bulletin
Mater. Res. Innovations	Materials Research Innovations
Mater. Sci.	Materials Science
Mater. Sci. Eng., A	Materials Science and Engineering A
Mater. Sci. Eng., B	Materials Science and Engineering B
Mater. Sci. Eng., C	Materials Science and Engineering C
Mater. Sci. Eng., R	Materials Science and Engineering Reports
Mater. Sci. Forum	Materials Science Forum
Mater. Sci. Semicond. Process.	Materials Science in Semiconductor Processing
Mater. Sci. Res. Int.	Materials Science Research International
Mater. Sci. Technol.	Materials Science and Technology
Mater. Struct.	Materials and Structures
Mater. Today	Materials Today
Mater. Trans., JIM	Materials Transactions, JIM
Materialwiss. Werkstofftech.	Materialwissenschaft und Werkstofftechnik
Matrix Biol.	Matrix Biology
Meas. Sci. Technol.	Measurement Science and Technology
Mech. Compos. Mater.	Mechanics of Composite Materials

Mech. Compos. Mater. Struct.	Mechanics of Composite Materials and Structures
Mech. Mater.	Mechanics of Materials
Mech. Time–Depend. Mater.	Mechanics of Time Dependent Materials
Med. Chem. Res.	Medicinal Chemistry Research
Mendeleev Commun.	Mendeleev Communications
Met.–Based Drugs	Metal–Based Drugs
Met. Ions Biol. Syst.	Metal Ions in Biological Systems
Met. Sci. Heat Treat.	Metal Science and Heat Treatment
Metab. Eng.	Metabolic Engineering
Metall. Mater. Trans. A	Metallurgical and Materials Transactions A: Physical Metallurgy and Materials Science
Metall. Mater. Trans. B	Metallurgical and Materials Transactions B: Process Metallurgy and Materials Processing Science
Metall. Trans. A	Metallurgical Transactions A
Metall. Trans. B	Metallurgical Transactions B
Metalloved. Term. Obrab. Met.	Metallovedenie Termicheskaya Obrabotka Metallov
Methods Biochem. Anal.	Methods of Biochemical Analysis
Methods Enzymol.	Methods in Enzymology
Microb. Comp. Genomics	Microbial and Comparative Genomics
Microbiol. Res.	Microbiological Research
Microchem. J.	Microchemical Journal
Microelectron. Eng.	Microelectronic Engineering
Microelectron. J.	Microelectronics Journal
Microporous Mater.	Microporous Materials
Microporous Mesoporous Mater.	Microporous and Mesoporous Materials
Microscale Thermophys. Eng.	Microscale Thermophysical Engineering

Microsc. Microanal.	Microscopy and Microanalysis
Microsc. Res. Tech.	Microscopy Research and Technique
Mikrochim. Acta	Mikrochimica Acta
Mine Water Environ.	Mine Water and the Environment
Miner. Eng.	Minerals Engineering
Miner. Metall. Process	Minerals and Metallurgical Processing
Miner. Process. Extr. Metall. Rev.	Mineral Processing and Extractive Metallurgy Review
Mini–Rev. Med. Chem.	Mini – Reviews in Medicinal Chemistry
Mod. Drug Discovery	Modern Drug Discovery
Mod. Phys. Lett. A	Modern Physics Letters A
Mod. Phys. Lett. B	Modern Physics Letters B
Modell. Simul. Mater. Sci. Eng.	Modelling and Simulation in Materials Science and Engineering
Mol. Cell. Biochem.	Molecular and Cellular Biochemistry
Mol. Cryst. Liq. Cryst. Sci. Technol., Sect. A	Molecular Crystals and Liquid Crystals Science and Technology Section A
Mol. Cryst. Liq. Cryst. Sci. Technol., Sect. C	Molecular Crystals and Liquid Crystals Science and Technology Section C
Mol. Mar. Biol. Biotech,	Molecular Marine Biology and Biotechnology
Mol. Interventions	Molecular Interventions
Mol. Microbiol.	Molecular Microbiology
Mol. Pharmacol.	Molecular Pharmacology
Mol. Phys.	Molecular Physics
Mol. Reprod. Dev	Molecular Reproduction and Development
Mol. Supramol. Photochem.	Molecular and Supramolecular Photochemistry
Mon. Not. R. Astron. Soc.	Monthy Notices of the Royal Astronomical Society
Monatsh. Chem.	Monatshefte fur Chemie
MRS Bull.	MRS Bulletin

MRS Internet J. Nitride Semicond. Res.	MRS Internet Journal of Nitride Semiconductor Research

以 N 字母开头的期刊 — **Journals beginning with N letters**

Nachr. Chem. Tech. Lab.	Nachrichten aus Chemie Technik und Laboratorium
Nano Lett.	Nano Letters
Nanostruct. Mater.	Nanostructured Materials
Nat. Biotechnol.	Nature Biotechnology
Nat. Prod. Lett.	Natural Products Letters
Nat. Prod. Rep.	Natural Products Reports
Nat. Prod. Sci.	Natural Product Sciences
Nat. Struct. Biol.	Natural Structural Biology
Nat. Toxins	Natural Toxins
NATO ASI Ser., Ser. A	NATO ASI Series, Series A Life Sciences
NATO ASI Ser., Ser. B	NATO ASI Series, Series B: Physics
NATO ASI Ser., Ser. C	NATO ASI Series, Series C Mathematical and Physical Sciences
NATO ASI Ser., Ser. E	NATO ASI Series, Series E Applied Physics
NATO ASI Ser., Ser. G	NATO ASI Series, Series G Ecological Sciences
NATO ASI Ser., Ser. H	NATO ASI Series, Series H Cell Biology
Naunyn–Schmiedeberg's Arch. Pharmacol.	Naunyn–Schmiedeberg's Archives of Pharmacology
NDT and E Int.	NDT and E International
Neft. Khoz.	Neftyanoe Khozyaistvo (Petroleum Industry)
Neorg. Mater.	Neorganicheskie Materialy
Neurochem. Int.	Neurochemistry International
Neurochem. Res.	Neurochemical Research
New Compr. Biochem.	New Comprehensive Biochemistry
New Diamond Front. Carbon Technol.	New Diamond and Frontier Carbon Technology

New J. Chem.	New Journal of Chemistry
New Polym. Mat.	New Polymeric Materials
NMR Biomed.	NMR in Biomedicine
Nucl. Eng. Des.	Nuclear Engineering and Design
Nucl. Fusion	Nuclear Fusion
Nucl. Instrum. Methods Phys. Res., Sect. A	Nuclear Instruments and Methods in Physics Research Section A
Nucl. Instrum. Methods Phys. Res., Sect. B	Nuclear Instruments and Methods in Physics Research Section B
Nucl. Phys. A	Nuclear Physics A
Nucl. Phys. B	Nuclear Physics B
Nucl. Technol.	Nuclear Technology
Nucleic Acids Res.	Nucleic Acids Research
Numer. Heat Transfer, Part A	Numerical Heat Transfer Part A
Numer. Heat Transfer, Part B	Numerical Heat Transfer Part B
Nuovo Cimento Soc. Ital. Fis., A	Nuovo Cimento della Societa Italiana di Fisica A
Nuovo Cimento Soc. Ital. Fis., B	Nuovo Cimento della Societa Italiana di Fisica B
Nuovo Cimento Soc. Ital. Fis., C	Nuovo Cimento della Societa Italiana di Fisica C
Nuovo Cimento Soc. Ital. Fis., D	Nuovo Cimento della Societa Italiana di Fisica D

以 O 字母开头的期刊　　　　　Journals beginning with O letters

Oil Gas J.	Oil and Gas Journal
Opt. Commun.	Optics Communication
Opt. Express	Optics Express
Opt. Lett.	Optics Letters
Opt. Mater.	Optical Materials
Opt. Spectrosc.	Optics and Spectroscopy
Opt Spektrosk.	Optika i Spektroskopiya
Opt. Zh.	Opticheskii Zhurnal

Org. Electron.	Organic Electronics
Org. Geochem.	Organic Geochemistry
Org. Lett.	Organic Letters
Org. Mass Spectrom.	Organic Mass Spectrometry
Org. Prep. Proced. Int.	Organic Preparations and Procedures International
Org. Process Res. Dev.	Organic Process Research and Development
Org. React. Mech.	Organic Reaction Mechanics
Organohalogen Compd.	Organohalogen Compounds
Organomet. Chem.	Organometallic Chemistry
Origins Life Evol. Biosphere	Origins of Life and Evolution of the Biosphere
Oxid. Met.	Oxidation of Metals
Ozone Sci. Eng.	Ozone Science and Engineering
以 P 字母开头的期刊	**Journals beginning with P letters**
Part. Part. Syst. Char.	Particle and Particle Systems Characterization
Part. Sci. Technol.	Particulate Science and Technology
PCCP	Physical Chemistry Chemical Physics
Perspect. Drug Discovery Des.	Perspectives in Drug Discovery and Design
Pestic. Biochem. Physiol.	Pesticide Biochemistry and Physiology
Pestic. Outlook	Pesticide Outlook
Pet. Sci. Technol.	Petroleum Science and Technology
Physical Review E: Statistical	Physics, Plasmas, Fluids, and Related Interdisciplinary Topics
Phys. Rev. Lett.	Physical Review Letters
Phys. Scr.	Physica Scripta
Phys. Status Solidi A	Physical Status Solidi A
Phys. Status Solidi B	Physical Status Solidi B
Physica A	Physica A
Physica B	Physica B

Physica C	Physica C
Physica D	Physica D
Physica E	Physica E
Physiol. Biochem. Zool.	Physiological and Biochemical Zoology
Physiol. Chem. Phys. Med. NMR	Physiological Chemistry and Physics and Medical NMR
Physiol. Plant.	Physiologia Plantarum
Phytochem. Anal	Phytochemical Analysis
Pharm. Chem. J.	Pharmaceutical Chemistry Journal
Pharm. Pharmacol. Commun.	Pharmacy and Pharmacology Communications
Pharm. Pharmacol. Lett.	Pharmaceutical and Pharmacological Letters
Pharm. Res.	Pharmaceutical Research
Pharm. Technol.	Pharmaceutical Technology
Pharmacol. Res.	Pharmacological Research
Phase Transitions	Phase Transitions
Philos. Mag. A	Philosophical Magazine A
Philos. Mag. B	Philosophical Magazine B
Philos. Mag. Lett.	Philosophical Magazine Letters
Philos. Trans. R. Soc. London, Ser. A	Philosophical Transactions of the Royal Society of London, Series A
Philos. Trans. R. Soc. London, Ser. B	Philosophical Transactions of the Royal Society of London, Series B
Phosphorus, Sulfur Silicon Relat. Elem.	Phosphorus Sulfur Silicon and the Related Elements
Photochem. Photobiol.	Photochemistry and Photobiology
Photosynth. Res.	Photosynthesis Research
Phys. Chem. Chem. Phys.	Physical Chemistry Chemical Physics
Phys. Chem. Glasses	Physics and Chemistry of Glasses
Phys. Chem. Liq.	Physics and Chemistry of Liquids

Phys. Chem. Miner.	Physics and Chemistry of Minerals
Phys. Fluids A	Physics of Fluids A
Phys. Fluids B	Physics of Fluids B
Phys. Lett. A	Physics Letters A
Phys. Lett. B	Physics Letters B
Phys. Med. Biol.	Physics in Medicine & Biology
Phys. Rev. A: At. Mol. Opt. Phys.	Physical Review A: Atomic, Molecular, and Optical Physics
Phys. Rev. B: Condens. Matter	Physical Review B: Condensed Matter
Phys. Rev. C: Nucl. Phys.	Physical Review C: Nuclear Physics
Phys. Rev. D: Part. Fields	Physical Review D: Particles and Fields
Polym. Int.	Polymer International
Polym. J.	Polymer Journal
Polym. Mater. Sci. Eng.	Polymeric Materials Science and Engineering
Polym. Networks Blends	Polymer Networks and Blends
Polym. Plast. Technol. Eng.	Polymer – Plastics Technology and Engineering
Polym. Polym. Compos.	Polymers and Polymer Composites
Polym. Prepr. (Am. Chem. Soc., Div. Polym. Chem.)	Polymeric Preprints (American Chemical Society, Division of Polymer Chemistry)
Polym. React. Eng.	Polymer Reaction Engineering
Polym. Recycl.	Polymer Recycling
Polym. Test.	Polymer testing
Powder Diffr.	Powder Diffraction
Powder Metall.	Powder Metallurgy
Powder Metall. Met. Ceram.	Powder Metallurgy and Metal Ceramics
Powder Technol.	Powder Technology
Prep. Biochem. Biotechnol.	Preparative Biochemistry and Biotechnology

Prepr. – Am. Chem. Soc., Div. Pet. Chem.	Preprints – American Chemical Society, Division of Petroleum Chemistry
Prepr. Pap. – Am. Chem. Soc., Div. Fuel Chem.	Preprint Papers – American Chemical Society, Division of Fuel Chemistry
Proc. R. Soc. London, Ser. A	Proceedings of the Royal Society of London Series A
Proc. R. Soc. London, Ser. B	Proceedings of the Royal Society of London Series B
Process Biochem.	Process Biochemistry
Process Control Qual.	Process Control and Quality
Process Saf. Environ. Prot.	Process Safety and Environment Protection
Process Saf. Prog.	Process Safety Progress
Prog. Biophys. Mol. Biol.	Progress in Biophysics and Molecular biology
Prog. Biotechnol.	Progress in Biotechnology
Prog. Chem. Org. Nat. Prod.	Progress
Prog. Colloid Polym. Sci.	Progress in Colloid and Polymer Science
Prog. Cryst. Growth Charact. Mater.	Progress in Crystal Growth and Characterization of Materials
Prog. Energy Combust. Sci.	Progress in Energy and Combustion Science
Prog. Heterocycl. Chem.	Progress in Heterocyclic Chemistry
Prog. Ind. Microbiol.	Progress in Industrial Microbiology
Phys. Rev. E: Stat. Phys.,	Physical Review E: Statistical Physics,
Plasmas, Fluids,	Plasmas, Fluids, and Related Interdisciplinary Topics
Plant Physiol. Biochem.	Plant Physiology and Biochemistry
Planta Med.	Planta Medica
Plasma Chem. Plasma Process.	Plasma Chemistry and Plasma Processing
Plasma Phys. Controlled Fusion	Plasma Physics and Controlled Fusion
Plasmas Polym.	Plasmas and Polymers

Plasma Sources Sci. Technol.	Plasma Sources Science and Technology
Plast. Eng.	Plastics Engineering
Plast. Rubber Compos. Process. Appl.	Plastics Rubber and Composites Processing and Applications
Platinum Met. Rev.	Platinum Metals Review
Plat. Surf. Finish.	Plating and Surface Finishing
Pol. J. Chem.	Polish Journal of chemistry
Polycyclic Aromat. Compd.	Polycyclic Aromatic Compounds
Polym. Adv. Technol.	Polymers for Advanced Technologies
Polym. Bull.	Polymer Bulletin
Polym. Compos.	Polymer Composites
Polym. Degrad. Stab.	Polymer Degradation and Stability
Polym. Eng. Sci.	Polymer Engineering and Science
Polym. Gels Networks	Polymer Gels and Networks
Prog. Inorg. Chem.	Progress in Inorganic Chemistry
Prog. Lipid Res.	Progress in Lipid Research
Prog. Mater Sci.	Progress in Materials Science
Prog. Nucl. Magn. Reson. Spectrosc.	Progress in Nuclear Magnetic Resonance Spectroscopy
Prog. Org. Coat.	Progress in Organic Coatings
Prog. Pap. Recycl.	Progress in Paper Recycling
Prog. Polym. Sci.	Progress in Polymer Science
Prog. React. Kinet.	Progress in Reaction Kinetics
Prog. Solid State Chem.	Progress in Solid State Chemistry
Prog. Surf. Sci.	Progress in Surface Science
Prot. Met	Protection of Metals
Protein Eng.	Protein Engineering
Protein Sci.	Protein Science

Przem. Chem.	Przemysl Chemiczny
Pure Appl. Chem.	Pure and Applied Chemistry

以 Q 字母开头的期刊   Journals beginning with Q letters

Quant. Struct.–Act. Relat.	Quantitative Structure–Activity Relationships
Quim. Anal. (Barcelona)	Quimica Analitica
Quim. Nova	Quimica Nova

以 R 字母开头的期刊   Journals beginning with R letters

Radiat Eff. Defects Solids	Radiation Effects and Defects in Solids
Radiat. Phys. Chem.	Radiation Physics and Chemistry
Radiat. Prot. Dosim.	Radiation Protection Dosimetry
Radiat. Res.	Radiation Research
Radiochim. Acta	Radiochima Acta
Rapid Commun. Mass Spectrom.	Rapid Communications in Mass Spectrometry
Rapra Rev. Rep.	Rapra Review Reports
React. Funct. Polym.	Reactive and Functional Polymers
React. Kinet. Catal. Lett.	Reaction Kinetics and Catalysis Letters
Recl. Trav. Chim. Pays–Bas	Recueil des Travaux Chimiques des Pays–Bas Journal of the Royal Netherlands Chemical Society
Refract. Ind. Ceram	Refractories and Industrial Ceramics
Regul. Toxicol. Pharm.	Regulatory Toxicology and Pharmacology
Rep. Prog. Phys.	Reports on Progress in Physics
Res. Chem. Intermed.	Research on Chemical Intermediates
Res. Commun. Mol. Pathol. Pharmacol.	Research Communications in Molecular Pathology and Pharmacology
Res. Microbiol.	Research in Microbiology
Rev. Anal. Chem	Reviews in Analytical Chemistry
Rev. Chem. Eng.	Reviews in Chemical Engineering
Rev. Chim.	Revista de Chimie

Rev. Comput. Chem.	Reviews in Computational Chemistry
Rev. Environ. Contam. Toxicol.	Reviews of Environment Contamination and Toxicology
Rev. Gen. Therm.	Revue Generale de Thermique
Rev. Metall. / Cah. Inf. Tech.	Revue de Metallurgie / Cahiers d' Informations Techniques
Rev. Physiol., Biochem. Pharmacol.	Reviews of Physiology Biochemistry and Pharmacology
Rev. Roum. Chim.	Revue Roumaine de Chimie
Rev. Sci. Instrum.	Review of Scientific Instruments
Rheol. Acta	Rheologica Acta
Rubber Chem. Technol.	Rubber Chemistry and Technology
Russ. Chem. Bull.	Russian Chemical Bulletin
Russ. J. Appl. Chem.	Russian Journal of Applied Chemistry
Russ. J. Bioorg. Chem.	Russian Journal of Bioorganic Chemistry
Russ. J. Coord. Chem.	Russion Journal of Coordination Chemistry
Russ. J. Electrochem.	Russian Journal of Electrochemistry
Russ. J. Gen. Chem.	Russian Journal of General Chemistry
Russ. J. Nondestr. Test.	Russian Journal of Nondestructive Testing
Russ. J. Org. Chem.	Russian Journal of Organic Chemistry
Russ. Metall.	Russian Metallurgy
以 S 字母开头的期刊	**Journals beginning with S letters**
S. Afr. J. Chem.	South African Journal of Chemistry
SAMPE J.	SAMPE Journal
Scand. J. Metall.	Scandinavian Journal of Metallurgy
Sci. China, Ser. B	Science in China, Series B Chemistry
Sci. China, Ser. E	Science in China, Series E Technological Sciences
Sci. Prog.	Science Progress

Sci. Technol. Weld. Joining	Science and Technology of Welding and Joining / font>
Sci. Total Environ.	Science of the Total Environment
Scripta Mater.	Scripta Materialia
Semicond. Sci. Technol.	Semiconductor Science and Technology
Sens. Actuators, A	Sensors and Actuators, A
Sens. Actuators, B	Sensors and Actuators, B
Sep. Purif. Methods	Separation and Purification Methods
Sep. Purif. Technol.	Separation and Purification Technology
Sep. Sci. Technol.	Separation Science and Technology
Silic. Indus.	Silicates Industriels
Smart Mater. Struct.	Smart Materials and Structures
Soil Biol. Biochem.	Soil Biology and Biochemistry
Sol. Energy Mater. Sol. Cells	Solar Energy Materials and Solar Cells
Solid State Commun.	Solid State Communications
Solid State Ionics	Solid State Ionics
Solid State Nucl. Magn. Reson.	Solid State Nuclear Magnetic Resonance
Solid−State Electron.	Solid State Electronics
Solvent Extr. Ion Exch.	Solvent Extraction and Ion Exchange
Spectrochim. Acta	Spectrochimica Acta
Spectrochim. Acta, Part A	Spectrochimica Acta, Part A
Spectrochim. Acta, Part B	Spectrochimica Acta, Part B
Spectrosc. Eur.	Spectroscopy Europe
Spectrosc. Lett.	Spectroscopy Letters
Spectrosc. Prop. Inorg. Organomet. Compd.	Spectroscopic Properties of Inorganic and Organometallic Compounds
Speculations Sci. Technol.	Speculations in Science and Technology
Spill Sci. Technol. Bull.	Spill Science and Technology Bulletin

Springer Ser. Chem. Phys.	Springer Series in Chemical Physics
Springer Ser. Solid–State Sci.	Springer Series in Solid–State Sciences
Struct. Bond.	Structure and Bonding
Struct. Chem.	Structural Chemistry
Stud. Nat. Prod. Chem.	Studies in Natural Products Chemistry
Stud. Surf. Sci. Catal.	Studies in Surface Science and Catalysis
Supercond. Sci. Technol.	Superconductor Science and Technology
Superlattices Microstruct.	Superlattices and Microstructures
Supramol. Chem.	Supramolecular Chemistry
Supramol. Photosensit. Electroact. Mater.	Supramolecular Photosensitive and Electroactive Materials
Supramol. Sci.	Supramolecular Science
Surf. Coat. Int.	Surface Coatings International
Surf. Coat. Technol.	Surface and Coatings Technology
Surf. Eng.	Surface Engineering
Surf. Interface Anal.	Surface and Interface Analysis
Surf. Rev. Lett.	Surface Review and Letters
Surf. Sci.	Surface Science
Surf. Sci. Rep.	Surface Science Reports
Surf. Sci. Spectra	Surface Science Spectra
Synth. Commun.	Synthetic Communications
Synth. Met.	Synthetic Metals
Synth. React. Inorg. Met.–Org. Chem.	Synthesis and Reactivity in Inorganic and Metal–Organic Chemistry

以 T 字母开头的期刊 | **Journals beginning with T letters**

Tappi J.	Tappi Journal
Tetrahedron Lett.	Tetrahedron Letters
Tetrahedron: Asymmetry	Tetrahedron: Asymmetry

THEOCHEM	THEOCHEM Journal of Molecular Structure
Theor. Exp. Chem.	Theoretical and Experimental Chemistry
Theor. Chem. Acc.	Theoretical Chemistry Accounts
Theor. Found. Chem. Eng.	Theoretical Foundations of Chemical Engineering
Thermochim. Acta	Thermochimica Acta
Thin Solid Films	Thin Solid Films
Tissue Eng.	Tissue Engineering
Top. Appl. Phys.	Topics in Applied Physics
Top. Biol. Inorg. Chem.	Topics in Biological and Inorganic Chemistry
Top. Catal.	Topics in Catalysis
Top. Curr. Chem.	Topics in Current Chemistry
Top. Inorg. Chem.	Topics in Inorganic Chemistry
Top. Fluoresc. Spectrosc.	Topics in Fluorescence Spectroscopy
Toxicol. Appl. Pharmacol.	Toxicology and Applied Pharmacology
Toxicol. Environ. Chem.	Toxicological and Environmental Chemistry
Toxicol. Lett.	Toxicology Letters
Toxicol. Sci.	Toxicological Sciences
Tr AC, Trends Anal. Chem.	TRAC Trends in Analytical Chemistry
Trace Elem. Electrolytes	Trace Elements and Electrolytes
Trans. Inst. Met. Finish.	Transactions of the Institution of Metal Finishing
Trans. Inst. Min. Metall., Sect. A	Transactions of the Institution of Mining and Metallurgy Section A
Trans. Inst. Min. Metall., Sect. B	Transactions of the Institution of Mining and Metallurgy Section B
Trans. Inst. Min. Metall., Sect. C	Transactions of the Institution of Mining and Metallurgy Section C
Transition Met. Chem.	Transition Metal Chemistry
Trends Biochem. Sci	Trends in Biochemical Sciences

Trends Biotechnol.	Trends in Biotechnology
Tsvetn. Met. (Moscow)	Tsvetnaya Metally
以 U 字母开头的期刊	**Journals beginning with U letters**
Ukr. Khim. Zh.	Ukrainskii Khimicheskii Zhurnal
Ukr. Fiz. Zh.	Ukrainskii Fizicheskii Zhurnal
Ultrason. Sonochem.	Ultrasonics Sonochemistry
Usp. Khim.	Uspekhi Khimii
以 V 字母开头的期刊	**Journals beginning with V letters**
Vib. Spectrosc	Vibrational Spectroscopy
以 W 字母开头的期刊	**Journals beginning with W letters**
Waste Manage. (Oxford)	Waste Management
Waste Manage. Res.	Waste Management and Research
Water Environ. Res	Water Environment Research
Water Res.	Water Research
Water Resour. Res.	Water Resources Research
Water Sci. Technol.	Water Science and Technology
Water, Air, Soil Pollut.	Water, Air, and Soil Pollution
World J. Microbiol. Biotechnol.	World Journal of Microbiology and Biotechnology
以 X 字母开头的期刊	**Journals beginning with X letters**
X–Ray Spectrom.	X–Ray Spectrometry
以 Z 字母开头的期刊	**Journals beginning with Z letters**
Z. Anorg. Allg. Chem.	Zeitschrift fur Anorganische und Allgemeine Chemie
Z. Kristallogr.	Zeitschrift fur Kristallograhie
Z. Kristallogr. – New Cryst. Struct.	Zeitschrift fur Kristallograhie – New Crystral Stuctures
Z. Meta Ilkd.	Zeitschrift fur Meta Ilkunde

Z. Naturforsch., A: Phys. Sci.	Zeitschrift fur Naturforschung A: Journal of Physical Sciences
Z. Naturforsch., B: Chem. Sci.	Zeitschrift fur Naturforschung B: Journal of Chemical Sciences
Z. Naturforsch., C: Biosci.	Zeitschrift fur Naturforschung C: Journal of Biosciences
Z. Phys. A: Hadrons Nucl.	Zeitschrift fur Physik A: Hadrons and Nuclei
Z. Phys. B: Condens. Matter	Zeitschrift fur Physik B: Condensed Matter
Z. Phys. C: Part. Fields	Zeitschrift fur Physik C: Particle Fields
Z. Phys. D: At., Mol. Clusters	Zeitschrift fur Physik D: Atoms, Molecules and Clusters
Z. Phys. Chem.	Zeitschrift fur Physikalische Chemie
Zh. Fiz. Khim.	Zhurnal Fizicheskoi Khimii
Zh. Neorg. Khim.	Zhurnal Neorganicheskoi Khimii
Zh. Obshch. Khim.	Zhurnal Obshchei Khimii
Zh. Org. Khim.	Zhurnal Organicheskoi Khimii
Zh. Prikl. Khim.	Zhurnal Prikladnoi Khimii

参考文献
References

1. 葛驰，朱雷. 对万方数据库的浅析 [J]. 医学图书馆通讯. 1998（04）

2. 刘志松. 关于电子图书验收问题的探讨——以广州图书馆方正 Apabi 为例 [J]. 图书馆学研究. 2007（08）

3. 庄善洁等主编. 现代信息资源检索与利用 [M]. 哈尔滨工程大学出版社. 2010

4. 冯攀，王江红. 美国外国医师执业资格认证管理的启示 [J]. 中国卫生法制. 2015（01）:51–53

5. 朱建国. 美国执业医师培训考试制度对我国高职高专医学教育的启示 [J]. 卫生职业教育. 2013（03）:7–8

6. 陈梁. 美国医师执照考试及对中国医学教育和执业医师考试的启示 [J]. 中国高等医学教育. 2012（09）:18–19+51

7. 冯攀. 加拿大医师能力框架对我国制定执业医师能力标准的启示 [J]. 中国医院管理. 2013（04）:61–63

8. 韩玉，李鸿鹤，曲波，张阳，伦施斯. 英国 PLAB 考试新进展及对我国执业医师资格考试的启示 [J]. 中国高等医学教育. 2013（09）:54–56

9. 何惧，何佳，陈声宇. 美国医师执照考试简介及中美医师资格考试比较 [J]. 中国考试. 2005（10）:53–56

10. 贺加. 香港执业医生的管理及启示 [J]. 中国高等医学教育，2004.4：60–61

11. 汪勤俭，贺加. 英国医师执业注册、考试及启示 [J]. 中国医院管理，2004.4:63–64

12. 宫城岛明. 世界各国的国家医师考试现状 [J]. 国外医学教育分册，1994，15（3）:132–136

13. What's USMLE? [EB/OL].[2016.3.5].http://www.usmle.org/

14. About the NBME[EB/OL].[2016.3.25]. http://www.nbme.org/about/index.html

15. Register for your United States Medical Licensing Examination[EB/OL].[2016.4.12].https://www.fsmb.org/

16.About the USMLE[EB/OL].[2016.4.12].https://www.kaptest.com/medical-prep/usmle/usmle-prep-course/step-1-qbank

17.Resources for USMLE,Board Certification& Nursing[EB/OL].[2016.4.30]. http://www.uworld.com/

18. Pratice Materials[EB/OL].[2016.5.5]. http://www.usmle.org/practice-materials/index.html

19.USMLE-Rx 360 Step1[EB/OL].[2016.6.15].https://www.usmle-rx.com/https://www.usmle-rx.com/content/step-1-prep

20. Step 2 Qmax[EB/OL].[2016.7.5].https://www.usmle-rx.com/content/step-2-ck-prep

21. Examinations[EB/OL].[2016.8.4]. http://mcc.ca/examinations/

22. 丁香园考试交流区 [EB/OL].[2016.8.5].http://www.dxy.cn/bbs

23.Journals and databases[EB/OL].[2016.8.20].https://www.nice.org.uk/

24. Publications & resources[EB/OL].[2016.9.18].http://www.hkcog.org.hk/hkcog/pages_4_81.html

25. AMC MCQ Examination[EB/OL].[2016.8.15]. http://www.amc.org.au/assessment/mcq-exam

26. Guides &Booklets[EB/OL].[2016.8.17]. https://www.mcnz.org.nz/news-and-publications/guides-and-booklets/

27. Gernal Medical Council[EB/OL].[2016.10.23].http://www.gmc-uk.org/